JEWISH PARLIAME

JEWISH PARLIAMENTARIANS

GREVILLE JANNER
and
DEREK TAYLOR

VALLENTINE MITCHELL
LONDON • PORTLAND, OR

First published in 2008 by Vallentine Mitchell

Suite 314, Premier House,
112–114 Station Road, Edgware,
Middlesex HA8 7BJ, UK

920 N.E. Avenue, Suite 300,
Portland, Oregon 97213 3786
USA

www.vmbooks.com

British Library Cataloguing in Publication Data

Janner, Greville
  Jewish parliamentarians
  1. Jewish legislators - Great Britain - History 2. Jewish
  legislators - Great Britain - Biography 3. Great Britain -
  Politics and government - 20th century
  I. Title II. Taylor, Derek
  328.4'1'0923924

ISBN 978 085303 819 1 (cloth)
ISBN 978 085303 817 7 (paper)

Library of Congress Cataloging-in-Publication Data

The Pears Foundation is producing a DVD looking at the history
of Jewish MP's. For more information on this DVD
please email the Foundation on contact@pearsfoundation.org.uk.

Printed by Biddles Ltd. King's Lynn, Norfolk

Contents

List of Plates

1. Lionel de Rothschild
2. Sir David Salomon
3. Sir Francis Goldsmith
4. Sir George Jessel
5. Samuel Montagu
6. Rufus Isaacs
7. Herbert Samuel
8. Sir Philip Magnus
9. Alfred Mond
10. Walter Rothschild
11. Manny Shinwell
12. Robert Gee
13. Leslie Hore-Belisha
14. Marion Phillips
15. Barnett Janner
16. Leo Abse
17. James de Rothschild
19. Sir Ivan Lawrence
19. Phil Piratin
20. Joel Barnett
21. Harold Lever
22. Sir Henry d'Avigdor Goldsmid
23. Sir Keith Joseph
24. Sheila Faith
25. Leon Brittan
26. Nigel Lawson
27. Helen Hayman
28.Malcolm Rifkind
29. Michael Howard
30. Oona King
31. David Miliband
32.Ed Miliband

10 DOWNING STREET
LONDON SW1A 2AA

THE PRIME MINISTER

On Friday, July 23rd 1858, Queen Victoria gave the Royal Assent to the Oaths Act. Two hundred years after being allowed to live in Britain again, Jews were finally able to sit as MPs in House of Commons, using words for their Oath allegiance which did not conflict with their religious beliefs.

The House of Commons made a very wise decision when they passed the Act. Over the years, as this book recounts, Jewish MPs have made major contributions to the work of our governments and have been appointed to many political offices.

There have never been more than some 400,000 Jews in Britain, but this comparatively small community has always supported our country admirably and has shown that an ethnic and religious group can do so without sacrificing their historical traditions.

As this remarkable book describes, our energetic minority of Jewish citizens have done – and still do – great work in our parliament. So I congratulate the authors for compiling this remarkable and unique book.

May 2008

Acknowledgements

The authors would like to thank the following for all their help and cooperation in the production of this book:

The staff of the House of Lords Library; Erla Zimmels and the Jews College Library; Richard Burton and the Jewish Chronicle; Stewart Cass and Vallentine Mitchell, Heather Marchant, Ben Grabiner, Maureen Gold and Valerie Taylor. Little has been specifically written on the subject before, but we would like to acknowledge Geoffrey Alderman's book *The Jewish Community in British Politics* (Clarendon Press, 1983).

1 1858–1880: The Pioneers

One of the unwitting foster parents of Jewish emancipation in Britain was the inventor of the water closet. It seems an odd device to associate with the passing of the Oaths Act in 1858, which enabled Jews to swear their allegiance to the Crown in language they found acceptable, but then 1858 was exceptional. This was a very hot summer occuring at the close of a centuries-long cold spell which has been called a mini-Ice Age, but nobody knew at the time that it had ended. The summer of 1858 was so hot, however, that it became known as the year of the Great Stink.

The problem with the oath in question was simple enough. For centuries, Members of Parliament had sworn an oath of fealty to the monarch when they took their seat in the House. It didn't concern the Jews because they'd been thrown out of the country in 1290. From the time of James I at the beginning of the seventeenth century, these Oaths of Supremacy and Allegiance included the words 'on the true faith of a Christian'. The 'true faith' referred to was not, of course, Christianity as against Judaism. It was Protestantism as against Catholicism. Anyone who followed the Catholic doctrine was inadmissible to the House of Commons.

When Charles II allowed the Jews return to England in 1661, he didn't alter the parliamentary oath and there were other grounds for Jews not even being allowed to vote. This state of affairs continued until 1829 when the Catholics were emancipated; they could now sit in parliament. But the Jews still couldn't, and so in 1830, to liberalize the situation, a bill was introduced into the Commons to allow them to do so. This was defeated. There were then fourteen more bills in the next twenty-five years, all of which went through the Commons – but as fast as the Commons passed them, the Lords vetoed them. As the years went by, the pace of introducing such bills quickened and they came before the Commons in 1848, 1849, 1851, 1853, 1854, 1856 and 1857.

The leaders of the Jewish community in early Victorian times came primarily from a few families connected by marriage. They became known as 'the Cousinhood' and they were rich, originally Orthodox in their religious practices, and some were increasingly resentful of anything which prevented them from exercising the rights of an enfranchised citizen. The community was divided into two groups, or factions: those who had originally come from Holland in the seventeenth century were called the Sephardim; those from Germany and Eastern Europe, most of whom arrived some years later, were called the Ashkenazim.

In London, the synagogues were almost all located in the East End where the immigrants had first arrived at the docks from the continent, but in 1840 a few of the rich men decided to set up a synagogue in the West End of London. They also made some minor changes in the traditional Orthodox ritual and their West London Synagogue of British Jews is now part of what is called the Reform movement. At the time there weren't many significant differences between the two groups, but any changes are normally considered by the Orthodox to be for the worse, and the West London (Reform) Synagogue changed a great deal from the middle of the twentieth century, so producing Sephardi, Ashkenazi and Reform – three groups.

Did the Jews have the same rights as any other British citizen? In many ways, no. In the time of the Stuarts, the Jews looked to the monarch to decide their rights and the law courts argued over many statutes which might have been detrimental to Jewish interests if they had been applied. There was a Stuart law, for example, which actually made attending synagogue a crime, but it was agreed by the King that the Jews didn't have to obey the statute. Allowances were made over the years, barriers were broken down and, when the Oath Act was passed, it overturned the last important hurdle to Jews having equal rights with all their fellow citizens.

Nowadays, when some ethnic communities in Britain have few or weak central organizations, the Jews are an example of how successfully to approach the problem of relating to government. From the end of the eighteenth century, the body which represented the Jewish community with the Crown and the authorities was the Board of Deputies of British Jews, established in 1760. When legislation was suggested which would adversely affect the Jewish community, the Board of Deputies made representations to have the offending clauses changed. From early in Queen Victoria's reign, the president of the Board of Deputies was a retired City magnate, the very charitable Sir Moses Montefiore, who was a friend of Victoria. Any Orthodox Jew could be elected to the Board of Deputies – but only Orthodox Jews – so members of the West London (Reform) Synagogue were barred.

As the years went by, the Board could point with satisfaction to the passing of the Jewish Municipal Relief Bill in 1845 which allowed Jews to be elected to every municipal office. In the course of time they would be able to go to Oxford and Cambridge, become lawyers and take government office.

Many of the rules which held them back had their origins in Christian oaths. This was the sticking point for religious Jews. The man who was primarily responsible for the agitation to change the official form of words for MPs was David Salomons. A successful banker, stockbroker and Lloyds underwriter, Salomons was also one of the Cousinhood, having married Jeannette Cohen who was the niece of a Rothschild and also of Moses Montefiore. But this family connection was not an unmixed blessing.

Sir Moses was not at all sure that he wanted Jews in parliament and the vast majority of the Jewish community was completely indifferent, just wanting to get on with their lives in peace. Montefiore's motivation had nothing to do with the pros and cons of emancipation: he was concerned that a Jewish MP might not be able to carry out his religious duties as thoroughly as he had before his election. It was – and still can be – a considerable problem. For example, as the Jewish Sabbath is a Saturday, surgeries that MPs conduct in the constituencies on that day are held on their Sabbath. There are also a very large number of rules for the Orthodox about what you should do on Saturday and holding a surgery makes it almost certain that you will break some of the prohibitions. When there were important votes on Saturday – the second reading of the Parliamentary Reform Act in 1866, for example – Jewish MPs had to choose between their God and their constituents. They would all choose their constituents, but many would feel unhappy doing so. So it was not surprising that many of the original Jewish MPs came from the ranks of the West London Synagogue, whose members were less troubled by the demands of the Orthodox regulations.

It didn't help the case of those who wanted Jews to be in parliament just like anyone else that there were restrictions as to who could be a member of their own Board of Deputies. If, however, it was to be a case of both bodies being open to all, or neither, then Montefiore would have far preferred to abandon the fight for parliamentary status.

In 1847, Lionel de Rothschild was persuaded to stand as a candidate for one of the seats allotted to the City of London. There were nine candidates competing for four seats and Rothschild came in third, which was good enough to get him elected. It wasn't unexpected. His father, Nathaniel, was in his day one of the most powerful men in the City, as head of the great Rothschild bank. So Lionel went to the House but refused to take the Oath on the New Testament, as a matter of conscience, and withdrew from the Chamber. He then resigned his seat in 1849, stood again at the resulting by-election, was again successful but again wouldn't take the oath on the Gospels and couldn't take his seat. No one would give way. He was elected again in 1852 and in 1857, with the same result.

The problem of the Oath obviously only affected religious Jews: baptized Jews had taken seats in the House on a number of occasions before. In 1770 Samson Gideon won Cambridge and in 1802 Sir Menassah Lopes took Romney. He supported Pitt between 1804 and 1806 and Lord Liverpool from 1812 to 1819. His sister's son, Ralph Franco, won Westbury in 1814, but then it was a Lopes borough – in those days, you could buy the few official voters for hard cash in many constituencies. In 1818, Ralph Bernal won Lincoln and David Ricardo, the famous economist, won Portarlington in 1819. All these members had abandoned Judaism. Benjamin Disraeli had been baptized when he was a child and, like the other proselytes, took the existing oath when he was elected for Maidstone in 1837. Disraeli was officially a Christian, even if he still suffered from racial abuse throughout his career.

Jews do not recognize the conversion of their co-religionists, because over the centuries conversion has, too often, been forced upon them; therefore a converted Jew may still be buried in a Jewish cemetery and married in a Jewish synagogue. What alone defines his or her status as a Jew is the religion of the mother. If she is Jewish, then so are her children, and so they will remain, according to Jewish law. In this book we have included all the MPs who can be considered Jewish on this traditional view, as well as a few 'doubtful' cases – the difficulty being that some conversions to Judaism are not universally accepted within the Jewish community.

In 1858, the House of Lords decided on a compromise over the Oath, proposed by Lord Lucan (who had been ignominiously involved in the Charge of the Light Brigade during the Crimean War). Arguing in support of Jewish emancipation did not present any physical risks, such as charging Russian guns, but it could still do Lucan's reputation no good. It was nevertheless agreed that the Lords would let the Commons do what they liked about their own Oath of Supremacy and Abjuration. For the Upper House, the ancient wording would stand – and it did till 1885. This cleared the way for the Commons to pass the Oath Act, which would make it possible for Rothschild not to be obliged to commit himself to Christianity. There might, however, still have been a lot of opposition to the bill in the Commons, and it might not have passed.

Which brings us to the flush toilet. Prior to its invention, all sewage went into pits or was carried away from London by barge, but by 1858, just a few years after the mass production of flush toilets had started, about 200,000 WCs were pouring sewage into the Thames. In 1858, there came that hot dry summer, which did indeed create a great stink – north, south, east and west of the river. The atmosphere in the Houses of Parliament, right on the bank of the Thames, became really oppressive. The Commons considered relocating to Hampton Court, and some pessimists went so far as to suggest a location as far away as Oxford. The curtains for the windows of the Houses of Parliament facing on to the river had to be soaked in chloride of lime and the windows in committee rooms remained shut, in spite of the heat. But it was still almost impossible to work in the buildings.

The complaint of one MP on 7 June was recorded in Hansard: 'It was a notorious fact that Hon. Gentlemen sitting in the Committee rooms and in the library were utterly unable to remain there in consequence of the stench which arose from the river'. The second reading of the Oaths Bill took place on Friday 16 July. The day before the temperature had reached 86 degrees; now it was still 70 degrees, even in the open air. Objections were made that the passing of the bill would 'destroy the Christian character of Parliament'. Passing it would, however, let the members escape into the fresh air, and the bill was approved by 156 to 91, a majority of 65. Happily, only 40 per cent of the members had turned up to vote.

The following Tuesday came the third reading of the bill. Objections were again raised: could it not be put off for three months, asked one MP, knowing that this would kill the proposal? How about an adjournment to the next day, asked another? The debate dragged on. It was coming up to one o'clock in the morning when a weary House at last agreed to the adjournment. On the next day the bill finally passed by 129 to 55. This time only 30 per cent of the House had turned up. Still, the job was done and the bill received the royal assent on Friday 23 July 1858. The following Monday, Rothschild finally made his point. He was allowed by a special resolution of the House to omit the inappropriate words. The resolution was passed by 69 votes to 37. This time, less than 20 per cent of the House voted. In accordance with the Jewish tradition, Rothschild covered his head before swearing his oath of allegiance to God alone. The need for a special resolution on each occasion was replaced by a Standing Order in 1860.

These voting figures compare with those which had been cast only a few years before in 1847 on a similar bill to remove Jewish disabilities. The voting on the first reading was 256–186, on the second 227–204, and on the third 234–173. Admittedly, it had then been a far more contentious piece of legislation. Benjamin Disraeli had just been made Leader of the Conservative rump in the Commons after his party had split over the repeal of the Corn Laws. Everyone knew that Disraeli had been born a Jew. So when he stood up in parliament to advocate removing Jewish disabilities, he was taking a considerable risk that his political career would come to a speedy halt, because his party certainly wasn't behind him. The leader of the Tory Party, the Earl of Derby, was dead-set against Jewish emancipation, and so were his followers.

Nevertheless, Disraeli spoke up for the Jews amid increasing uproar. He finished his speech with these brave words:

> I cannot sit in this House with any misconception of my opinion on this subject. Whatever may be the consequences on the seat I hold . . . I cannot, for one, give a vote which is not in deference to what I believe to be the true principles of religion. Yes, it is as a Christian that I will not take upon me the awful responsibility of excluding from the legislature those who are from the religion in the bosom of which my Lord and saviour was born.

He sat down amid stony silence and only he and one other member of his party voted to accept the bill. It still passed but, like its predecessors, was killed in the Lords. It was resistance like this on the part of the Tory members which led to the majority of Jewish electors initially supporting the Liberals. Indeed, for many years it was considered to be letting the side down if a Jew voted Tory – as many did because there were a number of other issues of concern besides representation. For instance, the Liberal Party's views on economic management did not meet with the approval of the House of Rothschild and while they would sit in the Commons as Liberals, for many years they didn't always think like Liberals, and eventually wouldn't vote like them.

It does appear that what might well have interested the members of the Commons far more in 1858 was how to deal with that enduring sewage stench. The Metropolitan Board of Works was eventually instructed to levy rates and borrow money to deal with the effluent. Which is how Sir Joseph Bazalgette finally got agreement to produce the Embankment, three new bridges across the river and an underground system of sewers which still does a perfectly adequate job for London today.

Religious Jews had difficulty with the Christian forms of the old oaths and the early Jewish MPs came from religious backgrounds. There were then about 25,000 Jews in the United Kingdom. The Rothschilds were all nominally Orthodox, though some were more Orthodox than others. When Sir David Salomons was elected in 1859, he was a stalwart of the West London Synagogue, but still a religious Jew, who observed most of the tenets of the Orthodox community.

Over time, this situation would change. Many of the nearly 200 Jewish MPs elected over the next 150 years were Jews by birth, but had little connection with the community. Rather, the Jewish strain which often remained within them became a commitment to Jewish ideals. For instance, Sir John Simon was one of the early Jewish MPs, winning Dewsbury in 1870. He was far ahead of his time in wanting to end capital punishment. When, in 1965, another Jewish MP, Sidney Silverman, introduced a Private Member's Bill which did finally lead to its abolition, he was following in Sir John's wake. He was also following in the footsteps of the Jewish judges who had, effectively, abolished capital punishment in biblical times. But to convict at that time, you had to have two eye witnesses to the murder – and you had to have warned the murderer in advance that what he was about to do was wrong! So although many Jewish MPs have abandoned their faith over the years, they have often found it less necessary, as we shall see, to forget the teachings of the sixth-century Talmud.

Jews have sat in the House of Commons in every parliament since 1858. They have been appointed to almost every major office of state (see the Epilogue). They have always had a greater percentage of MPs than would have been the case if there had been proportional religious representation. Even in 1860 when they had just three MPs, this represented 0.5 per cent of the Commons when they only represented 0.2 per cent of the population. At their peak in 1974, they had forty-six MPs – 7 per cent of the Commons – when they represented under 3 per cent of the population. And those elected often punched above the weight of their numbers.

After Lionel de Rothschild was allowed to take his seat he was re-elected a further five times, but during his eighteen years in the chamber, he never spoke once! It was alleged that he wielded far more influence through his office in the City than he could in parliament. The Rothschilds were indeed immensely powerful because of their ability to raise loans for foreign governments. If you wanted to fight a war in those days, you would probably need the Rothschilds to raise the money to pay for it. This was certainly how the British financed their campaigns in the Crimean War.

From 1857 to 1945 there was always a Rothschild in the House of Commons, except between 1922 and 1929; seven Rothschild MPs in all. It did help, of course, to have the wherewithal to support yourself while working in the interests of your constituents. MPs were not paid a salary until 1911, which meant that those elected had to have independent wealth or be financially supported by friends or relatives. The result was that the Victorian Jewish MPs, like all the others, were well-to-do, and becoming an MP was out of the question for the poor. In 1911 MPs were granted £400 a year (equivalent to £28,000 now). By contrast, at the beginning of 2008, MPs receive a salary of £60,675, plus an additional £90,505 (maximum) for staff, as well as up to £21,339 for running their offices and £23,083 for overnight stays on their parliamentary duties. There is an additional £10,000 in communication costs, car allowances and expenses to cover fifteen journeys each year for their partner. MPs also receive staff training expenses, a contribution to security costs and centrally provided insurance. All such expenses had to be paid for personally by a Victorian MP.

Lionel de Rothschild was not concerned about the money and neither were the other two Jewish Members elected in 1859. One was his brother, Mayer Amschel, and the other Sir David Salomons. Mayer Amschel represented Hythe in Kent and it was generally accepted that this constituency could always rely on financial support from the Rothschild family. Indeed, they donated £12,000 a year to the Hythe Conservative Party over a long period. When the constituency lost the Rothschild donation, they elected a Sassoon with the same result. The other Rothschild bailiwick was Aylesbury, which boasted the stately homes of various Rothschilds, and where the whole area benefited greatly from the charitable largesse of the family.

The third of the Jewish MP triumvirate in 1859 was Sir David Salomons, who was elected for Greenwich, and in 1860 Sir Francis Goldsmid was elected for Reading in a by-election. The Goldsmids were bullion brokers. The firm had been founded in 1671 by Moses Mocatta and in 1783 became Mocatta and Goldsmid. Nine generations of the two families had run the firm and it became one of five companies fixing the price of gold every day from 1919 onwards. In their time, great uncles Benjamin and Abraham Goldsmid had raised much of the money that the British government needed to fight the Napoleonic wars. There were to be five Goldsmids in the Commons, serving from 1860 to 1900 and from 1955 to 1974, a grand total of fifty-nine years. The last two were twentieth-century major generals. In 1865, Lionel Rothschild was joined by his son, Nathaniel, elected for Aylesbury at the age of 25. In the same year Francis Goldsmid welcomed his brother, Frederick, who won Honiton, but Frederick died soon after and his son, Julian, was elected in his place.

The older generation had prepared the way and Nathaniel Rothschild and Julian Goldsmid settled down to make their marks in parliament. Nathaniel kept his seat at every election over the next twenty years, until he was made the first Jewish peer in 1885. He played a prominent part in the Commons up until his death in 1915; Julian continued in the Commons until he died in 1896.

If Jews were now allowed to sit in the House of Commons, the obvious question was: whom did they represent? Were they a Jewish lobby, or MPs who merely happened to be Jews? In reality, very few constituencies had sufficient Jewish electors to make the religion of the candidate an issue. When Sir John Simon was elected for Dewsbury in 1865 there wasn't even one Jew living in the town. Where there were a number of Jewish voters in a constituency with a small electorate they might make a difference, but this rarely happened. Even if the Jewish MPs had been prepared to vote in a bloc, their impact would have been insignificant, and in any case this never occurred. Every party had its Jewish supporters. The East End of London was, of course, the main centre of Jewish population in the UK, but its inhabitants were rarely entitled to vote. From the 1880s onwards, as thousands arrived as refugees, large numbers were not even naturalized. Even so, the Jewish MPs took their responsibility to represent all their electorate very seriously.

There would always be critics who saw Jewish MPs as part of a cabal with a secret agenda to take over the world. The Russian secret police gave voice to this monstrous calumny in 1903 with the publication of *The Protocols of the Elders of Zion*, but only the very gullible were taken in by it. The truth was that the Jewish MPs didn't even agree on the right approach to communal matters. It was well said within the community that if you got three Jews together, you would soon have four political parties.

The election of 1868 was the first of William Gladstone's four terms as Prime Minister. Lionel de Rothschild was beaten but was returned unopposed at a by-election in 1869. When the Commons assembled after the 1868 election there were five Jewish Liberal MPs: Francis Goldsmid, Nathaniel Rothschild, David Salomons, Sir John Simon and a new name, George Jessel, who had won Dover. The convention of Jews always standing as Liberal candidates was broken in 1874 when Saul Isaac, a truly colourful Jewish Conservative, was elected for Nottingham. Isaac was followed by another Jewish Tory, Baron Henry de Worms, who was related to the Rothschilds.

The debt the Jewish electorate felt towards the Liberal Party was severely undermined in 1878 as a consequence of the massacre of Bulgarian Christians by the Turks. Gladstone, the Liberal leader, went on the warpath up and down the country, condemning Turkey, yet he did not seem to be similarly concerned over the murder of Jews by the Bulgarians, another horrific crime. What sharpened the difference of opinion between Gladstone and the Jewish community even further was the fact that Turkey had in former times welcomed a Jewish presence. Twenty thousand Jews had taken refuge in the Ottoman Empire, on the invitation of the Sultan, when they were expelled from Spain in 1492. The Turks had treated them far better than had many of the Christian states of Europe. As Sir John Simon wrote to *The Times*, 'Is all sympathy reserved for the (Christian) "subject races" and none to spare for the unhappy Jewish people?' Simon was prophetic when he warned the Liberal Party that their policies were alienating the Jewish community.

The first Jewish MPs were highly respectable as well as being pillars of their community but, naturally, they were very inexperienced parliamentarians when they first sat in the House. The story of the Jewish MPs is told in the following pages; an MP's name is given in bold on first being elected. Those who were elected and admitted between 1858 and 1880, after the passing of the Oath Act, were:

1858   **Lionel de Rothschild, David Salomons** (Liberal)
1859   Lionel de Rothschild, **Mayer Amschel Rothschild**, David Salomons (all Liberal)
1860   **Francis Goldsmid** (Liberal)
1865   Francis Goldmid, **Frederick Goldsmid**, Lionel de Rothschild, Mayer Amschel Rothschild, **Nathan Rothschild**, David Salomons, **J d'A. Samuda** (all Liberal)
1866   **Julian Goldsmid** (Liberal)
1868   Francis Goldsmid, **George Jessel**, Mayer Amschel Rothschild, Nathan Rothschild, David Salomons, J d'A. Samuda, **John Simon** (all Liberal)
1869   Lionel de Rothschild (Liberal)
1870   Julian Goldsmid (Liberal)
1874   Francis Goldsmid, Julian Goldsmid, **Farrer Herschel, Saul Isaac**, Lionel de Rothschild, Nathan Rothschild, J d'A. Samuda, John Simon (all Liberal except Isaac, Conservative)

LIONEL DE ROTHSCHILD 1808–1879

In 1847, Lionel de Rothschild was elected to the Commons as a Liberal for the City of London, and refused to take the oath in the prescribed form. The discussions which ensued on Jewish emancipation went on for the next eleven years. Never let it be said that the House of Commons fails to examine the minutiae of its rules. In 1849, Rothschild resigned his seat and then stood again in the by-election which he had precipitated. He was elected again, and when again called upon to swear, he asked to do so on the Old Testament. This was agreed. When, however, he left out the words 'upon the true faith of a Christian' he had gone too far and was again asked to leave. When finally, after he had been elected in two more contests, the Oath Act was passed in 1858, he covered his head, took the oath on the Old Testament and added, 'So help me God'. The principle of a more tolerant and plural democracy had finally prevailed.

Rothschild was re-elected in 1859 and 1865 but finally lost his seat in 1868. Could it have been because he had supported the Liberal candidate in the neighbouring constituency of Tower Hamlets? The problem with that gentleman was that he was a Jew who had converted to Christianity. Had Rothschild alienated sufficient Jewish voters to lose his own seat? He stood again in 1869 and was elected unopposed, but finally lost the seat in 1874 when the Conservatives came to power under Disraeli.

Rothschild did good by stealth. His generosity was legendary but carried out quietly. He gave handsomely to relieve the starvation in Ireland caused by the potato famines. To mark his election in 1858, he endowed the largest scholarship at the City of London School. He supported both Jewish and Christian causes. Rothschild had been educated at the University of Göttingen and in 1836 he took over the family bank from his father when he was only 28. He raised loans for governments all over the world, including the Americans and the Russians. He raised £16 million for Irish famine relief. In 1874 he lent Disraeli money to buy shares in the Suez Canal, which gave Britain control of the waterway for the next eighty years. Rothschild was a serious power in the land.

For the last twenty years of his life he was crippled by osteoarthritis, which made him very irascible. His temper in parliament was not improved by his party leader, Gladstone, who believed that income tax should be abolished: Rothschild violently disagreed. He believed that the country, like any good citizen, should be able to balance its books. Even so, when in 1869 Gladstone recommended him to the

Queen for a peerage, which Victoria refused to countenance, the Prime Minister referred to 'his amiable and popular character'. Communally, he was president of the largest synagogue, a member of the Jewish Board of Deputies, a major benefactor to the Jews' Free School, a council member of the United Synagogue, and much more. Socially, he was a member of Brooks and the Reform Club.

Rothschild died in 1878. He was one of the first to be buried in the new Willesden cemetery and his estate amounted to £2.7 million (about £188 million today). He died on 3 June. His horse, St Bevys, won the Derby on 4 June. Now that is really bad luck – mind you, the time of three minutes and twenty seconds was the slowest since 1856 and no horse since has ever won in a slower time.

MAYER AMSCHEL ROTHSCHILD 1818–1874

Mayer Amschel Rothschild, commonly known as 'Muffy', weighed in at sixteen stone and was devoted to horse riding and racing. In 1871 he won £25,000 (£1,500,000 today) in prize money on the Flat. This was largely from Flavonius winning the Derby and Hannah winning the Oaks, the 1,000 Guineas *and* the St Leger. Muffy didn't leave much for the other horse owners that year.

The jovial Muffy was Lionel's brother and had been educated at both Leipzig and Heidelberg Universities before going on to Trinity and then Magdalen College in Cambridge: he was in fact the first Jew to attend an English university as a student. Isaac Abendana was only one of the Jews who had been on the academic staff at both Oxford and Cambridge in the late-seventeenth century, but Anglicans alone had been permitted to become students. Meyer Rothschild worked in a number of the branches of his family banking empire but he was never particularly attracted to the financial world. He also found time to become High Sheriff of Buckinghamshire in 1847 and was elected as MP for Hythe in 1859, serving the constituency until his death, fifteen years later.

Hannah Rothschild, Meyer's mother, decided that rural life would be more healthy for her sons and bought considerable tracts of the countryside around Aylesbury which she divided between them. Muffy used his acreage to build Mentmore, one of the great stately homes of England. He and his wife had only one child, their daughter Hannah, and as sole heiress she carried on the political tradition of the family by marrying the Earl of Rosebery, who became Prime Minister in 1894. Nathaniel took over as the Rothschild MP for Aylesbury in 1865 and Muffy died in 1874. He is buried in the family plot at Willesden cemetery. Hannah is too, much to Rosebery's disappointment.

DAVID SALOMONS 1797–1873

Together with Lionel Rothschild, David Salomons was the moving spirit in the campaign to achieve political emancipation for the Jews. He was elected MP for Greenwich in 1851 and created a furore by coming to the floor of the House, refusing to take the oath, returning three days later and not only sitting down but taking part in the debate on whether he should be admitted. He voted three times. The proposal to admit him was defeated and he was removed very courteously by the serjeant-at-arms. Six months later he was prosecuted for voting in the House when not qualified to do so and fined £500 (£30,000 today). He appealed and lost, though the judges said that they regretted having to confirm the fine as they recognized that the original oath hadn't been designed for the Jews at all.

When emancipation was achieved, Salomons won Greenwich again and sat for the constituency until he died in 1873. He had been fighting the battle for Jewish equality long before his efforts to storm the walls of the Commons. In 1835 he became the first Jewish Sheriff to be elected in the City of London, but he wasn't allowed to take up that office until the passing of the Sheriffs' Declaration Act in 1836. In 1835 he was elected an alderman, but couldn't take that oath either and was disbarred. He was re-elected in 1847 and the passing of the Religious Opinions Relief Act enabled him finally to take up the office. In 1855 he became the City's first Jewish Lord Mayor.

Salomons was born into the Cousinhood as his aunts were the wives of Sir Moses Montefiore and Nathan Mayer Rothschild. He grew up to be a successful banker and stockbroker. A man of many talents, he had studied for the Bar and was accepted in 1849, and although he didn't practise, he did sit as a JP. As a member of the community, Salomons was a pillar of the West London Synagogue of British Jews. He was twice president of the Board of Deputies, in 1838 and 1846, supportive of a wide range of Jewish organizations and held in very high regard by the whole community. Salomons was also a founder of the London and Westminster Bank, now the Natwest. So he certainly wouldn't have needed a salary as an MP, had it been available, which it wasn't.

FRANCIS GOLDSMID 1808–1878

Francis Goldsmid was one of the real pioneers of Jewish municipal and parliamentary equality. He was a member of the great banking family and in 1833 became the first Jew to be called to the Bar, becoming a QC in 1858. He wrote a number of pamphlets, including *Remarks on the Civil Disabilities of the Jews*, which had a wide circulation and helped move the emancipation campaign forward. Goldsmid was a Liberal, lost Great Yarmouth in 1847 but was successful when standing for Reading in 1860. He represented the constituency until his death in 1878. He used his seat in parliament to make a number of appeals on behalf of oppressed Jewish communities in Russia, Poland, Serbia and Romania and was known as 'the member for Jewry' in the House and the press.

Goldsmid was also a founder of the oldest Jewish school still extant, the Jews' Free School, and he was a major supporter of the new University College London, where he endowed the Chair of Applied Mathematics. He also gave University College Hospital a lot of financial support. In his own county, he was Deputy Lieutenant for Berkshire. Apart from being the president of the West London Synagogue of British Jews, Goldsmid was elected vice-president of the Anglo Jewish Association in 1871. Goldsmid died in 1878 at the age of 70 as the result of a railway accident. He was succeeded by his nephew, Julian, as he had no children. The Orthodox synagogue in Reading is in Goldsmid Road.

FREDERICK GOLDSMID 1812–1866

Since, in his youth, Jews were not allowed to go to Oxford or Cambridge, Frederick was fortunate that his father, Isaac Lyon Goldsmid, bought the site for University College London for £30,000 (about £2 million today) in 1827, though it was only ten years later that the College was allowed to award degrees. One of the first Jews to be admitted to the college, Goldsmid went on join the family company of bullion merchants. He was the brother of Francis Goldsmid and the father of Julian Goldsmid.

He suffered poor health but managed to father a son and five daughters and to be well known for his charity work, in particular, spending much time on the Metropolitan Association for Improving the Dwellings of the Labouring Classes. He was president of the Jews' Hospital and worked on many other charitable committees, such as those supporting UCL and UCH. He won Honiton for the Liberals in 1865 but died in 1866 after a four-day illness, at the age of 54.

NATHAN ROTHSCHILD 1840–1915

Nathan Rothschild was the first Jew to take the simpler form of the Oath of Allegiance intended to cover all faiths. He was the Liberal member for Aylesbury from 1865 to 1885 when he was recommended to the Queen for a peerage. In 1869 Victoria had turned down the suggestion that his father, Lionel de Rothschild, be made a peer, but she accepted his son. Rothschild became head of the family bank after his father died in 1879. Among the bank's most influential loans in his time was the one which created the British South Africa Company and the de Beers diamond conglomerate. Both were vital to Cecil Rhodes and after Rhodes' death, Rothschild helped set up the Rhodes Scholarship scheme at Oxford University. He also helped stave off a major crisis in the City when in 1890 Barings was about to collapse after making unwise investments in South America. Rothschild chaired the committee of bankers who bailed Barings out – Northern Rock could have used Rothschild over a century later.

In the tradition of the Rothschilds, Nathan was extremely charitable. In 1900 the Jews' Free School was the largest in the country with over 4,000 pupils. The Rothschilds saw to it that the school remained solvent and the Rothschild family colours remain those of the school to this day. Although Rothschild started his political life as a Liberal, he became a Liberal Unionist in 1886 as he opposed Home Rule for Ireland. From that position he eventually went over to the Conservative Party. It could not be said that Rothschild found change easy; in his time he opposed the introduction of death duties, old age pensions and women's suffrage. When Lloyd George raised income tax from 5p to 6p in 1909 Rothschild spoke at a rally of 1,000 City merchants and called Lloyd George's measure 'a Robbers' budget'.

In the House, Lloyd George recalled that Rothschild had been in favour of eight Dreadnought battleships when the government had felt that it could only afford four. 'And now,' said the Chancellor, 'Rothschild doesn't even want to pay for them. Lord Rothschild's ancestors had to make bricks without straw but that is nothing compared to making Dreadnoughts without money.' Rothschild was the undisputed head of the Jewish community after he became the first Jewish peer, but the kind of dressing-down that Lloyd George gave him always made the community wish that their co-religionists would keep a low profile on contentious issues before parliament if they didn't affect them personally or communally. Rothschild died in 1915 at the age of 75. By this time there were still only four Jews in the House of Lords.

JOSEPH D'A. SAMUDA 1813–1885

Joseph d'Aguilar Samuda was a Sephardi Jew – his family originated in Spain and Portugal. He started off his business life in his father's counting house but he didn't stay long. With his brother, he set up as a builder of marine engines, based, not as most were, in Derby or Glasgow, but on the Isle of Dogs, close by London docks. The brothers moved on to shipbuilding, constructing everything from royal yachts and riverboats to steamships for the navy, Samuda himself often superintending the construction. In 1860 he was a founder of the Institute of Naval Architects and wrote a major treatise on the adaptation of atmospheric pressure to drive locomotion on railways. His firm also built railway lines.

Samuda was elected Liberal MP for Tavistock in 1865 and in 1868 was returned for Tower Hamlets, which he represented until 1880. When he spoke in the House on the subjects he knew, some of his speeches were described as 'treasure-houses of technical and political knowledge'. He left the Jewish faith and is buried in the Kensal Green cemetery. His name is still to be found on the Samuda Estate on the Isle of Dogs and shortly before his death he was hard at work raising money for the local London Hospital and helping a favourite charity, the Merchant Seaman's Orphan Asylum. He died at 72.

JULIAN GOLDSMID 1838–1896

Julian Goldsmid had eight daughters and – like all the MPs at the time – didn't receive a salary as an MP. Fortunately, he didn't need the money as Mocatta and Goldsmid, the family bullion merchants, were able to provide an income for the whole clan. Whether paid or not, Goldsmid was a ferocious worker and always determined to succeed at anything to which he set his hand. Goldsmid went to University College London and became a barrister. He was passionate about being an MP and during his career he won Honiton in 1866, Rochester in 1870 and St Pancras South in 1885, all for the Liberals. He also lost Mid Surrey in 1870 and Sandwich in 1880. Indeed he was so involved in the Commons that he was made Deputy Speaker and was said to preside over the proceedings as if they were a board meeting of his company. Like a number of other Jewish MPs, he became a Liberal Unionist when the party split over the Home Rule Bill.

Within the Jewish community, he was president of the Anglo-Jewish Association when it was at its most influential, and chairman of the Russo-Jewish Committee from its foundation in 1882 until 1894. He also found time to be the Honorary Colonel of the 1st Sussex Artillery Volunteers, chairman of the Submarine Telegraph Company, chairman of Imperial and Continental Gas and treasurer of University College. And these were just a few of his activities. It was a very full life but in 1895 his health worsened, his beloved wife died and he followed in 1896, at the age of only 58.

GEORGE JESSEL 1824–1883

Jessel was a lawyer. Of about 200 Jews who have served as MPs, he was the first of over forty members of the legal profession, most of them barristers. He was called to the Bar in 1847 although, as a Jew, he couldn't officially be a member for some years. No one objected to his practising, however. Jessel was not celebrated as a great speaker but, having been elected Liberal MP for Dover in 1868, he made two excellent contributions to the debate on the Bankruptcy Bill in 1869. As a result, in 1871 Gladstone appointed him Solicitor General, the first Jew to become a government minister and also the first to be made a Privy Councillor. He was appointed Master of the Rolls and served in that judicial role for ten years, before dying from diabetes and chronic heart disease when he was only 59. He was the first Jew to be a judge and the last judge to have the right to sit in the Commons.

Jessel's main contribution as a judge was the speed with which he dealt with cases. He was so fast that he often helped other judges to clear their lists. He never reserved a judgement in Chancery, even in one action which occupied twenty-two days with 150 witnesses. It was known as 'the Epping Forest case' and the papers went back to the time of the thirteenth century and King John. Nothing fazed Jessel. In his time the fusion of law and equity was completed in the Judicature Acts and it was generally agreed that this would not have been possible without him. In court he certainly didn't suffer fools gladly and was respected as both forceful and direct.

Jessel was the son of a Jewish diamond merchant. He went to a Jewish school and on to University College London. In 1844, he was a gold medallist at the University in mathematics and natural philosophy; in 1846 he was invited to be a fellow of the College. At his peak as a barrister, he averaged £25,000 a year (equivalent to about £1.5 million today). An impressive career.

JOHN SIMON 1818–1897

John Simon was the first Jewish judge in Britain. He was made a ser-jeant-at-law in 1864, a title which no longer exists. It enabled him to sit on the bench, which he did on many occasions. Initially he had wanted to become a *chazan* (cantor) and conduct services in syna-gogue, but his father persuaded him that the law was a better career. Simon was born in Jamaica where the family had lived since the reign of Charles II. He was educated in Liverpool and at University College London. The College had been kick-started by Jewish philanthropy and had always allowed Jews to study under its auspices. In 1842 Simon was the second Jew to be called to the Bar, nine years after Francis Goldsmid. When Simon was back in Jamaica he had been responsible for the restoration of representative government on the island and, when it was very unfashionable, he always supported the rights of black people.

When Simon was at school in Liverpool, his headmaster was David Woolf Marks, the first minister of the breakaway synagogue set up in the West End and called the West London Synagogue of British Jews. It developed into the foremost Reform synagogue in the country and Simon helped Marks with a new version of the liturgy. Their basic belief was that the Written Law to be found in the Pentateuch was perfect and that therefore there was no need for the Oral Law, which had been built on its foundations. Today, the Written Law is also con-sidered to be optional by the Reform movement.

As one of the early Jewish MPs, Simon was conscious that eman-cipation had been a cause that its opponents were unhappy to lose. As he remembered in the *Jewish Chronicle* in 1891, 'The opposition was relentless, virulent and marked in some instances by bitter religious animosity'. The question of the right of children not to attend state schools on the Sabbath was important to the Commons and Simon ensured that this would apply to the Jewish Saturday as well. Unlike Samuel Montagu, Simon supported Gladstone against the Turks, but he attacked the Prime Minister when nothing was done to help the persecuted Jewish communities in Eastern Europe, particularly in Romania and Serbia. He organized a massive protest demonstration at the Mansion House, but in this he was not supported by Rothschild and Salomons. Many MPs were still wary of using their position in the Commons to promote such action.

So persistent was Simon in the interest of his co-religionists that, like Francis Goldsmid, he became known as 'the Member for Jewry'. Gladstone was not amused and passed him over for a knighthood in

1880, but Simon was granted the accolade in 1886. His agitation on behalf of Jewish communities was not without its cost in other ways, and he lost a number of clients for his chambers in Liverpool. Another of Simon's failed crusades was his effort to induce more upper-class Jews to become ministers of religion, but he did succeed in getting a measure passed through parliament which enabled 'aged couples' over 60 to live together in workhouses.

Having benefited from the change in the form of the Oath that Jews had to take, Simon supported William Bradlaugh, an atheist who also wanted to affirm. Bradlaugh fought for this right for many years and was elected four times for Northampton in the 1880s without being able to take his seat. He did vote on one occasion, and where-as Salomons had been fined £500 for this offence, Bradlaugh was fined £1,500. Eventually he got his way and it is now permissible to affirm rather than take any form of religious oath. Simon was elected five times for Dewsbury, but in 1888 he was too ill to continue in the Commons, though he only died in 1897 at the age of 79. He remained a great humanitarian until the end.

FARRER HERSCHEL 1837–1899

Breach of promise is taken very seriously in Judaism, and the penalties for the retracting male are severe. So they used to be in British law until Farrer Herschel, the junior member for Durham, carried a resolution in the House in 1879 making damages dependent on the lady having suffered financially. Gladstone noticed his intervention and in 1880 made him Solicitor General. Herschel's father, the Rev. Ridley Haim Herschell, was Jewish but was also a founder of the British Society for the Propagation of the Gospel among the Jews. What his son's views on being included in this book would be are no longer ascertainable, although he did make a mild attempt to divorce himself from his ancestors by dropping the second 'l' in his surname. Since he served as Lord Chancellor on two occasions in 1886 and from 1892 to 1895, it would be a pity to leave out someone so distinguished: PC, GCB, DLC, LL.D, DL and JP.

Herschel was called to the Bar in 1860, but he wasn't very successful. He even thought of moving to Shanghai where the Consular Courts were less competitive. He stayed on the Northern Circuit in the end and took silk in 1872. His speeches to the jury were considered his strongest point, though he didn't address the Commons very often. Having a very good memory, he seldom used notes. He was the Recorder of Carlisle from 1873 to 1880 and Chancellor of London

University in 1893. He died in Washington in 1899 where he was helping to settle boundary disputes between America and Canada. President McKinley and the judges of the American Supreme Court attended the funeral service and a British warship brought his body home. He is buried in the parish church at Tincleton in Dorset. He was only 62.

SAUL ISAAC 1823–1903

When Saul Isaac stood in 1873 as Conservative candidate for Darlington he was not popular with the Jewish community. The Conservatives had fought tenaciously against the emancipation of the Jews. *Punch*, the comic magazine, commented, 'A Tory Jew! Why not? Or short or tall, he'll stand out proud among 'em like King Saul'.

Isaac was brought up in the great naval town of Chatham and in his youth learned about service supply contracts. With his brother, Sam, he formed a company which became the largest European suppliers to the Confederacy in the American Civil War: military materiel went out and cotton came back. His ships ran the Union blockade successfully but, unfortunately for Isaac, the Confederacy paid in bonds. When the Union won, the bonds were worthless. Both brothers went bankrupt but, prudently, much of their wealth was held in their wives' names. So Sam went on to build the Mersey Railway Tunnel and Saul bought a colliery in Nottingham. When he became an MP, he was the first Jew to be elected as a Conservative, the first to support Disraeli and the first to be elected to the very exclusive Carlton Club.

In parliament, Isaac devoted his maiden speech to trying to get the Education Act amended to make religious education mandatory in schools. This became law in the Education Act in force at his death in 1903, at the age of 80. He was also responsible for saving the City Livery Companies, which were threatened with dissolution by a bill that had every chance of being passed in the Commons without opposition. At a crucial moment in the debate, Isaac made an impassioned speech on behalf of the Guilds, called for a division and saw the measure defeated. The City Livery Companies continue to this day, but their debt to Saul Isaac has no memorial.

Isaac clearly didn't fit the mould of Jewish MPs drawn from the Cousinhood but he played a full part in the Jewish community. He helped create the Bayswater Synagogue, was a strong supporter of the new United Synagogue and did much charitable work for the Jews' Hospital and Orphan Asylum. Finally, however, his risky approach to business did him no favours and he died in comparative poverty.

2 1880–1906: The New Influx

When Czar Alexander II was assassinated in 1881 by Ignacy Hryniewiecki, his death became an excuse for an outbreak of virulent anti-Semitic pogroms. In fact, Hryniewiecki was a Polish nationalist student and not Jewish at all, but that made no difference. As similar pogroms broke out in other Eastern European countries, a large number of Jews decided they had to leave. To the approximately 35,000 Jews who lived in Britain in 1880, there would be added another 200,000 by 1914. The community was completely transformed by this huge influx. The majority of Jews who originally fled their native lands headed for America. But because the cost of passage via London was cheaper, a large number finished up in England if they couldn't afford the onward journey. They went to live primarily in the East End of London.

From the point of view of the Cousinhood, who had been running the community for years, the newcomers posed a threat to their continued hegemony because of their sheer weight of numbers. If positions of power were ever going to be decided through Jewish universal suffrage, members of the Cousinhood might not gain and retain authority anything like as easily as they had done for years. The policy, soon adopted by the veteran community, was to discourage immigrants from coming if they could, and try hard to anglicize them if they couldn't.

But there was another side to the coin. Jews have always stuck together to try to alleviate the misfortunes of their brethren, and the Cousinhood had no intention of abandoning that philosophy. If there was mistreatment of Jews on the continent, then a number of Jewish MPs would now raise the subject in the House. They would ask the government to make representations on behalf of the oppressed. They would try to get the greatest nation in the world to put pressure on overseas governments to ameliorate the condition of their Jewish communities. There was much need for this. The anti-Jewish atrocities were not just to be found in Russia, Romania and Poland; many other countries were equally at fault, to greater and lesser degrees.

It was not a new initiative for the British government. When Palmerston had been Foreign Secretary forty years earlier, after a blood-libel allegation against Jews in Syria, he had told the embassies in the Middle East to look after the interests of the Jewish communities in the countries where they were posted. Apart from the humanitarian aspect, the realpolitik argument was that this might enable the UK to have an excuse for interfering in the internal affairs of the local governments. The French used this stratagem on behalf of Catholic communities and the Russians for the Russian Orthodox Church congregations. In 1851, Palmerston ordered the blockade of Greece to obtain compensation for a Jewish merchant, David Pacifico, whose possessions had been looted in an attack on his home three years before. The Foreign Secretary deployed a naval force larger than Nelson had needed to win the Battle of the Nile.

The massive new influx of Jews affected parliament in three ways – two relatively unimportant, but the other rather more so. The less important results were that a very few constituencies in the country could theoretically be won now if the Jewish electors voted as a body, which they seldom did. Seats like Whitechapel and Leeds North East could muster substantial numbers of Jewish electors. Another result was that the Jewish community was now represented by a total number of MPs more in line with its own size. It had been thought in Jewish circles that for six MPs to represent 35,000 people was likely to be considered excessive.

The more important result was a steadily more vociferous call as years went by for parliamentary legislation to reduce the flood of immigrants to a number which people believed could be more easily absorbed. There were demands for an Aliens Act. Many Jews did come to Britain to improve their economic prospects, but then they always had. The seventeenth-century influx from Holland might have been seeking sanctuary but most Ashkenazi Jews from Europe had come to better themselves. Now, however, a lot of the Jewish immigrants were definitely refugees and the community was torn in its emotions towards them. On the one hand, they wanted to help their persecuted brethren; on the other, they feared the newcomers would undermine their carefully nurtured image of solid, respectable British citizenry. The new migrants were foreign, mostly Yiddish speaking, unaccustomed to British cultural norms, and very poor.

They therefore posed several threats to Jews already established in Britain. First, they spoiled the image that the Jewish community had been trying to foster for over 200 years of being more English than the English. Most veteran Jews aped their local neighbours, hoping to achieve a lower profile as a result. If their heads didn't appear above the parapet, there was less likelihood that anti-Semites would take a potshot at them. Second, the newcomers aroused discord among their neighbours as rents rose where they lived, when demand for housing, no matter how defective, outstripped supply.

Third, they were prepared to work for very little, just to keep body and soul together. As a consequence, accusations of undercutting wages were soon to be put about by the press and workers' leaders. The accusations were true, in that Jewish immigrants would work for a pittance to stay alive. But it was not true that this would greatly affect the local work force because the Jews normally worked in industries where there was little Christian expertise at the time, tailoring and cigar making being just two examples. This didn't stop the agitation for parliament to act to prevent more immigration.

Fourth, the high standard of religious observance of a sizeable proportion of the newcomers put a critical spotlight on the steadily declining standards of the veteran community. Worse, from the immigrants' point of view, the leadership of that veteran community allowed lapses in observance which would debar them from office in more religious circles. Many of the newcomers would set up far more observant congregations. Their criticism of the standards of observance of the veteran community might be considered an attempt to prove their superiority in at least spiritual, if not financial, matters. The fact was that many of them did observe far more of the rules laid down in the Talmud.

The *Jewish Chronicle* was itself concerned about the standard of observance of Jewish MPs. In 1885 it said:

> Every movement and every vote of theirs will be identified with the community, and the latter morally held responsible for their public acts . . . What if it should be our misfortune to be represented by men only nominally Jews . . . without Jewish feeling, and without Jewish convictions . . . Would it not be better for the Jewish community not to have any of its members in Parliament than to be represented by men of this kind.

It was a consideration, and the point could also have been made that Russell's Parliamentary Reform Bill had been passed in 1866 by five votes, and all six Jewish MPs had voted for it.

After the death of Sir Moses Montefiore in 1884, Nathaniel Rothschild became the head of the Jewish community, just as the refugees started to arrive in large numbers. The serving Jewish MPs were still mainly drawn from the Cousinhood; they would all support the community's charitable endeavours to help the immigrants but they too usually wanted to discourage more from coming. It wasn't easy for the core 35,000 Jews, most of whom were, themselves, relatively or even very poor, to find the funds that were often desperately needed.

By contrast, the leadership of the immigrant Jews in the East End was totally fragmented. Initially, they had organized themselves into small communities linked to the towns from which they originally came. There then emerged an MP who would lead them against the Cousinhood, even though he belonged to it. This was Samuel Montagu, and he would serve as Liberal MP for Whitechapel, in the heart of London's East End, from 1885 to 1900. The opposition to Montagu from the embattled leadership of the community was headed by Rothschild.

It wasn't just a question of religion or leadership of the community. Rothschild had left the Liberal Party over the question of Home Rule for Ireland in 1886. He didn't agree with Gladstone's efforts to secure the measure and other Jewish MPs followed his lead. Montagu, on the other hand, remained closely allied to Gladstone. Even though Montagu was an early Zionist, the Turks ruled in the Holy Land and Gladstone hated the Turks for the massacres of Christians in Bulgaria. The Conservative Prime Minister, Lord Salisbury, thought differently. He was more concerned about thwarting Russian ambitions to take over from the Turks and particularly to gain access for the Russian fleet through the Dardanelles into the Mediterranean. Salisbury supported the Ottoman Empire and Rothschild supported Salisbury.

Another cause of dissension between Montagu and Rothschild was their differing views on the best way to finance the country's trade. Samuel was a bullion merchant and Rothschild was a banker. Samuel wanted cheap money to help the British economy expand. Rothschild was content with Britain only using gold as its standard specie. This meant in the 1880s that trading with countries that used silver as well as gold was more difficult. Interest rates tended to fluctuate and while this was no problem for bankers, it could play havoc with trade.

Chancellors of the Exchequer from both political parties would seek Montagu's expert advice. Gladstone had another reason for keeping in with the bullion merchant. Montagu was one of the comparatively few very rich men left in the party after the split over Home Rule. Montagu helped finance the Liberals from that time. The battle within the Jewish community, plus the differing views over bimetallism, led to Rothschild trying to unseat Montagu in

Whitechapel and the united approach of the Jewish MPs in the community coming under considerable strain.

In 1905, the future prospects of the Conservative Party were looking bleak. The government needed to pass measures which they considered to be in the country's interest and which would be popular into the bargain. The Aliens Act, in their opinion, fitted both criteria, so after the measure had been discussed for years without reaching a conclusion, a bill was proposed. Nobody was in much doubt that one of the bill's main objectives was to reduce the flow of Jewish immigrants into the country. Equally, the government knew that pogroms were continuing against the Jews in Eastern Europe and that Britain was one of the only countries where they could seek sanctuary.

The Jewish MPs were particularly aware that this was the case: when the bill came up for its third reading, how were they to vote? Four voted to approve the bill – Herbert Jessel (Unionist – St Pancras South), Francis Lucas (Conservative – North Suffolk, and the son of the vice-president of the United Synagogue), Harry Marks (Conservative – Thanet, and the son of the minister of the main Reform Synagogue) and Gustav Wolff (Conservative – Belfast East). Four voted against the bill – Maurice Levy (Liberal – Loughborough), Herbert Samuel (Liberal – Cleveland), Stuart Samuel (Liberal – Whitechapel, and the successor to his uncle, Sir Samuel Montagu) and Louis Sinclair – (Conservative, Romford). So seven of the eight MPs voted for their parties. Only Louis Sinclair refused to support the government. Four abstained – Ben Cohen (Conservative – Islington East), Rufus Isaacs (Liberal – Reading), Walter Rothschild (Unionist – Bucks, and the son of the president of the United Synagogue) and Edward Sassoon (Unionist – Hythe). Three were effectively Conservatives but balked at the measure. One was a Liberal with a glittering career ahead of him.

It was a bill which addressed the crunch question: would you vote for what your party thought was best for the country or would you put the interests of your co-religionists first, particularly as they were in dire peril? Since what was at stake was not imperilling the nation – the provisions of the Aliens Bill would be used very sparingly – the pressure on those who supported or abstained on the measure must have been great indeed.

Jewish MPs elected between 1880 and 1906 were:

1880 **Arthur Cohen, Benjamin Cohen,** Farrer Herschel, Nathan Rothschild, John Simon, **Sydney Woolf, Henry de Worms** (all Liberal except Sydney Woolf and Henry de Worms, Conservative)

1880   Julian Goldsmid (Liberal)

1882   **Lewis Isaacs** (Conservative)

1885   Arthur Cohen (Liberal), **Lionel Cohen** (Conservative), Julian Goldsmid (Liberal Unionist), Lewis Isaacs (Conservative), **Alfred Jacoby** (Liberal), **Samuel Montagu** (Liberal), John Simon (Liberal Unionist), Henry de Worms (Conservative)

1885   **Ferdinand de Rothschild** (Liberal Unionist)

1886   Arthur Cohen (Liberal), Lionel Cohen (Conservative), Julian Goldsmid (Liberal Unionist), Lewis Isaacs (Conservative), Alfred Jacoby (Liberal), Samuel Montagu (Liberal), Ferdinand Rothschild (Liberal Unionist), John Simon (Liberal Unionist), Henry de Worms (Conservative)

1891   **Herbert Leon** (Conservative), **Sydney Stern** (Conservative)

1892   Benjamin Cohen (Conservative), Julian Goldsmid (Liberal Unionist), Alfred Jacoby (Liberal), Herbert Leon (Conservative), Samuel Montagu (Liberal), Ferdinand de Rothschild (Liberal Unionist), Sydney Stern (Liberal), **Arthur Strauss** (Liberal), Henry de Worms (Conservative)

1892   **Gustav Wolff** (Conservative)

1895   Benjamin Cohen (Conservative), Julian Goldsmid (Liberal Unionist), Alfred Jacoby (Liberal), **Harry Marks** (Conservative), Samuel Montagu (Liberal), Ferdinand Rothschild (Liberal Unionist), **Harry Samuel** (Conservative), Arthur Strauss (Liberal Unionist), Gustav Wolff (Conservative), Henry de Worms (Conservative)

1896   **Herbert Jessel** (Liberal Unionist)

1897   **Louis Sinclair** (Conservative)

1898   **Sigismund Mendl** (Liberal)

1899   **Walter Rothschild** (Unionist), **Edward Sassoon** (Unionist)

1900   Benjamin Cohen (Conservative), Alfred Jacoby (Liberal), Herbert Jessel (Unionist), **Maurice Levy** (Liberal), **Francis Lucas** (Conservative), **Henry Norman** (Liberal), Walter Rothschild (Unionist), **Stuart Samuel** (Liberal), Edward Sassoon (Unionist), Louis Sinclair (Conservative), Gustav Wolff (Conservative)

1902   **Herbert Samuel** (Liberal)

1904   **Rufus Isaacs** (Liberal), Harry Marks (Conservative)

What sort of men had been elected to join the Old Guard?

ARTHUR COHEN 1830–1914

One of the eighteenth-century founders of the Jewish Cousinhood of influential families was Levi Barent Cohen, and Arthur Cohen was his grandson. The leader of British Jews for much of the nineteenth century was Sir Moses Montefiore; Cohen was his nephew. He was therefore well connected and expensively educated in Frankfurt and at University College London. When Cohen wanted to go on to Cambridge, however, he was turned down by both Trinity and Christ College because he was a Jew. Prince Albert, the Cambridge Chancellor, intervened to get him into Magdalene and he became president of the Union in 1852 and fifth wrangler in the Mathematics Tripos, but he still couldn't take his degree until 1860 when the Tests Act was repealed. Cohen must have been particularly pleased to be asked to become Counsel to the University in 1879, a position he held until his death thirty-five years later.

Cohen was called to the Bar in 1857, took silk in 1874 and was chairman of the Bar Council in 1893. When he was eligible for promotion to the higher courts, he was expected to pass through on the nod. Everybody liked Cohen, except the Lord Chief Justice, a Jew who had converted to Christianity and who made the decisions. It was sourly joked at the time that all the LCJ would give Cohen was a Pass-over. Cohen never became a High Court judge, though as a great international lawyer he represented his country in a number of important cases, notably the Geneva Arbitration and the USS *Alabama* compensation dispute.

Communally, he played a full part as president of the Board of Deputies from 1880 to 1895, at which point his daughter was felt to have let the side down by marrying out of the faith and Cohen resigned. 'I am sure I only did my duty in resigning', he wrote. He was also vice-chairman of the seminary, Jews' College, but was not re-elected to that office in 1901.

Discriminated against by both sides, Cohen made his own position clear in a 'beautifully modulated voice of extraordinary timbre'. He said, 'a man . . . must be of sluggish temper and dull of intellect who is not proud to own allegiance to a faith at once so ancient and so young'. Late in his life he was commended by the then Lord Chief Justice, Lord Alverston: 'There is no man more entitled to esteem and regard by reason of his high character and great abilities'. At over 70,

Cohen was still in harness, chairing the Royal Commission on Trade Unions in 1903 and the Shipping Commission in 1906. Cohen's parliamentary career was something of an interruption to his brilliant career as an advocate and administrator. He was elected in 1880 for Southwark and served until 1888. He died in 1914 at the age of 84.

BENJAMIN COHEN 1844–1909

Ben Cohen was another member of the Cousinhood, like Arthur Cohen a grandson of one of the founding fathers, Levi Barent Cohen. He was also a brother-in-law of Samuel Montagu. His father was an important pillar of the London Stock Exchange who specialized in foreign loans. Cohen was extremely active in Jewish community affairs, president of the Orphan Society and for thirteen years president of the Board of Guardians. He was also a vice-president of the United Synagogue and a warden of the prestigious Bayswater Synagogue. As early as 1865 he had founded the Stepney Jewish Schools at the request of the Chief Rabbi, Nathan Marcus Adler. In the wider context, he became a member of the London County Council in 1888 and represented the City of London until 1901. He also took a keen interest in one of the first Cambridge colleges for women, Newnham, and was one of their major benefactors.

With such a high profile, Cohen would have seemed an ideal candidate for the Conservative club, the Junior Carlton, but he was very conscious that, as a Jew, he might be blackballed. When, however, he was proposed by the Earl of Iddesleigh and seconded by Sir Stafford Northcote, Cohen sailed in. He died after a long illness only a few years later at the age of 65.

Ben Cohen's parliamentary career ended in a blaze of anything but glory. He was one of the four Conservative MPs who voted for the Aliens Act in 1905 and his East Islington seat was won by the Liberals at the general election shortly afterwards. The Jewish electors would not have been pleased with his vote; Balfour's government was facing defeat in 1905 in any case. The Aliens Act was a measure which it was hoped would be a vote winner, but it did them little good. Campbell-Bannerman was victorious in 1906 with a stunning 399 seats. The Conservatives lost 246, the worst result for them until 1997.

SYDNEY WOOLF 1844–1892

Sidney Woolf won Pontefract for the Conservatives in 1880, retired from the House in 1885 and was re-elected to the seat from 1892 to

1895. In 1890 he took silk. The family business was producing earthenware and they were major employers in the Pontefract area. In London, he was a member of the independent orthodox Western Synagogue. Woolf's lasting claim to fame was that he was the father-in-law of Virginia Woolf. He had nine children altogether before he died in 1892 at the early age of 48.

HENRY DE WORMS 1840–1903

When Worms stood for the Conservatives in 1867 he was roundly condemned in the Jewish press for supporting a party which had opposed emancipation. He lost – but won Greenwich in 1880 and represented Toxteth from 1885 to 1895. He was then created Lord Pirbright. Deeply involved in Jewish organizations, Worms was treasurer of the United Synagogue in 1872 during its very early days and vice-president from 1880 to 1882. He then rather spoiled his image within the community by attending the wedding of his daughter in a church as it was widely expected at the time that such a union would divorce the child from its parents. As a consequence, in 1886 Worms was forced to resign from his presidency of the prestigious Anglo-Jewish Association, a position he had held since 1873. To add insult to injury, he was not invited to join other Jewish leaders in offering loyal greetings to Edward VII on his accession to the throne. Pirbright was severely disgruntled – he was one of only a handful of Jewish peers at the time – and when he died in 1903, he left instructions that he was to be buried in a Christian cemetery.

Worms was a great-grandson of the founder of the Rothschild banking dynasty, Mayer Amschel Rothschild of Frankfurt. He was called to the Bar in 1863 and had gone on to become a tea planter and one of the most expert commodity merchants in the City. It was a sound qualification for his appointment as parliamentary secretary to the Board of Trade in 1885 and he also served as Under-Secretary to the Colonies from 1888 to 1892. He had a reputation as a bore, but if you were interested in his pet subjects, such as sugar bounties, he could be eloquent. Especially in 1888, when he served as the British plenipotentiary and president of the international conference on the topic. He left no male heir and his peerage died with him.

LEWIS ISAACS 1830–1908

Educated at the Royal Lancaster Grammar School and University College London, Lewis Isaacs was a notable architect. He started as the architect and surveyor for the Holborn Board of Works in London and designed the Holborn Town Hall, Holborn Viaduct Station, Paddington Baths and the East Library at Gray's Inn. He went on to obtain, among other commissions, the design of the Northumberland Avenue, Carlton and Coburg Hotels at a time when creating a new hotel was regarded as the peak of an architect's career.

Isaacs was elected Conservative member for the Walworth Division of Newington in 1882 and sat until 1892. He was a strong supporter of the fair trade movement and a founder of the 40th Middlesex Volunteer Corps. The Volunteers were somewhat like the Territorial Army today, and he served in the Corps for thirty years, retiring as a major. He was also Mayor of Kensington from 1902 to 1904; he died in 1908.

LIONEL COHEN 1838–1887

Lionel Cohen was Sir Benjamin's older brother, and was financed all his life by the profits from Louis Cohen and Co., bankers and brokers. The company was highly respected in matters of foreign trade but was eventually dissolved when it was overtaken by larger institutions. In his time, Cohen sat on Royal Commissions on the depression in trade, gold and silver, and endowed schools.

Both Lionel and Benjamin were also related to Henry de Worms, and Lionel's brother-in-law was Samuel Montagu. In communal matters, the Jewish establishment worked closely together. When he was only 27, Lionel had founded the Jewish Board of Guardians, which was designed to ameliorate poverty in the community. In 1870 he helped to bring all the major synagogues together by creating the United Synagogue organization. He felt it needed a Rothschild as president but he took the role of vice-president. He was known for his 'matchless energy, grasp of detail and power of original and constructive thought', wrote the *Jewish Chronicle*.

Cohen was particularly keen to see a Jewish boarding house attached to one of the good public schools. At the time, Clifton College in Bristol was seeking a charter. Cohen offered to help them to obtain it and when the charter was granted, the Jewish boarding house also came into being. He worked hard for the Conservative Party, serving as vice-president of the National Union of Conservative Associations. Like Nathan Rothschild, he was in favour of free trade and against Home Rule for Ireland. Lionel Cohen's political life was very brief. He was elected for Paddington South in 1885 and again in 1886. He died of a heart attack in 1887.

ALFRED JACOBY 1852–1909

Sir Alfred James Jacoby was Liberal MP for Mid Derbyshire from 1885 and was Member of Parliament for his constituency until his death in 1909. He was born of German Jewish stock but became a Unitarian. He was a lace manufacturer in Nottingham and served on its council for some years; he campaigned for Home Rule for Ireland. A conscientious MP, Jacoby worked hard to obtain an eight-hour day for the local Nottingham miners. In the Commons, he was for many years chairman of the Kitchen Department and much admired for the standard of food and drink available in its restaurants and bars. A reporter for the *New York Times* wrote at his death in 1909, 'Jacoby was the spoiled child of the House of Commons and for himself everybody loved him'. He left £52,000, nearly £4 million today.

SAMUEL MONTAGU 1832–1911

In many ways, Samuel Montagu was a one-off. To begin with, his real name was Montagu Samuel but he chose to use his names the other way round. Next, he was extremely religious, following all the rules. He befriended the refugees who fled from pogroms to the East End of London and persuaded the vast majority of the small communities to join together as a Federation of Synagogues. He wanted them to be a counterbalance to the growing socialist influence in the East End, and yet Montagu also supported East End trade unions, where the Jewish community was strongly represented.

A self-made man, Montagu was a bullion merchant and one of the most powerful individuals in the City. He was so experienced in many financial matters that chancellors from both political parties would seek his views, but he could also hold a Jewish refugee audience enthralled in his Whitechapel constituency because he could address them in the only language they all knew – Yiddish.

Montagu won Whitechapel consistently from 1885 to 1900, when he handed it over to his nephew, Stuart Samuel. He also helped the careers of his son, Edwin Montagu and his nephew, Herbert Samuel. As a Liberal, Montagu's influence in the party partially rested on his handsome contributions to party funds after the Liberals had split over Irish Home Rule. Many of their richer supporters went over to the other side.

Montagu was a powerful advocate of free trade and was particularly anxious to break down the barriers caused by different monetary systems internationally. Many nations only accepted gold as a reserve

currency while others accepted both gold and silver. Until gold started to be mined in South Africa there was often a shortage of the
metal, which led to fluctuations in interest rates and currencies. These
were bad for international trade as the manufacturer didn't know
what his goods would earn him in his own currency.

Within the Jewish community the immensely wealthy Montagu represented the poor but now numerous East End Jews against the far
smaller but considerably richer older community, led by Lord
Rothschild. Although Jewish MPs of all parties normally worked har-
moniously on matters affecting their own community, Rothschild vs
Montagu was an exception. His Lordship tried to unseat Montagu,
which he was fully entitled to do as a Conservative – Rothschild was a
banker who showed little concern for the effect of interest rates on
trade: high interest rates usually increase the profits for bankers.
Montagu was a Liberal who believed in the importance of free trade to
the nation and the two men clashed on religious, political and economic grounds. In 1907 Prime Minister Campbell-Bannerman made
Montagu a peer, and as Lord Swaythling he served in the Upper House
until his death in 1911 at 79.

FERDINAND DE ROTHSCHILD 1839–1898

When Nathan Rothschild went to the Lords in 1885 another member
of the family took over the Aylesbury seat for the next thirteen years.
This was Ferdinand James von Rothschild. He was born in France but
came from the Austrian branch of the family – hence the von. Indeed,
in the ranks of the Austrian nobility he held the hereditary title of
baron. Rothschild went to Cambridge and there became a friend of
the Prince of Wales. Shortly afterwards he moved from Vienna to
London and was known thereafter as Ferdinand de Rothschild.

In England, Ferdinand was a banker with the family firm and he married his cousin Evelina in 1866. Sadly their first son was stillborn and his
wife died the next day. In her memory Rothschild built, equipped and
endowed the Evelina Hospital for Sick Children in Fulham Palace Road
in South London, which is now part of the Guy's Hospital NHS Trust.
Ferdinand de Rothschild is best known for his great house, Waddesdon,
now owned by the National Trust; it looks like a sixteenth-century
French chateau and Rothschild filled it with Renaissance objets d'art. He
bequeathed these to the British Museum when he died in 1898, still in
harness as an MP. In Orthodox Jewish homes a small scroll is pinned to
the right-hand door of every room, containing an extract from the Bible.
There are no pinholes on the right-hand doors of Waddesdon.

HERBERT LEON 1850–1926

Before Bletchley Park became famous for housing the cryptographers who broke the German wartime codes, the house belonged to Sir Herbert (Sammy) Leon. Leon was the son of the founder of Leon Bros, a stock exchange firm headquartered in the West End of London. He went into the company, made a fortune dealing in stocks and shares and became its senior partner. He was also part proprietor of the *Daily News*. Leon was a good friend of David Lloyd George and was elected Liberal MP for North Bucks in a by-election in 1891. He won the seat again in 1892 but was beaten in 1895 and never stood again. He remained an ardent anti-socialist in retirement. He opened Bletchley Park for a Liberal rally in 1910 and from this emerged the annual Bletchley Show. In 1911 he was made a baronet by the grateful Liberals and decided to become Sir Herbert rather than Sir Sammy. His daughter married another Jewish MP, Sir Herbert Raphael.

Leon was a popular man in Buckinghamshire; he bred shorthorn cattle and chaired the county council finance committee. He was chairman of the Rationalist Press Association. He died in 1926 at 76 and left instructions that there were to be no prayers or flowers at his funeral, and that his ashes were to be scattered. Sir Herbert did not retain any connection with the Jewish community in later life.

SYDNEY STERN 1845–1912

Stern was the eldest son of Viscount de Stern of Portugal, which was remarkable as Jews had only been allowed to live in Portugal from 1800. His mother was a Goldsmid and he went into the family banking firm. No one could accuse Stern of not trying: he was beaten in elections for parliament in 1880, 1884, 1885 and 1886. He finally won Stowmarket as an Independent in 1892 but only stayed in the Commons for three years before being elevated to the House of Lords as Baron Wandsworth. He left his house as a home for aged Jews and it is now known as Nightingale House. Stern was an extremely charitable man and when he died he left over £1.5 million – over £1 million of which went to charity. A keen sailor, Stern was a member of the Royal Yacht Squadron. He was unmarried and died in 1912 at the age of 66.

ARTHUR STRAUSS 1847–1920

Arthur Strauss was the son of a Mayence immigrant and his father sent him to university in Germany. He became a tin merchant in

Cornwall, eventually operating several smelting works; he introduced the tin ticketing machine, which was a boon for his miners. Strauss was a Unionist, first elected to the House for Camborne from 1895 to 1900. He lost his seat but was elected in January 1910 as the member for Paddington North. In that contest the main opposition was from a newly formed 'League of Gentlemen' who made little secret of being anti-Semitic. Strauss stood for the seat again as an Independent Liberal in 1918 but was not successful. He died in 1920 at the age of 73.

GUSTAV WOLFF 1834–1913

Jewish immigrants arrived in Britain throughout the nineteenth century. At the time of the Great Exhibition in 1851, Prince Albert appointed his university friend, Chief Rabbi Nathan Marcus Adler, to the Exhibition organizing committee. In the same year, Mr and Mrs Moritz Wolff arrived in Liverpool. Their son, Gustav, went to college in the city and was apprenticed as an engineer. In 1860, he met Edward Harland and was asked to become the manager of the Queen's Island Shipping Yard, which Harland was buying. The price was £5,000 but at that time the yard only employed 200 men. Wolff accepted the offer and, after two years, persuaded Harland to take him on as a partner. Wolff was dynamic and the renamed company, Harland and Wolff, went from strength to strength. One of Wolff's major coups was a deal to build all the ships for the White Star Line. This was very lucrative business and when Wolff eventually died in 1913 the company had 15,000 employees. Shortly after he retired in 1908 Harland and Wolff built the *Titanic*.

In 1892 Wolff stood for parliament as Conservative for Belfast East. Because he was highly regarded as an employer he won the seat easily and represented the constituency for the next eighteen years. He even retained it in the 1906 election when the Conservative Party was routed by the Liberals. In those five elections, Wolff was unopposed every time. Wolff died in 1913 at nearly 80. He was active in the House up to the age of 76. He never married but was elected a member of the Carlton Club, the Junior Carlton and the Garrick, which were every bit as comfortable as a substantial residence. Wolff did a great deal for the Irish economy and was influential in developing their rope industry. When he died, the flag flew at half mast on Belfast Town Hall.

HARRY MARKS 1855–1916

Harry Hananel Marks was the son of David Woolf Marks, the first rabbi of the 1840 breakaway West London Synagogue of British Jews. This became the first Reform synagogue many years later. The first Hananel was an eleventh-century rabbi who wrote a distinguished commentary on the Babylonian Talmud. Marks fils was educated at University College School and l'Athenée Royale in Brussels. He became a journalist, working in America from 1871 to 1883. Returning home and seeing a gap in the market, he founded and edited the *Financial News*. He served on the London County Council from 1887 to 1898 and was elected as Conservative member for the St George's division of Tower Hamlets in 1895. He retired from the House in 1900 but won Thanet in a by-election in 1904 and held it until 1910, when he decided to step down again.

Marks was a strong advocate of tariff reform and Colonial Preference. He was also in favour of curbing alien immigration, inevitably a contentious issue in his constituency. Indeed, his attacks on 'pauper aliens' were widely resented in the East End, but Thanet remained unaffected. During the First World War Marks joined the Buffs as a major when he was 59 but he died in 1916 at the age of 61.

HARRY SAMUEL 1853–1934

Harry Samuel's mother was a niece of Sir Moses Montefiore and thus definitely a member of the Cousinhood. Samuel went to Eastbourne College and St John's College, Cambridge. He joined the family firm of Montefiore and Co., and became a partner. In 1884 he decided to devote his life to public works and retired from the company. He also had a commission in the 1st Middlesex Volunteers, Royal Engineers. Samuel was in business at a time when British manufacturing was under increasing pressure from overseas competition. His well-publicized view was that if business was bad, wages had to come down. If the unions struck, he warned that this would force a lot of companies into bankruptcy. He was in favour of protecting home industries by import duties. Britain was, however, a major trading nation and retaliatory import duties by other countries would have damaged the British economy more than protection would underpin British firms.

Samuel was a Conservative Unionist, elected for Limehouse in 1895. He was knighted in 1903 but lost his seat in the Liberal landslide of 1906. It was said at the time that he was sadly missed. He recovered to win the Norwood division of Lambeth in the second election of 1910. He was made a Privy Councillor in 1916. He was elected to parliament as a Conservative for Limehouse in 1895 and stayed until 1906. Communally, Samuel was a warden of the main Reform synagogue, the West London Synagogue of British Jews, and vice-president of the Anglo-Jewish Association. He retired from the Commons in 1922 and died in 1934 at the age of 81.

HERBERT JESSEL 1866–1950

Herbert Jessel was the second son of George Jessel, Britain's first Jewish minister. He went to Rugby School and New College, Oxford and became a Captain in the 17th Lancers. He served in India from the ages of 21 to 24. He married within the Cousinhood, Maud, the fifth daughter of Sir Julian Goldsmid, so he was related to the House of Commons on two sides. He succeeded his father-in-law in 1895 in the St Pancras South seat and served the constituency until 1906 as a Unionist. He was re-elected in 1910 as a Conservative and remained the MP until 1918.

Jessel was a highly active parliamentarian. Notably, he carried the Old Age Pension Act through the Commons in 1911 and when he succeeded to the title of Lord Jessel in 1936, he steered the Road Traffic (Driving Licence) Act through the Lords. So if you have a pension or a driving licence, Jessel is one of your benefactors. As a trained soldier, Jessel spent the First World War in action and was mentioned in dispatches twice. He retired from the army as a colonel in 1919, and died in 1950. His son served as Deputy Speaker in the House of Lords from 1963 to 1977 but when he died in 1990, the title became extinct.

LOUIS SINCLAIR 1861–1928

Louis Sinclair was born in Paris and educated at University College School in London and on the continent, but by the time he was 17 he had taken himself off to Australia. Sinclair first worked for the *Melbourne Argus* but then got involved in sugar and railways to such good effect that he was able to retire at the age of 25. By 1897 he was back in London and was elected for Romford as a Conservative from 1897 to 1906. While he was in parliament, he formed the Commercial Committee of the House of Commons in 1899 and initiated Anglo-French parliamentary visits. This helped develop the 'Entente Cordiale' between Britain and France. When Sinclair lost his seat he continued to promote commercial committees in other

European capitals and eventually became the permanent honorary secretary of the Commercial International Parliamentary Congress. During the war, he served in the Royal Automobile Club Transport Service. He died at the age of 67 in 1928.

SIGISMUND MENDL 1866–1945

Sigismund Mendl did not sit in the House for long. Educated at Harrow and Trinity College, Oxford, he was initially a barrister. A Liberal, he was beaten in the 1892 and 1895 elections but was successful in 1898. He lost his Plymouth seat in 1900 and made no attempt to become an MP again. Mendl eventually became a grain merchant and between 1909 and 1912 and again from 1915 to 1919 was president of the London Corn Trade Association. His ships, *Nina* and *Rosina*, were familiar sights off the coast of Cornwall. He served on the War Office Advisory Commission on War Contracts from 1915 to 1918, when he was knighted. Afterwards he continued a highly successful business career until he died in harness in 1945 when nearly 80. As chairman of the National Discount Company he reported to the shareholders only a few months previously that deposits had reached £81 million (equivalent to £2.4 billion today).

WALTER ROTHSCHILD 1868–1937

Walter Rothschild, in due course the second Lord Rothschild, represented Aylesbury – where else? – from 1899 to 1910. Rothschilds would represent Aylesbury for nearly sixty years, from 1865 to 1923. Walter was Nathaniel's son and took over the family seat when his uncle Ferdinand died. Walter went to Magdalen College, Cambridge, which was then one of the smartest colleges, both academically and socially. He went on to work for the family bank for ten years but developed a great interest in zoology.

Rothschild was the author of numerous scientific papers. He went on an expedition around the world to find new species and funded research into lesser-known species. He was fascinated by the cassowary, which is a large, flightless Australasian bird, and had sixty-five specimens stuffed for £2,000 (the equivalent today of about £140,000). He knew how to popularize zoology, harnessing zebras to draw his carriage at home and occasionally driving them through London. There is still today a species of giraffe named after him – *Giraffa Camelopardis Rothschild*. He opened his zoo at Tring to the public in 1892, but in 1932 the unmarried Rothschild had to sell his enormous collection of birds to the American Museum of Natural History – partly because he was being blackmailed by an aristocratic former mistress. The rest of the collection is now the Walter Rothschild Zoological Museum, a division of the Natural History Museum, still located in Tring. He kept the cassowaries and they are still on display in the museum.

Rothschild kept up the original family allegiance to the Liberal Party. He was instrumental in encouraging the government to pass the Balfour Declaration in 1917. When some leaders of the Jewish community wrote to *The Times* condemning the idea, Rothschild and the Chief Rabbi replied with a letter of rebuttal warmly supporting it. It was indeed to Rothschild himself that Balfour eventually wrote, spelling out the government's commitment to a National Home for the Jews. Walter went to the Lords in 1915 when Nathaniel died, and passed away in 1937.

EDWARD SASSOON 1856–1912

The Sassoons were Jewish merchants who had gone to India from Persia. They made vast fortunes in the subcontinent and in the middle of the nineteenth century moved on to more sophisticated surroundings in London. Some became friends and financial supporters of Edward VII when he was Prince of Wales and having great difficulty in balancing his books. The Sassoons were very much part of the Marlborough House set which gathered round the future monarch. Edward Sassoon's father, Albert, was particularly close to the Prince.

Edward Sassoon, like his father, was a very religious man. He was from the ranks of the Sephardim who had first reached England in reasonable numbers during Cromwell's time. There had been very few Jews in England until then, though two of Queen Elizabeth's doctors were Jewish. Sassoon served as president of the Elders, the ruling committee of the Sephardim. He was also vice-president of the Jewish religious educational centre, Jews' College, and he was a strong supporter of the Anglo-Jewish Association. This was a body of rich Jews who set themselves up to represent their co-religionists and to do all they could for those communities overseas who were having trouble with their governments – which in Europe meant a large number. The AJA did much good work, but it was not a democratic organization.

Sassoon married Aline Caroline de Rothschild after he graduated from London University and served in the Middlesex Yeomanry (Duke of Cambridge's Hussars). With that background, it was no surprise that he succeeded in being selected for the Hythe constituency in 1899 on behalf of the Liberal Unionist Party. He would be its MP until he died in 1912 at the early age of 56. A family mausoleum 'in the Indian style' was built behind his house in Brighton, where Sassoon was buried, but it was emptied and sold in 1933. It is now a Private Members Club.

MAURICE LEVY 1859–1933

Maurice Levy was born in Leicester and was 'privately educated' before becoming a student at University College London. He became chairman of Hart and Levy, wholesale clothiers and woollen merchants in London. It was just the sort of company that benefited enormously from the influx of refugee Jews who scratched a living out of the tailoring industry; Hart and Levy provided the cloth.

Levy divided his life between London and Leicestershire. He was elected Liberal MP for Loughborough in 1900 and remained in the House until 1918. He vigorously opposed the Aliens Act in 1905, but to no avail. He was knighted in 1907. During the First World War he served in the Ministry of Munitions and after he lost his seat, he became High Sheriff of Leicestershire from 1920 to 1927. He was always very much a Leicester man and enjoyed hunting and shooting even though he wasn't 'to the manor born'. Although he was a member of the New West End Synagogue, he left instructions that he was to be cremated, which is not permitted according to Orthodox Jewish law. He died at the age of 74 in 1933, not a good year for past and present Jewish MPs since Sir Philip Magnus and Bertram Straus died in the same year.

FRANCIS LUCAS 1850–1918

Francis Lucas was the Conservative Unionist member for Lowestoft from 1900 to 1906. He was deputy chairman of the Alliance Assurance Company and a keen supporter of the Victorian Army Volunteers. Lucas spent forty-one years in the reserve forces, including six as the commander of the Harwich Volunteer Brigade from 1900 to 1906. He was the son of the vice-president of the United Synagogue and played a full part in communal affairs. He was treasurer of the Jewish Board of Guardians for twenty years and served on the committee of the Jews' Free School. He was standing for Kennington in the 1918 election when he developed influenza on the hustings, dying of heart failure at the age of 68.

HENRY NORMAN 1858–1939

Henry Norman was born in Leicester and studied theology and philosophy at Leipzig and Harvard Universities. He became a journalist and spent years in the east. From 1892, he was the Assistant Editor of the *Daily Chronicle*. In 1900 he stood for Wolverhampton South as a Liberal, won and held the seat until 1910. From then until 1923 he sat for Blackburn and in 1915 he was knighted. In 1918 he became a Privy Councillor. One other field in which Norman specialized was wireless telegraphy where he was a real pioneer. He died in 1939 at the age of 81. He had little contact with the Jewish community.

STUART SAMUEL 1856–1926

The obituarist in the *Sunday Times* wrote of Stuart Samuel, 'A man of sweeter nature or of broader sympathies I never met'. He contrasted this width of vision with another element of Samuel's character: 'One of the most Orthodox Jews I ever met'. That was Stuart Samuel, following his faith at all times but equally concerned for others. Samuel was the brother of Herbert Samuel. He went to University College School but joined the family bullion business at an early age. When his uncle, Samuel Montagu, gave up the Whitechapel seat, he saw to it that his nephew succeeded him and Samuel sat for the constituency for almost all of sixteen years. The gap occurred when a common informer accused him of voting in the House on a bill when his firm had the task of buying silver for the Indian government. By an old Act, this was illegal and a select committee of the Privy Council ruled that he had to relinquish the seat. He won the by-election which resulted. In court, however, he was fined £25,000 (over £1.5 million today). The case came up at the time of the Marconi scandal (see below the entries for Herbert Samuel and Rufus Isaacs) in which his brother was involved, and which could well have been a factor.

Communally, there was hardly a Jewish charity in which Samuel did not take an interest. He held office for the Jewish Deaf and Dumb Home, the Jewish Working Men's Club and the Jewish Homes for Incurables and he became president of the Board of Deputies. This last appointment was after the former president's unauthorized opposition to the Balfour Declaration led to his repudiation by the Deputies and his resignation. Samuel wasn't a Zionist either, which tended to prove that lack of consultation, rather than Zionist fervour, had swayed a lot of the Deputies. Samuel was a member of the independent Orthodox Western Synagogue and highly regarded throughout the community. He died in 1926, at the age of 70.

HERBERT SAMUEL 1870–1963

When Herbert Samuel was made a peer, he became Viscount Samuel of Carmel and Toxteth, the former in the Holy Land and the latter in Liverpool. For his motto he chose: 'Turn not aside'. Those choices summed him up perfectly. Samuel was born in Toxteth and educated at University College School in London and Balliol College, Oxford where he gained a first-class degree. He was the son of Samuel Montagu's brother, so the family bullion firm made it unnecessary for him to work for a living. He could devote himself to working in the public interest and he was elected Liberal MP for Cleveland in 1902. He won the seat in every election until 1918. Stuart Samuel, his cousin, was an MP and Jack Brunel Cohen would marry Stuart Samuel's daughter and be elected for Liverpool Fairfield after the First World War. Another cousin, Edwin Montagu, Samuel Montagu's son, was also in the Cabinet for a number of years. The family were certainly well represented, though on political grounds they didn't always see eye to eye.

Samuel became Under-Secretary at the Home Office when the Liberals won power and introduced an important bill to protect minors from exploitation which became known as the Children's Charter. In 1909 he was made Chancellor of the Duchy of Lancaster by Prime Minister Asquith, and became a Privy Councillor. In 1910 he was appointed Postmaster General.

Herbert Samuel was not religious but his wife was devout, so the family attended synagogue regularly and Samuel went on high holy-days. But not being an observant Jew was no protection against anti-Semitism. In 1912, the Marconi Company was awarded a wireless station contract. A government committee had recommended Marconi as the favoured supplier and Samuel's permanent secretary had advised him to approve the recommendation. The problem was that Rufus Isaacs and David Lloyd George had bought shares in the American parent company just before the details of the contract were announced. They were accused of insider trading, but Samuel's name was dragged in solely because he was a Jew. He had not bought shares and only acted on advice. It was a thoroughly nasty and groundless accusation, as was eventually accepted.

In 1916 Samuel was made Home Secretary but when the Liberals split as Lloyd George ousted Asquith, Samuel didn't turn aside from his old leader. He was offered a ministry by Lloyd George but refused to serve under him. When the 1918 election took place, like most of the Asquithians, he lost his seat, but he wasn't out of work for long. In 1920, he was invited to become the first High Commissioner for Palestine. He served in that position for five years and, in trying to reconcile the irreconcilable, was criticized by both sides but acted with firm fairness.

Back in Britain, he wanted to retire but agreed to chair important government enquiries. He regained his appetite for politics and won Darwen for the Liberals in 1929. In 1931, the Liberal leader Lloyd George was ill and Samuel was consulted by George V on what kind of government would be best for the country in the depths of the Slump. Other leaders recommended either a Conservative or a Labour administration, but the King felt Samuel made a better case for a National Government and he invited Ramsay Macdonald to form one.

Samuel led the Liberals from 1931 to 1935 and was made a Viscount in 1937. He supported Chamberlain's policy of appeasement in the hope of avoiding another world war. He became well known during the war as a member of the Brains Trust, a highly popular radio programme at the time. Samuel led the Liberal Party in the House of Lords from 1944 to 1955 and presided over the dinner in 1956 to mark the tercentenary of the Jews being allowed to return to live in England. Lord Hill, an excellent speaker in the Lords, described Samuel's contributions as 'serene, wise and witty'. On one occasion, a Tory peer paused while delivering a long and tedious speech and observed, 'The noble Viscount opposite appears to be asleep'. Samuel opened one eye and said 'Unfortunately not'! Samuel died at 93, in 1963.

RUFUS ISAACS 1860–1935

The first Attorney General to sit in the Cabinet, Lord Chief Justice, Viceroy of India, the British Ambassador to the United States, Lord Warden of the Cinque Ports, Foreign Secretary and Leader of the Liberal Party, Rufus Isaacs was the a son of a fruit merchant in London's Spitalfields market. He also finished up as a marquis – the highest rank in the peerage ever reached by a Jew. Yet Isaacs started as a runaway ship's boy when he was 16, going on to work in the Stock Exchange in his early 20s. In the meantime, he had attended both Brussels and Hanover Universities. He then studied hard at Law and was called to the Bar when he was 27.

A high-profile legal case of 1904 established Isaacs' career. An individual named Whitaker Wright was accused of promoting gold mines of doubtful value, and when charged with fraud, Isaacs prosecuted. The case received tremendous publicity and Isaacs won with the help of a biased judge (whose behaviour presumably made it more difficult for the defence to convince the jury); Whitaker Wright got seven years and immediately took cyanide to avoid the sentence. It was also in 1904 that Isaacs stood for the Liberals in a by-election in Reading, which he won, going on to represent the constituency for the next nine years.

In 1906 the Liberals finally won office and Campbell-Bannerman offered Rufus Isaacs the post of Solicitor General. He accepted, giving up what was then the largest practice at the Bar. He was appointed Attorney General in 1912 and became the first holder of that office to sit in the Cabinet. Isaacs was one of the major players in the Liberal Cabinet but his career was nearly ruined in 1912 when he was involved in a scandal about alleged insider trading. It was said that he bought shares in a Marconi company when he knew that a subsidiary was about to win a major government contract; David Lloyd George was also involved. The arguments raged indecisively and when everything calmed down accusations of a whitewash by the government were pretty widespread, but there was no prosecution.

In 1913 Isaacs was appointed Lord Chief Justice and retained that position even though he went to America as British Ambassador from 1918 to 1919, primarily to conduct some delicate negotiations. He was 61 years old when he resigned as Lord Chief Justice to become Viceroy of India. In 1922, he was again involved in controversy when he imprisoned Mahatma Gandhi for disobedience. Isaacs served five years as Viceroy before returning home. In the Macdonald National Government of 1931 Isaacs served as Foreign Secretary for three months, with Anthony Eden as his under-secretary, but his health worsened and he stood down. Isaacs died at 75, in 1935.

There can be no question that Isaacs lent lustre to the Jewish community of his time. He was also anxious to do what he could to help the Zionist cause. In collaboration with Alfred Mond and Herbert Samuel, both of whom had also received peerages, he was a founding chairman of what has become the Israel Electric Corporation. The Reading power station in Tel Aviv is named after him. Altogether, a remarkable life: first Marquis, GCB, GCSI, GCVO, PC, KC.

The Liberals won by a landslide in 1906 and with a manifesto which promised major changes in the way the country was run. Eighteen Jewish MPs were elected, the largest number ever, of whom only three were Conservatives. Two more won by-elections soon after. The government had a majority in the Commons of over 300 but Tory peers dominated the House of Lords. Over the next four years the Lords rejected every major piece of legislation that had been passed in the House of Commons. This eventually led to constitutional crisis and a reduction in the powers of the Lords.

For Jewish MPs, a prime concern was the effect of the Aliens Act which the Balfour government had passed during its last year in office. Many had voted for it in spite of the fact that the main object of the bill was to reduce the volume of Jewish immigration. Their co-religionists needed a safe haven, but many of the Jewish MPs considered it was in the social and economic interests of their country to remove the United Kingdom as a possible choice for the refugees. As a result of the bill, there was a decline in the number of Jews entering the UK, but, if you had been guaranteed a job and were in good health, there was still an excellent chance of finding refuge.

It was in the aftermath of the Liberal landslide of 1906 that Jewish MPs started to make real progress up the greasy pole of politics. Two of them – cousins Herbert Samuel and Edwin Montagu – would become members of the Cabinet and seriously important politicians. But it has to be remembered that their national responsibilities would be of far greater importance to them in the future than their involvement in questions of major interest to the Jewish community. Montagu's performance as Minister of Munitions in 1916 affected the country far more than his opposition to the Balfour Declaration. Herbert Samuel, as Home Secretary, did more important work than he did as High Commissioner for Palestine in the 1920s. Jewish politicians recognized where their responsibilities lay.

It was also during this period that more Jewish members were elected who came from outside the Cousinhood. The most powerful families in the community still provided the majority of Jewish MPs – Rothschild, Sassoon, Samuel et al. – but Rufus Isaacs, the Strausses and Charles Henry came from outside the magic circle. The problem for anyone other than a wealthy individual remained the necessity of private means in order to support himself as a Member of Parliament. It was also at this time that MPs began to receive payment.

In 1908, to mark the fiftieth anniversary of the passing of the Oath Act, a major dinner was arranged to which leaders of the political parties were invited. Asquith, the Prime Minister, couldn't attend, but sent his congratulations. Nor could Balfour, Leader of the Conservative opposition, but who said in his letter regretting his absence,

> Every one of the 50 years which have elapsed since 1858 has given us fresh proof – if fresh proof were necessary – of the patriotism, the generosity and the public spirit of the great community who in that year were too tardily admitted to the full rights of citizenship.

In August 1911, 250 years after Charles II officially allowed the Jews to live in England again, those who had always proclaimed that anti-Jewish riots could happen in Britain had their one and only piece of positive evidence. There were, in fact, two instances in Wales – one in Tredegar and another up the road in Ebbw Vale. In Tredegar, the disturbances took place on the Saturday and Sunday nights of 19 and 20 August. Eighteen Jewish-owned shops were looted. The town had been going through desperate economic times and some Jewish landlords were widely regarded as charging exorbitant rents for their poor tenants. In addition, some of the Jews who owned factories were accused of paying in tokens which could only be used in company shops – the infamous 'truck system'.

There were far more important reasons for the economic deprivation of the areas concerned, but on this occasion the Jews were made the scapegoats by the rioters. The largest non-Jewish employer in the town reported to the Home Office, 'I know of no other reason other than this [rack renting] which would give rise to the feeling against the Jews, many of whom are respectable citizens and who have been in business in Tredegar for very many years'. The Chief Constable wrote later, 'The present state of general unrest is too favourable an opportunity to be missed for attacking the Jews. The advance in prices owing to the railway strike has also caused ill feeling.'

During the looting, no Jews were hurt but many Jewish families left their homes to shelter in the houses of non-Jewish friends, who were horrified at the disturbances and supportive of their neighbours. Unlike Russia, where the police would often stand by and watch – and sometimes lend a hand – the local magistrates did their duty, read the Riot Act and called out the troops to help the police. The constabulary waded in with their batons, much to the disgust of one councillor, a Miners' Federation sponsored representative, who said the police were too brutal. But then it had happened before, only that was thirty years previously when Catholics were the ones accused of disturbing the peace of the workers by undercutting wages. On Monday 21 August troops of the Worcester Regiment arrived in Tredegar from Cardiff to keep order, and so on Tuesday the looters moved and started again a few miles up the road in Ebbw Vale. That outbreak was halted by the same force. Come the weekend it was all over.

It didn't, of course, prevent one publication – the *Jewish World* – appearing with a blazing headline: 'An All-British pogrom in South Wales', though that wasn't the general reaction. Most Jewish and non-Jewish pundits fell over backwards to protest that the riot was not even anti-Semitic. They insisted that it was just a coincidence that all the Christian shops had their windows broken and all the Jewish shops were looted. The Jewish victims received a lot of sympathy locally but at least one of their leaders was less supportive. Lord Rothschild, when asked to approach the government during the riots, said of his co-religionists, 'They are a bad lot and probably deserve what they are getting'. The Tredegar Council agreed to set aside £12,500 as restitution, though only £6,000 was eventually needed. At Ebbw Vale the sum was slightly larger at £7,500, adding 1p to the rates. All the authorities behaved impeccably throughout. It is no wonder that very Orthodox Jews still refer to Britain as the Kingdom of Mercy.

Throughout this period the number of British Jews who supported the Zionist aim of obtaining a National Home for the Jews was increasing. Even so, it was an uphill struggle. The majority of the leaders of the community shunned Zionism as a distraction, the support of which could cast doubt on their loyalty to Britain. In the early days just about the only Jewish public figure on the side of Theodor Herzl, the founder of the movement, was the spiritual head of the small Sephardi community, Moses Gaster. But then Gaster was born in Romania and knew from first-hand experience how badly a permanent refuge was needed.

The government did discuss with Herzl the possibility of a National Home in Uganda, but the idea fizzled out. Zionism was actively frowned upon in the major Jewish organizations such as the Board of Deputies and the Anglo-Jewish Association. Only about 5 per cent of the community were active Zionists at the outbreak of the First World War.

When the Great War broke out, many Jews flocked to the colours, but for many members of the community there was a serious snag. They were being asked to fight on the side of an alliance which included the Russians. The refugee element of the Jewish population had excellent reasons for hating the Russians. Literally hundreds of thousands of Russian Jews died between 1880 and 1920 as a result of the enormities of both Czarist and Bolshevik Russia. They would far rather have fought alongside the Turks, who had always treated their Jewish subjects very well, but who were now on the opposite side. Many Jews had become Bolsheviks solely to oppose the Czar, though others supported the Communist philosophy. This led to general accusations that all the Jews were Bolsheviks, an accusation as stupid as the blood libels of centuries past. Anti-Semites have never been very interested in logical arguments.

Of more importance from the government's point of view was the fact that American Jewry felt the same way as the Jews in the East End of London. American Jewry also had good reason to hate the Russians, and in 1916 President Wilson was dithering about whether to come into the war on the Allied side or to stay neutral. It was at this point – and with the war going extremely badly – that Balfour, the Foreign Secretary in the Coalition Government, took soundings on whether it would help to sway American opinion if the Jews were promised a National Home in Palestine when the Allies won.

As ever, the Jewish MPs were no more united in their opinion on this topic than they were on any other subject. Edwin Montagu, for example, was very much against the proposition. He felt that to support such a move would raise doubts as to whether the Jewish community was loyal to Britain or to a home in Palestine. Lord Rothschild, the unofficial head of the community, was in favour. He had just inherited the title from his father in 1915 and was concerned that the heads of the two major Jewish organizations – the Board of Deputies and the Anglo-Jewish Association – had written to *The Times* opposing the idea. Rothschild felt that it should have been discussed with him first and he didn't want to set a precedent of Rothschild views being ignored, now that his father was dead.

When the Board of Deputies met to be asked to ratify their president's letter, they narrowly defeated the proposition. They explained that this was not because they were Zionists – very few were – but because they, too, had not been consulted before the letter was written! With the opposition of the Board of Deputies neutralized and Rothschild and the Chief Rabbi coming down in favour, Balfour made the Declaration and sent it in writing to Rothschild.

Jewish MPs elected between between 1906 and 1918 were:

1906 **Charles Henry** (Liberal and Labour), Rufus Isaacs (Liberal), **Arthur Lever** (Liberal), Maurice Levy (Liberal), **Philip Magnus** (Unionist), Harry Marks (Conservative), **Edwin Montagu** (Liberal), **Alfred Mond** (Liberal), **Horatio Myer** (Liberal), Henry Norman (Liberal), **Herbert Raphael** (Liberal), Walter Rothschild (Liberal), Herbert Samuel (Liberal), Stuart Samuel (Liberal), Edward Sassoon (Unionist), **Bertram Strauss** (Liberal), **Edward Strauss** (Liberal), Gustav Wolff (Conservative)

Jan   **Charles Goldman** (Conservative), **Frank Goldsmith** (Conservative)

1910 Charles Henry (Liberal and Labour), Rufus Isaac (Liberal), Herbert Jessel (Liberal Unionist), Maurice Levy (Liberal), **Ignatius Trebitsch-Lincoln** (Liberal), Philip Magnus (Unionist), Alfred Mond (Liberal), Edwin Montagu (Liberal), Henry Norman (Liberal), Herbert Raphael (Liberal), **Lionel Rothschild** (Unionist), Harry Samuel (Unionist), Herbert Samuel (Liberal), Stuart Samuel (Liberal), Edward Sassoon (Unionist), **Arthur Strauss** (Unionist), Edward Strauss, (Liberal)

Dec   All the MPs elected in January 1910 were returned in the December 1910 election except Trebitsch-Lincoln. The only newcomer was **Felix Cassel** (Conservative)

1911 **Leopold Amery** (Conservative), **Maurice de Forest** (Conservative)

1912 **Philip Sassoon** (Unionist)

1913 **Sam Samuel** (Unionist)

1916 **Percy Harris** (Liberal)

CHARLES HENRY 1860–1919

Charles Henry was an Australian, born in Adelaide, but his family came to England and he was educated at St Marylebone School, King's College London and the University of Göttingen. The family business was metal broking. Henry was highly patriotic. In 1914, at the outbreak of the First World War, he had a ship loaded with copper berthed in a German port. He brought it back to London and sold the contents to the government at the pre-war price, losing £60,000 pounds on the deal (£4 million today).

Elected as Liberal MP for Wellington in 1906, Henry served the constituency until 1918 when he won the Wrekin. During the war the government used his expertise to negotiate supplies of metal in Sweden and other neutral countries. He equipped a home for wounded soldiers in Berkshire at his own expense. He was knighted in 1916. Henry was also president of the Jewish Soup Kitchen but refused to provide support for Russian emigrant Jews who wouldn't volunteer for the army.

A committed anti-Zionist, after the Balfour Declaration Henry became treasurer of the League of British Jews, which opposed the Zionist lobby. He was also on the council of the Anglo-Jewish Association and a member of the South Hackney Synagogue. His ashes are buried at the Willesden cemetery. Henry lost his only son in battle and never fully recovered from the blow. When he died in 1919 at the age of 59 there was an article in the *London Evening News* which summed up the public's feeling towards him: 'When I hear people abusing Jews, I always think of Sir Charles Henry and wish there were more of them.'

ARTHUR LEVER 1860–1924

Arthur Lever was yet another ex-University College schoolboy who became a Jewish MP. It was always a good school but its attraction for Jewish parents was that it allowed boys to practise their religion in peace without problems about taking time off school for the Sabbath or attending chapel. Its forward-looking attitude reflected in part the considerable financial support the school had received from the Cousinhood at its foundation.

Lever's original name was Levy. He was elected as a National Liberal for Harwich in 1906 but lost the seat in January 1910. He was made a baronet in 1911 and won Hackney Central in 1922. During the war he was with the Royal Fusiliers in France from 1917, having served as the deputy director for recruiting in the South East Region; he left the service with the rank of colonel. Now Colonel Sir Arthur Levy Lever, he served on the London War Pensions Committee and retired in 1923, dying in 1924 at the age of 64. He took no part in Jewish affairs, and his family firm was Levy & Hart, clothing manufacturers in Leicester.

PHILIP MAGNUS 1842–1933

An elite university education is an excellent way to produce the future leaders that a country requires, but there is equally a need to help those who are less academically gifted. Sir Philip Magnus must be credited for the advanced education of hundreds of thousands of such students over the last 120 years. It was Magnus who created the City & Guilds of London Institute for the Advancement of Further Education in 1880. He was knighted for this achievement in 1886, and served for many years as the City and Guilds secretary and director.

Magnus was born in 1832 and went to the University College School in Hampstead, going on on to UCL and finally studying theology at Breslau University. Between the ages of 24 and 38 he was one of the two ministers at the West London Synagogue, at the same time becoming a lecturer in Applied Mathematics at UCL – Jewish ministers of religion always had day jobs until about the sixteenth century, so there was ample precedent for Magnus having two occupations.

Magnus was a fine speaker and wrote many books. He deserved his reputation as a distinguished educationalist. He took a great interest in developing the oral teaching of people with problems of hearing and speech and was president of the Jewish Deaf and Dumb Home. He stood for parliament in 1906 for the London University seat, which he won as a Unionist but held from 1910 onwards as a Conservative. He retired from the City and Guilds in 1915 when he was over 70 and from parliament in 1922, when he was nearly 80.

Communally, Magnus was vice-president of the Board of Deputies and of the Anglo-Jewish Association. Although from a breakaway congregation himself, he was also vice-president of the Orthodox Jews College. There was however another side to Philip Magnus: he was a founder member of the Anti-Zionist League of British Jews, following the Balfour Declaration. He regretted that the Declaration had ever been approved. When the proposal was being discussed, and even though it would benefit foreign Jewish communities, the Declaration still received no support from Magnus. In 1917, he wrote a letter to the *Morning Post* condemning foreign Jews as Bolsheviks, and in 1919 he helped to stop a proposed Mansion House meeting to protest at Poland's appalling treatment of its Jews.

Magnus strongly believed that such British gestures cast doubt on the rock-solid loyalty of the Jewish community to the United Kingdom. In today's multicultural society, when almost any state visit can be guaranteed a demonstration against one policy or another, such a belief would be considered outrageous, but in those days it was more understandable. Magnus' views alienated the Chief Rabbi and he resigned from the Board of Deputies. The Board behaved churlishly, since Magnus received no vote of thanks for his sterling work over many years. He died at the age of 90 in 1933.

EDWIN MONTAGU 1879–1924

Edwin Montagu was the second son of Samuel Montagu, Lord Swaythling, but was very unlike his father: he had little interest in Judaism where his father had been rigidly Orthodox, and he was also strongly anti-Zionist. Calling the Balfour Declaration 'anti-Semitic', Edwin Montagu felt that the Jews had no right to rule in Palestine with, in his view, the local inhabitants reduced to subordinates. Montagu also felt that 'Turks and other Mohammedans in Palestine will be regarded as foreigners, just in the same way as Jews will hereafter be treated as foreigners in every country but Palestine'. That was the rub for Montagu: would not a National Home in Palestine reduce the status of Jews in the other countries where they lived? As this opposition was coming from a member of Asquith's War Cabinet it was difficult to contradict, but among the open opponents of Montagu's views were those of his cousin, Herbert Samuel, a moderate Zionist who had also served in the Cabinet.

Montagu had been elected as the Liberal member for Chesterton in 1906 and remained in parliament until 1922. He was the Under-Secretary of State for India from 1910 to 1914 and, as Secretary of State for India from 1917 to 1922, he was bitterly critical of General Dyer for the massacre of unarmed Sikh demonstrators in Amritsar. The general was never officially condemned. When he took over from Lloyd George as Minister of Munitions, Montagu was appointed to the War Cabinet. Unlucky in love and defeated on the Zionist issue, Montagu resigned from Parliament in 1922. He declined in spirit and died at the early age of 45.

ALFRED MOND 1868–1930

How odd that the man who created one of Britain's greatest chemical companies failed his Natural Sciences degree at Cambridge. But then Alfred Mond was not your typical scientist. His father was a German chemist who had built up a major company in Britain, called Brunner Mond, and as a migrant he was one of many who made substantial contributions to the British economy in the nineteenth century. Alfred, his son, switched to reading Law at Edinburgh University and became a barrister by the time he was 26. He never lost his guttural accent.

Mond first stood for Parliament as a Liberal and was elected for Chester in 1906. Four years later he switched to Swansea which he represented for the next thirteen years. He lost in 1923, changed to the Conservatives, and sat for Carmarthen from 1924 to 1928. Mond was knighted in 1910, became a Privy Councillor in 1913 and was one of the first Jews to serve in a Cabinet when he was appointed Minister of Health from 1921 to 1922. He went on to become Lord Melchett in 1928. This was largely due to his success in persuading four large chemical companies to come together in 1926 as Imperial Chemical Industries, one of the largest industrial corporations of its time. Mond was the first chairman.

In the 1920s most of the Jewish MPs were anti-Zionist, fearing that support for a National Home for the Jews would bring their loyalty to Britain into question. Mond was one of the few exceptions and became president of the British Zionist Federation and the first president of Technion, which was then the Israel Institute of Technology. There is even a town in Israel which he helped to found, called Tel Mond. At home he had a farm where he was noted as a pig breeder.

Throughout his life Mond had to overcome a degree of anti-Semitism, particularly on the hustings when he was fighting Carmarthen. He treated it with good humour and rose above the slanders. He died in 1930 and, apart from ICI, he is remembered for the fine collection of 'old masters' his father had collected and which Alfred gave to the National Gallery, paying to have them suitably displayed.

HORATIO MYER 1850–1916

Horatio Myer's father had come from the Rhineland and set up as a pawnbroker. His son was financed by the family when he went to London and decided to start a business selling beds. This developed into the well-known furnishing manufacturers, H. Myer & Co.

According to his Rabbi, Sir Hermann Gollancz, Myer was 'straight and honest to the core' and he was certainly devoted to his community, serving for many years as warden of the prestigious Bayswater Synagogue. In 1906 he was elected Liberal MP for Lambeth North and sat in the Commons until 1910. When he died in 1916, he left £47,000 (over £2 million today).

HERBERT RAPHAEL 1859–1924

Herbert Raphael followed a traditional Cousinhood lifestyle. Son of an eminent banker, educated at Trinity Hall, Cambridge, he read Law and was called to the Bar in 1883, but then decided to devote his life to public work. He could afford to, and a seat on the first London County Council got him started on his chosen career, but it was parliament that would give him the base he needed. The difficulty was that he was beaten twice at Romford and once at St Pancras North. He was finally elected for Derbyshire South as a Liberal in 1906 and represented the constituency until 1918.

Raphael owned 480 acres of land at Gidea Park on the eastern outskirts of London. With two other Liberal MPs, John Tudor Walters and Charles McCurdy, he built Romford Garden Suburb. He gave architectural opportunities to famous Arts and Crafts masters like Clough Williams-Ellis, who was also responsible for Portmeirion. Six of the buildings that were erected at Romford are now Grade II listed. He was knighted in 1911.

Raphael was rich but in 1914, at the age of 55, he still joined up as a private in the 2nd Sportsman's Battalion. By June 1915 he was a major and raised the 18th Kings Royal Rifle Corps (Arts and Crafts) Battalion. After the war he lost his seat but became a governor of Guy's Hospital and a trustee of the National Portrait Gallery. He might have devoted his old age to his favourite hobbies of fishing, shooting and golf but he died suddenly in 1924, at the age of 65.

BERTRAM STRAUS 1867–1933

Bertram Straus went to Harrow School and then spent nine years on St Marylebone Borough Council. He was a dedicated politician but lost three elections – in 1895, 1900 and 1905 – before he was eventually successful as a Liberal for Mile End in 1906, though he lost the seat in 1910 by a mere two votes. He applied to the High Court to have the result overturned but on a recount was declared to have lost the seat by four votes and had costs awarded against him.

During his time in the Commons, Straus introduced the Traffic Bill, which limited the speed at which cars could travel in built-up areas. So if you're convicted for speeding in town, it's Straus's fault! He served as secretary of the Liberal members in the House and defended Jewish interests against the effects of the Aliens Bill and trading legislation. For example, since Orthodox Jews closed their shops on the Sabbath, it was important to them to be allowed to open on Sunday, and this was agreed by statute. Straus was also active in the Jewish community. He was a member of the Board of Deputies for twenty-six years, representing the East London Synagogue, and was a founder of Bnai B'rith, which helped to support Jewish youngsters, among a host of other activities. In 1926, he became treasurer of the Board of Deputies. All of this was possible because he was the chairman of Virol, which sells a preparation of bone marrow. Virol was a favourite item in family life for many years, a means of supplementing children's diet, and its early pots and advertising are now collectors' pieces. The company's profits also helped to pay for his very fine collection of antique silver. Straus died at 66, in 1933.

EDWARD STRAUSS 1862–1939

Edward Strauss was educated at King's College London and first stood for parliament in 1906 as a National Liberal. He never changed his allegiance and his record over the next thirty-three years was: Played 11, Won 7, Lost 4. He won elections in 1906, 1910, 1918, 1922, 1927, 1931 and 1935. He lost in 1910, 1923, 1924 and 1929. The seats he stood for were always in Southwark. In his spare time Strauss was the managing director of a city firm, Strauss and Co., who were hop merchants. Strauss was very charitable and gave large donations to the poor, but he did not participate in Jewish communal affairs. He died in 1939 aged 77.

CHARLES GOLDMAN 1868–1958

Charles Goldman was born in the Cape Colony in South Africa. A friend of Cecil Rhodes, he worked in the mining industry. Goldman was attached to General Buller's army as a correspondent at the relief of Ladysmith during the Boer War. When he came to London he married the Hon. Agnes Mary Peel, Sir Robert Peel's granddaughter. From 1910 to 1918 he was the Unionist MP for Falmouth and Penryn. In 1919, he bought an estate in British Columbia which grew to be 300,000 acres. He died there in 1958 at the age of 90.

FRANK GOLDSMITH 1878–1967

Frank Goldsmith owned the Carlton in Cannes, one of the most famous hotels on the Riviera. He also owned forty-seven others, including the equally famous Hotel de Paris in Monte Carlo, and he was one of the founders of the King David Hotel in Jerusalem. Impressive, although he had enjoyed a good start in life. His grandfather had been a banker and consul to the Grand Duke of Tuscany. Goldsmith was the son of Adolf Goldschmidt and the father of Jimmy Goldsmith, frequent target for *Private Eye* and founder of the ill-fated Euro-sceptic Referendum party, another case of Orthodoxy-to-assimilation within three generations.

Goldsmith had a very successful career. After Magdalen College, Oxford, he was called to the Bar in 1902. He served his political apprenticeship on the Westminster City Council and the LCC until 1910 when he won Stowmarket for the Conservatives. Although he represented the seat until 1918, he effectively ended his parliamentary career when he joined up in 1914 and served in Palestine and Gallipoli as a major with the Sussex Yeomanry.

Goldsmith was particularly interested in education and special schooling for the disadvantaged. For the Jewish community, he was active as a member of the Emigration Committee of the Jewish Board of Guardians. Although the Aliens Act had made immigration into Britain more difficult for Russian Jews, it was certainly not impossible, especially for those who could provide a good case for asylum. Goldsmith moved to France after the war and was made a Chevalier of the Legion d'Honneur. He died in 1967 at the age of 89.

IGNATIUS TREBITSCH-LINCOLN 1879–1943

Among the nearly 200 Jews elected to parliament over 150 years, it would have been remarkable if there had been no crooks at all among them. In fact, the Jewish community produced three. The first was Ignatius Trebitsch-Lincoln who was elected for Darlington in 1910. Lincoln was a con man, a thief and a traitor to the country that elected him. He had enrolled in the Hungarian Royal Academy of Dramatic Art, so he was well trained to deceive the unwary. Fleeing to London, he gave up his Orthodox Judaism and was converted to Christianity on Christmas Day 1899. He then became a missionary, tasked with converting Canadian Jews, returning to England in 1903. Striking up an acquaintance with the Archbishop of Canterbury – Lincoln was extremely plausible – he was appointed a curate in Kent.

He then met Seebohm Rowntree, of chocolate fame, and became his private secretary. It was with Rowntree's support that he was adopted as the Liberal candidate for Darlington even though he was still a Hungarian national at the time. In the first 1910 election he beat a member of the Pease family who had held the seat for many years – six members had served in the Commons before the family bank went into liquidation in 1902. When Lincoln realized the implications of holding down an unpaid, though very prestigious job, and with his financial position worsening, he stood down before the second 1910 election.

In his subsequent career, Lincoln was involved in a number of highly suspect commercial ventures, all of which failed. He was then employed as a German spy, though when he fled to America in 1915 the Germans disowned him. The British government had him extradited for fraud and he was sentenced to three years in Parkhurst before being deported. Amazingly, he got involved in the 1920 right-wing Kapp Putsch in Germany, working as press censor until the movement collapsed. He followed this up by becoming a member of a variety of fringe revolutionary movements, afterwards selling his archives to whichever secret service offered the highest price.

Deported again, he ended up in China, became a Buddhist monk and rose to the position of abbot with his own monastery in Shanghai where initiates were obliged to hand over all their belongings to him when they were admitted; in his spare time, Trebitsch-Lincoln seduced the nuns. Switching to the Japanese, he also offered the Nazis his help in the Second World War. His offer was accepted and he worked for them until he died in 1943. Well, if you're going to have a rotten apple in the barrel, it might just as well be highly-coloured as plain.

LIONEL ROTHSCHILD 1882–1942

Lionel Rothschild was Leopold's son and went to Harrow and Cambridge. After university, in 1903 he joined the bank and also became a second lieutenant in the Royal Bucks Hussars. In 1910, he was elected unopposed for Aylesbury as the Conservative member after Walter Rothschild retired. He stayed in the House until 1923. Rothschild was extremely involved in Jewish communal life. He was a warden of the Great Synagogue from 1915 until his death and served on their Guild of Social Services from 1923. He was also president of the Memorial Council, treasurer of the Board of Guardians and eventually president of the United Synagogue. In the House he pressed the government to carry out its obligations under the Balfour Declaration.

Rothschild was also a friend of the King and Queen, entertaining them at his home and being invited to join them on the royal yacht. He was a great yachtsman himself and a fine gardener. During the Second World War, he opened the Jewish Temporary Shelter for members of the community whose homes had been destroyed by enemy action. He said in his speech:

> Today we are privileged to live in danger, to endure hardship, to make sacrifices for the preservation of our country and of civilization. Such is our privilege in common with our fellow citizens of every religious denomination. But, as members of the Jewish community we have an additional privilege: to strive, today and every day; to give, today and every day; to work, today and every day – each one of us – so that Jewish religious worship, Jewish religious education, and all else that is dear to us in our ancient traditions, may be preserved for us and for our children.

Rothschild died a few days after his sixtieth birthday in 1942.

ARTHUR STRAUSS 1847–1920

Arthur Strauss was born in Germany but came to Britain as a young child. He went to university in Germany and became a metal merchant. He owned several smelting works and it was said that three quarters of the tin exported from the area passed through the hands of his firms. Strauss was a Unionist and was first elected to the House for Camborne from 1895 to 1900, after facing down some opposition from within the party because of his foreign birth. He had previously lost an election in 1892, and would be defeated again in 1900 and 1903. He was elected again in January 1910, this time as member for Paddington North. He stood for the seat again as an Independent Liberal in 1918 but was not successful. Communally he was a member of the Bayswater Synagogue, though the *Jewish Chronicle* had commented when he was first elected that his name did not appear on any of their Jewish charity lists. In 1920, he was eventually buried in a Christian cemetery in Kensal Green.

FELIX CASSEL 1869–1953

Sir Ernest Cassel was one of the great Jewish nineteenth-century international financiers. His nephew was Felix Cassel who had brains as well as family connections. Felix was educated at Harrow and Corpus Christi, Oxford, where he achieved a First in Classical

Moderation and Jurisprudence. He was called to the Bar in 1894 and took silk in 1906. He then married Lady Helen Grimston, daughter of the Earl of Verulam, and moved out of the Jewish community.

Defeated as the Conservative candidate for Hackney Central in the first 1910 general election, he won St Pancras West in the second. From 1914 to 1916, he was in the 19th Battalion of the London Regiment and was then invited to become Judge Advocate General. This was a position in which he had to confirm death sentences on servicemen who had deserted or shown cowardice in the face of the enemy. As we now know, many of these unfortunate men were suffering mental breakdown, but they were shot anyway. In apportioning the blame after the war, the office of the Judge Advocate General was not criticized, but the memories must have given Cassel sleepless nights. He resigned from the Commons in 1916 but was knighted in 1920 and made a Privy Councillor in 1937. He died in 1953.

LEOPOLD AMERY 1873–1955

That Leopold Amery was Jewish was never in dispute. His mother was born Elisabeth Leitner but she divorced his father when the boy was 12. She then went off to Canada and became a farmer, having nothing to do with the family thereafter. As the *Dictionary of National Biography* delicately puts it, 'His Jewish connections were known but unremarked by his contemporaries'. Amery was a dedicated imperialist; he believed strongly that Imperial Preference was the best way of safeguarding Britain's trading position. He was first elected for Birmingham South in 1911 as a Conservative, finally losing his seat in 1945.

Amery became First Lord of the Admiralty in 1922 and Colonial Secretary from 1924 to 1929. He was also president of the Ski Club of Great Britain but chose to have no role in Jewish communal affairs. In public life, however, Amery helped to draft the Balfour Declaration and encouraged Jabotinsky in his efforts to form a Jewish Legion in the British army. When he left the Commons he became a director of, among other companies, Marks & Spencer. He turned down a peerage but was made Companion of Honour.

MAURICE DE FOREST 1879–1968

Maurice de Forest was the adopted son of Baron Hirsch, one of Edward VII's Marlborough House set and a very rich banker. De Forest went to Eton and Christ Church, Oxford before becoming a lieutenant in the Prince of Wales Own Norfolk Artillery. He was known as an advanced radical and was elected to the London County Council from 1910 to 1913. In 1911 he won North West Ham at a by-election as a Conservative but retired from the Commons in 1918. When the First World War broke out he joined the Royal Navy Voluntary Reserve as a commander. After the war he went abroad and in 1932 became a citizen of Liechtenstein. He died in 1968 at the age of 89.

PHILLIP SASSOON 1888–1939

When his father, Edward Albert, died in 1912, Phillip Sassoon, to the manor born, became the candidate and MP for Hythe and served the constituency for the next twenty-one years. Hythe had been a Rothschild enclave before Sassoon's father took the seat and Sassoon's mother was a Rothschild. Sassoon was a gilded youth and typical of a certain Jewish family progression where a very Orthodox grandfather makes the family fortune, the father establishes himself in the ranks of society, and the son leaves the religion far behind. Sassoon's sister, Sybil, even married the Marquis of Cholmondeley, who held the hereditary title of Lord Great Chamberlain of England.

Sassoon was not without talent. After Eton and Christ Church he became the youngest MP in the House when he entered it at 24. During the First World War, he was private secretary to Field Marshall Haig and in 1920, he fulfilled the same role for the Prime Minister, David Lloyd George. Between 1924 and 1929, and again from 1931 to 1937, he served in government as Under-Secretary of State for Air and must take some credit for the expansion of the RAF. Although Sassoon was regarded as one of the most eligible bachelors in Britain, he never married. He did give wonderful parties though. He died in harness in parliament in 1939 before the Second World War broke out; he was only 51. Born Albert Gustave David, Sir Phillip Sassoon ended his life as a Privy Councillor, GBE and CMG.

SAM SAMUEL 1855–1934

Sam Samuel was a seriously important businessman. With his brother, Marcus Samuel, Lord Bearsted, he founded Shell, of which he was a director for many years. He was also on the board of Lloyds Bank. He was Conservative member for Wandsworth from 1913 to 1918 and he was well known for his dinners at the House on the night after the budget. He invited the good and the mighty from the City to meet with the Chancellor, and an invitation was considered a great privilege. In 1919 Samuel won a by-election in Putney and stood for it again in 1922 when he met a hail of anti-Semitic opposition. It became so bad that he instituted an action for libel, but the voters were on his side and he won comfortably, remaining the constituency MP until his death. He spoke rarely but effectively. He was a bachelor and very much against extending the franchise to women.

Communally, he was equally well regarded. The obituarist in the *Jewish Chronicle* spoke for all when he wrote, 'He was the soul of generosity and never could he turn a deaf or uninterested ear to the appeal for help'. He was the president of the Jewish Soup Kitchen in succession to another Jewish MP, Sir Charles Henry. He did a lot of good work in the Holy Land, though he was not a Zionist, and said that he hoped Britain would 'clear out of Palestine'. He also gave large sums to finance the teaching of English abroad. Samuel was president of the Commercial Group of the House of Commons which had been founded by the Jewish MP, Louis Sinclair, and in 1926 presided over the International Meeting which was attended by over thirty countries. When he died in 1934, he was the oldest member of the House, at 79.

PERCY HARRIS 1876–1952

Percy Harris won six elections as a Liberal when his party was in decline – no mean achievement. His father, Wolf Harris, was a warden at the New West End Synagogue and Percy Harris was educated at Harrow and went on to Trinity Hall, Cambridge to read History. He was called to the Bar in 1899 when he was only 23. Harris was a great traveller and went round the world three times, living in New Zealand for three years. He was elected to the LCC in 1907, became deputy chairman in 1915 and served on it until 1934. Years later, in 1949, Labour and Conservatives held sixty-four seats each on the Council. Harris was the one Liberal and was soon called by the capital's press 'the most powerful man in London'.

During the First World War, he worked at the War Office and tried to ensure that the families of married men in the services were better able to cope with the absence of the main breadwinner. He was first elected for Harborough in a by-election in 1916, having been beaten in the 1906 and 1910 elections for the seat. He lost it again in 1918 but was elected for Bethnal Green South West in 1922, retaining the seat until 1945.

He was knighted in 1932, became the Liberal Chief Whip from

1935 to 1945 and Deputy Leader of the party during the years of the Second World War. He was always anxious not to waste public money and served on the Select Committee on National Expenditure. He was made a Privy Councillor in 1940 and died in 1952 at the age of 76. In his time he had been vice-president of the Jewish Norwood Orphanage, which would raise a future Labour MP, Reg Freeson, but Harris is buried in a churchyard in Chiswick.

At the end of the First World War, Jewish representation in parliament changed, and the Cousinhood would never again play as great a part as it had in the early days. There were however still very able Jewish MPs during the period – for example, three exceptional businessmen in Sam Samuel (Shell), Alfred Mond (ICI) and Isidore Salmon (Lyons). There were war heroes, like Robert Gee and Jack Brunel Cohen. There were elder statesmen in the House of Lords, like Herbert Samuel and Rufus Isaacs and debating stars in the Commons like Leslie Hore-Belisha. But it was no longer the case that the leaders of the community would also attempt to serve as members of parliament.

There was also a new breed of Jewish MPs emerging – socialists. Critics of the community had concentrated on the foreign origins of so many Jews before the war. Now they would claim that Communism was a Jewish conspiracy. The facts were quite simple. The working classes deserved a better deal and socialist manifestos were designed to achieve it for them; there were a great many working-class Jews who approved. Later, when the policy of the Nazi party and those who believed in National Socialism would be appallingly anti-Semitic, the Jews couldn't fight them off alone and their best allies available were the Communists. As a result of these factors a substantial number of Jews became socialists or Communists. Leading the socialist Jewish Labour MPs was Manny Shinwell who represented Linlithgow in Scotland, and he was the first of many.

There was also a perception within the community between the wars that Jews were more likely to be selected for winnable Liberal and Labour seats than for safe Conservative constituencies, though actual statistics hardly bear out this contention. Jewish candidates won 123 elections over these years. Of these, sixty-three won Conservative seats, thirty-eight Liberal and National Liberal and twenty-one Labour. The extra one was Independent.

It is true that there was a degree of anti-Semitism in the Conservative Party at the time, although it was usually no more antagonistic than to believe that a Jew was 'not one of us'. There was a belief that where Jewish candidates were prepared to divorce themselves from the community, they might stand a better chance of being accepted. Many followed that route. The irony was that anti-Semites often took little account of the Jewish candidate's own religious views. He might have forsworn the religion and even become converted to Christianity, but it made no difference for the anti-Semite. He had been born to Jewish parents and that was enough rope with which to hang him, in the eyes of the racists.

Obviously, it is not possible to know how many Jewish candidates failed to get elected because of their Jewish background. It is easy enough to put down failure to anti-Semitism, but there was also the party they represented and their own ability and personalities to take into account. When they stood their ground, like Alfred Mond, Isidore Salmon and Daniel Lipson, the country as a whole applauded them.

On the hustings, opponents are always likely to fasten on any perceived weakness in the other candidates, and a dislike of Jews and Judaism did motivate a proportion of the voters. After the Second World War, the famous *Times* Jewish columnist, Bernard Levin, was pondering an attitude which, if sufficiently extreme, could lead to the Holocaust. He wrote about anti-Semitism in Britain before the war: 'Decent society in those days was filled with people who had forgotten what anti-Semitism had led to, and who could not guess what it would lead to'.

Another running sore between the wars was the situation in Palestine. The British government during the First World War had made contradictory promises to the Arabs and to the Jews. The diplomatic chickens which had played their part in winning the war now came home to roost. The intransigence of both sides in the Middle East and the deployment of terrorism made the task of the British mandatory power in Palestine very difficult indeed. Inside the British Jewish community, there was no agreement on the right course to follow. There were large numbers of both Zionists and anti-Zionists within their ranks. It was only when the threat of Hitler and a second world war became more likely that the community as a whole turned to Zionism as the best hope of finding permanent asylum for the Jewish refugees.

The importance of the Jewish vote had become an issue after the passing of the bill to grant Universal Suffrage in 1928. As early as

1923, the *Jewish Chronicle* had told its readers, 'where any candidate ... expresses himself as opposed to Jewish interests, then it seems to us the duty of Jewish voters to withhold from him their support ... the constitutional idea of the suffrage is that each voter shall employ it in what he conceives to be his own true interests'.

The question was whether this would work out in practice, and the Whitechapel constituency in 1929 became a test case. The electorate had a substantial Jewish presence and an excellent Jewish candidate, Barnett Janner, was adopted by the Liberals to fight the seat. It was estimated that out of 37,000 voters, about 12,000 were Jews. To make matters worse for the government, they had issued a White Paper on a bill which would have had the effect of severely restricting Jewish immigration to Palestine. The Conservatives had held the seat with a majority of over 9,000 but in 1929, when all the votes had been counted, the majority had been slashed to 1,100. In the election of 1931, Janner won Whitechapel. The government had already taken note and abandoned the Palestine Bill. The problem of trying to help develop the National Home was that the accusation gained strength that the Jewish MPs were prepared to put the interests of their co-religionists ahead of their loyalty to the UK. This was the case even though a number of the Jewish MPs weren't Zionists at all. And in 1935, Janner lost Whitechapel to Labour.

The period also saw the further decline of the Liberal Party which had been the home of so many Jewish MPs from the beginning. As such a high proportion of the community were poor – a survey of East London suggested that nearly 14 per cent of the Jews in the area could be considered to be living in poverty – the Labour Party attracted a great deal of Jewish support; the Conservatives were generally seen as the party which represented the middle and upper classes.

Jewish MPs elected between 1918 and 1931 were:

1918   Leopold Amery (Conservative), **Jack Brunel Cohen** (Unionist), Charles Henry (Liberal), Philip Magnus (Unionist), Alfred Mond (National Liberal), Edwin Montagu (Liberal), Henry Norman (Liberal), Lionel Rothschild (Conservative), **Arthur Samuel** (Conservative), Sam Samuel (Conservative), Philip Sassoon (Conservative), Edward Strauss (National Liberal)

1919   **Thomas Myers** (Labour)

1922   Leopold Amery (Conservative), Jack Brunel Cohen (Conservative Unionist), **Walter de Frece** (Unionist), Percy

Harris (Liberal), Arthur Levy Lever (National Liberal), Alfred Mond (National Liberal), Henry Norman (Liberal), Lionel Rothschild (Conservative), Arthur Samuel (Conservative), Sam Samuel (Conservative), Philip Sassoon (Conservative), **Manny Shinwell** (Labour), **George Spero** (Liberal), Edward Strauss (National Liberal)

1923   Leopold Amery (Conservative), Jack Brunel Cohen (Conservative Unionist), **Leonard Franklin** (Liberal), Walter de Frece (Unionist), **Leslie Haden-Guest** (Labour), Percy Harris (Liberal), **Leslie Hore-Belisha** (National Liberal), **Henry Mond** (Liberal), Arthur Samuel (Conservative), Sam Samuel (Conservative), Philip Sassoon (Conservative), Manny Shinwell (Labour), **Henry Slesser** (Labour), George Spero (Liberal), **Joseph Sunlight** (Liberal), **Moss Turner-Samuels** (Labour)

1924   Leopold Amery (Conservative), Jack Brunel Cohen (Conservative Unionist), **Harry Day** (Labour), Walter de Frece (Conservative), **Sam Finburgh** (Conservative), **Robert Gee** (Labour), Percy Harris (Liberal), Leslie Hore-Belisha (National Liberal), **Frank Meyer** (Conservative), Alfred Mond (Conservative), **Isidore Salmon** (Conservative), Arthur Samuel (Conservative), Sam Samuel (Conservative), Philip Sassoon (Conservative)

1927   Edward Strauss (Liberal)

1928   Manny Shinwell (Labour)

1929   Leopold Amery (Conservative), Jack Brunel Cohen (Conservative Unionist), Harry Day (Labour), Walter de Frece (Conservative), Percy Harris (Liberal), Leslie Hore-Belisha (National Liberal), **Michael Marcus** (Labour), Henry Mond (Conservative), **Harry Nathan** (Liberal), **Marion Phillips** (Labour), **Jimmy Rothschild** (Liberal), Isidore Salmon (Conservative), Arthur Samuel (Conservative), Herbert Samuel (Liberal), Sam Samuel (Conservative), Philip Sassoon (Conservative), Manny Shinwell (Labour), George Spero (Liberal), Edward Strauss (Liberal), **George Strauss** (Labour)

JACK BRUNEL COHEN 1886–1965

The moment of a new member's maiden speech is a memorable event – standing before the House and trying to maintain its attention is nerve-racking. Jack Brunel Cohen asked if he could make his speech sitting down. The Speaker approved the request immediately and the House murmured its approval. Jack Cohen had lost both his legs at the Battle of Ypres in 1917. When he'd finished, members crossed the floor of the House and joined those on his side in congratulating him.

Cohen was a dedicated anti-Zionist and figured largely in the Society of British Jews set up to protest against the concept of a National Home, after the Balfour Declaration. As a patriotic Englishman, Cohen felt that support for Zionism might throw doubt upon the loyalty of the Jewish community in Britain. Intensely patriotic himself, his energetic post-war efforts were made on behalf of disabled servicemen. After the Second World War, when Ernest Bevin set up Remploy to provide work for severely incapacitated servicemen, Cohen served as chairman of the company. He was also treasurer of the British Legion for twenty-three years.

Cohen was elected for Liverpool Fairfield in 1918 and retired from parliament in 1931 after thirteen years representing the same constituency. He lived to be nearly 80 and, in his wheelchair, for years led the parade of Jewish Ex-Servicemen to the Cenotaph on the Sunday after Armistice Day. When he died, he left £300 to the sergeant who had saved his life in 1917 and £500 to the nurses of St Thomas' Hospital. It was specifically designated to buy them wine for Christmas.

ARTHUR SAMUEL 1872–1942

Arthur Samuel's father made a fortune in Canada during the nineteenth century and so his son got a good start in life. Samuel was always a Norwich man and went to Norwich Grammar School. He joined the family company but retired in 1912 to devote himself to public works. He was Lord Mayor of Norwich from 1912 to 1913. During the First World War he worked in the Ministry of Munitions and when the fighting finished, he was elected as the Conservative member for Farnham, after several previous disappointments. He remained its member until he was promoted to the House of Lords in 1937 as Lord Mancroft.

Samuel was an expert on trade and currency, and his scheme for trading between the Allied nations after the war was agreed at the

Paris Conference in 1916. In 1924 he was Minister for Overseas Trade until 1927 and was then made Financial Secretary to the Treasury. He supported the 'Come to Britain' movement which was the forerunner of the British Tourist Authority. Samuel's main argument during the Slump was that Britain should stop raising loans in the City for those foreign governments who were not going to pay the money back. Samuel held that although the cash produced might be spent on British exports they would be sold at too high a cost to the country. He summed up the causes of the Slump in five famous words: 'The decay of common honesty'. In Norwich, his bounty knew no bounds. He gave the George Borrow Museum to the city and donated large sums to the Norwich Hospital and other good causes. Communally, he took little part in Jewish community affairs but spoke up for the Jews on contentious issues in the House. He died at the age of 70, in 1942.

THOMAS MYERS 1872–1949

Thomas Myers went to elementary school and became a glassblower. He was an active trade unionist and served on the Thornhill Urban District Council from 1904 to 1910, moving on to the Dewsbury Borough Council from 1910 to 1920. In a by-election in 1919, he won Spen Valley for Labour but he was defeated in 1922 and then lost the next three elections. He continued in local politics as a Dewsbury councillor from 1935 to 1943 and was Mayor of the town in 1940/1. He died in 1949 aged 77.

SIR WALTER DE FRECE 1870–1935

There are some Jewish MPs who have no wish to be associated with the community. Sir Walter de Frece possessed many Jewish traits but divorced himself from his religious roots, which was a pity because he lent lustre to the organizations in which he was involved. He came from the world of theatre management, an industry with which Jews have always been associated. His father owned the Gaiety Theatres in Liverpool and Sheffield and had started the practice of putting on two shows a night. A Liverpool man, educated at its High School, the young de Frece went on to Brussels University before starting his own business, managing at his peak as many as twenty provincial theatres. He married Vesta Tilly, the immensely popular music-hall star.

Although really much too old to serve, de Frece joined the Sportsman's Battalion at the outbreak of the First World War but was invalided out as a major, so he turned his attention to providing entertainment for the forces and the munitions workers. He went on to work for the Ministry of Pensions and in 1919 was knighted for his efforts. At a by-election in 1920, he was elected the Coalition Unionist MP for Ashton-under-Lyne and won again in 1922 and 1923. In 1924 he moved to the Blackpool constituency as a Conservative and retired at the 1931 general election. He was made honorary colonel of the 9th Battalion, Manchester Regiment. The importance placed on charitable work in Judaism found a ready echo in de Frece. He raised a large sum for the Blinded Soldiers Fund after the war and was a trustee of the King's Fund for the Disabled. He moved to Monte Carlo in the 1930s, but in that balmy climate still managed to fall victim to pneumonia and dying at 64.

MANNY SHINWELL 1884–1986

Although Manny Shinwell maintained that he was not a practising Jew, he also said, 'We can justifiably be proud of being Jews'. Certainly, he was often enough attacked for his religion. In 1922, when he had just become the first Scottish Jewish MP for Linlithgow, an opposition MP greeted one of his remarks in a speech with the catcall 'Jew'. On another occasion an MP, Commander Bower, formerly the heavyweight boxing champion of the navy, shouted out 'Go back to Poland'. Shinwell crossed the house and slapped him round the head, bursting the commander's eardrum. As Chips Channon MP wrote, 'The crack resounded in the chamber . . . but the Speaker . . . refused to rebuke Shinwell'. Both MPs apologized and the commander went off to hospital; they became friends in later years. Shinwell was less aggressive when Lady Astor, the first woman MP, called out the same insult.

Shinwell was, above all, a fighter. He battled all his life for what he believed in, which marks out many Jews. Brought up in Glasgow in a Jewish family that had emigrated to Britain in 1868, he left school at the age of 11 and became a tailor. He was a strong trade unionist and was the assistant secretary of the National Union of Seamen just before the First World War, when he was immediately nicknamed Shinbad the Tailor. From 1916 to 1919, he was chairman of the Glasgow Trade Union Council and got five months in prison after taking part in a rowdy demonstration on behalf of his union.

In 1922, he left prison to be elected as one of the famous Ten Red Clydesiders and was Minister for Mines in the Labour government in 1924 and Financial Secretary to the War Office in 1929. He both nominated Ramsay Macdonald for Leader in the early days of the party and then, in 1935, stood against him because of Macdonald's decision to head the National Government. He beat the ex-Prime Minister by 20,000 votes.

Shinwell served in the House almost without a break from 1922 until he was made a peer in 1970. During his years in parliament he wrote the 1942 manifesto which brought Labour to power in 1945. In the Attlee government, he nationalized the mines in 1946 and was Minister of Defence from 1947 to 1951, getting on very well with the service chiefs.

In spite of his combative nature on behalf of the Labour party, Shinwell was publicly recognized in the House for his 'sterling patriotism' by as sound a judge as Winston Churchill. He was chairman of the Parliamentary Labour Party from 1964 to 1970 and made a Companion of Honour in 1965. In his old age Shinwell supported the Residential Centre for Jewish Deaf Children and the Jewish Secondary Schools Movement. When he finally died in 1986 at the age of 101 the Queen sent a message of condolence to the family.

GEORGE SPERO 1894–?

George Spero was born in the West Indies, the son of Isidore Spero. There had been a Jewish community in that part of the world for at least 300 years. When the family came to London, Spero went to London University, and first became a dentist, but moved on to be a doctor, surgeon and wireless manufacturer. During the First World War he served as a surgeon lieutenant in the navy from 1915 to 1917, and after the war, stood for parliament. He was beaten as a Liberal in 1922 and 1924 but won Stoke Newington in 1923. He switched to the Labour Party in 1925 and won Fulham in 1929, but he resigned in 1930. In the same year he sold his company but signed substantial cheques for his own use. In court £10,000 damages were awarded against him but Spero fled to America and was seen no more.

LEONARD FRANKLIN 1862–1944

Leonard Franklin came from the Samuel Montagu stable – his mother was Montagu's sister. He went to King's College London and was called to the Bar in 1894. He was a senior partner at Keysers, the foreign bankers. Throughout his life, Franklin was a hard worker for Jewish causes. He became treasurer of the Burial Society, chairman of the Associated Synagogues and a major benefactor of the Southend

Synagogue. He served as a warden at both the Hackney and New West End Synagogues.

Franklin was equally involved in the political world. He stood for parliament and was defeated in 1910, 1918 and 1922 but he won Hackney Central in 1923 for the Liberals, the last time the party won the seat. His political philosophy was summed up when he said: 'I am fully aware that we are sent to the House to represent our constituents, but this does not conflict with our duty of expressing the cause of our people and putting their case before the country.' This may or may not have been a contributing factor to his losing his seat in 1924. Franklin was an early advocate of proportional representation and was the inventor of the system known as percentage proportional representation. He died in 1944 at the age of 82.

LESLIE HADEN-GUEST 1877–1960

Leslie Haden-Guest was the first Jew to stand for election as a Labour candidate for an English constituency. He came from a well-to-do family in Oldham where his father was a surgeon, but the house was always full of Labour radicals and the lad was also much influenced by the poverty he saw all around him in the cotton towns. Haden-Guest was a doctor himself, having studied medicine at Owens College in Manchester and at the London Hospital in the East End. It wasn't easy for Jews to win places at teaching hospitals at the time, but because of its location the London Hospital had many Jewish benefactors, which made life easier for properly qualified Jewish candidates.

Haden-Guest served in the Boer War and both world wars. He won the Military Cross for his gallantry in saving casualties from the battlefield at Passchandaele. After the war, he went back to medicine in the East End and pioneered the School Medical and Dental Clinic Movement. In 1919, he turned his attention to politics and was elected to the LCC for Woolwich East. He came to the House as the Labour member for Southwark North in 1923. He went to Russia and talked to the main Communist leaders but this only made him very anti-Bolshevik.

Haden-Guest resigned his seat in 1927 because his party opposed the government's policy on China. For the next ten years he lost every election, joining and then leaving the Conservatives. Eventually, once more with Labour, he won Islington North in 1937 in a by-election. It was at this time that his son, David, was killed in the Spanish Civil War. Haden-Guest served his constituency until 1950. He was then made a peer and became a Lord-in-Waiting to the king; he was also a

Whip in the House of Lords. Haden-Guest was the founder of the Anglo-French Committee of the Red Cross. He worked extremely hard in the House of Lords when he was over 70 and was the chairman of the National Medical Manpower Commission. When he died at the age of 83, *The Times* pronounced his passing 'a considerable loss to British public life'.

LESLIE HORE-BELISHA 1893–1957

There was one major Jewish boarding house in an English public school at the turn of the twentieth century, Clifton College in Bristol, and one of its alumni was Isaac Leslie Hore-Belisha. The name Hore came from his mother's second marriage, as Leslie's father died in 1894 when he was only one year old. There is no doubt about it – Hore-Belisha was good. Whether as a major in the First World War, as president of the Oxford Union in 1919, or in the Commons from 1923 to 1945 as the member for his birthplace, Plymouth, Hore-Belisha shone. He was also called to the Bar in 1923 and became well known in the House as a flamboyant and brilliant speaker. Even as his Liberal Party declined, his own political star continued to rise. In the 1931 National Government, he was appointed Minister of Transport and during his three years in the job he created the black-and-white post with the orange globe at pedestrian crossings, still known as a Belisha Beacon.

Indeed, he did so well that Prime Minister Neville Chamberlain appointed him Secretary of State for War. This was a highly controversial office as the thinking of many senior officers was still rooted in the Great War of 1914 to 1918, rather than in a world where air power, submarines and tanks were to dominate future conflicts. Hore-Belisha recognized the likelihood of an approaching war and as a result wanted to introduce immediate conscription. He was promptly subjected to a whispering campaign that linked his policies with the fate of the Jews in Germany. Throughout the Second World War, Joseph Goebbels' propaganda machine laid the blame for its outbreak on a Jewish conspiracy, and some of the senior figures in the British armed forces took the same view.

Hore-Belisha introduced many reforms, such as improving the pay and pensions of ordinary soldiers. The officer ranks at the time gave undue consideration to birth, upbringing and family connections, and these were barriers to ambitious servicemen from poorer backgrounds. Hore-Belisha improved this situation but antagonized the old guard even more in the process. He was labelled a 'Bolshevik and warmonger' by many and nicknamed Horeb-Elisha (the golden calf in the book of Exodus was made in Horeb). Eventually, in January 1940, opposition to him within the War Office was sufficiently powerful to convince Chamberlain to dismiss Hore-Belisha from his government. He was briefly considered for the post of Minister of Information, but turned down because it was felt that to have a Jewish politician in that position at the time would be counterproductive.

Communally, Hore-Belisha was a member of the Elders of the Sephardi community and a representative on the Board of Deputies. Although Hore-Belisha tried to rescue his career when Churchill came to power as Prime Minister, the best he achieved was Minister for National Insurance in the 1945 caretaker government before Labour swept into office. In that election, Hore-Belisha was beaten by Michael Foot and although he fought Coventry in 1950, he was unsuccessful there too. Awarded a peerage by Churchill in 1954, he was leading a parliamentary delegation to France in 1957 when he dropped dead. It was a sign of the changing times that the Minister of Defence in the Attlee government was the working-class Manny Shinwell, who got on very well with the forces' chiefs.

HENRY MOND 1898–1949

Henry Mond was the son of Alfred Mond, the first Lord Melchett. He went to Winchester School and joined up in 1916, serving with the South Wales Borderers. He was wounded in action but survived and joined his father's company. When Alfred Mond put together what became ICI, Henry worked for the new company and eventually became the deputy chairman. He only resigned from the company in 1947, shortly before he died.

Mond's mother was Christian but he became very involved in Zionist activities and converted to Judaism in 1933. He was the honorary president of the Maccabi World Union, a Jewish Association devoted to sport. As he said in 1932, 'A physically fit Jew is essential if the great work of rebuilding the National Home is to be achieved'. He toured Europe promoting Maccabi and created the Maccabiah Games, which are the Jewish Olympics (in spirit, if not in the standards achieved). He was also honorary vice-president of the Zionist Federation of Great Britain and treasurer of the Children and Youth Aliyah, which encouraged young Jews to emigrate to Palestine. He was a vice-president of the World Jewish Congress and chairman of the Council of the Jewish Agency. When King George V celebrated his silver jubilee in 1935, it was Mond who raised the money to plant a vast forest in Palestine to celebrate the occasion.

He joined his father in parliament in 1923 when he won Toxteth East for the Conservatives and was elected for the constituency again in 1929. His only son was killed in the Second World War and Mond was ill for many years after. He died in 1949, when he was only 50.

HENRY SLESSER 1883–1979

Henry Schloesser changed his name to Slesser when the First World War broke out, at about the same time as the royal family changed theirs. He was Jewish, educated at Oundle and St Paul's before moving on to London University. He first took an apprenticeship in railway engineering but when his health broke down, he spent his recuperation studying for the Bar. As a barrister he took many cases defending workers and in 1912 he became standing counsel to the Labour Party; he was also a lecturer in Law at London University.

Although he didn't win Leeds Central in 1922 and was beaten twice more in 1923, he was finally elected for Leeds South East in 1924. He was appointed Solicitor General in Ramsay Macdonald's 1929 government. It was then necessary to make him both a King's Counsel (KC) and a Knight to hold the office. Both George Jessel and Rufus Isaacs were Jewish predecessors as Solicitor General. Like Jessel but unlike Isaacs, Slesser converted to Christianity. Slesser won again in 1929 but he was offered the position of a judge in the court of appeal and accepted. He retired from the court in 1940 and became a country gentleman in Devon until he died at the age of 96. He was happily married for 69 years. At least that is definitely a Jewish tradition.

JOSEPH SUNLIGHT 1889–1978

Joseph Sunlight was an architect like Lewis Isaacs. His father came to Britain to avoid military service in Russia which, for Jews, could be a twenty-year stint. The family name was Schimschlavitch but this was changed to Sunlight when the family settled in Manchester; Port Sunlight could have been the inspiration. Sunlight was apprenticed to an architect in 1904 and by 1907 had his own practice. He made a very large fortune by building more than 1,000 houses and many commercial buildings. He was the architect of the South Manchester Synagogue and of Sunlight House, which was notable in its time. Sunlight won Shrewsbury for the Liberals in 1923 but was defeated in 1924. He went back to his practice and to his great love of horse racing. He died in 1978 at the age of 89.

MOSS TURNER-SAMUELS 1888–1957

In 1923, when he was only 35, Moss Turner-Samuels won the Barnard Castle seat for Labour, but he lost it a year later. It would be another twenty years before he returned to parliament as the new Labour MP for Gloucester. He served the constituency for the next twelve years but died in office in 1957 when he was 69. It was odd that the next two MPs for the constituency were also Jewish – Jack Diamond (Labour) from 1957 to 1970 and Sally Oppenheim (Conservative) from 1970 to 1987. Few Jews live in Gloucester.

Turner-Samuels took silk in 1946 and had qualified as a solicitor and a barrister. He was a Geordie by birth, educated at Newcastle Grammar School, and, using another of his skills, he did a lot of both legal and political writing. As an Orthodox Jew he represented the Newcastle Old Hebrew Congregation on the Board of Deputies. Other notable Jewish barristers from Newcastle are Lord Taylor and Lord Woolf, both of whom became Lord Chief Justice.

Turner-Samuel was the soul of discretion but he still managed to get himself censured by the Masters and Benchers of the Middle Temple. The editor of the magazine of the Commons had decided in 1951 to do a series of articles on the professions of members. One of those they chose was Turner-Samuels and, although he hadn't written the article himself, the Benchers considered the offending piece to be an advertisement. And under no circumstances were barristers allowed to advertise. Turner-Samuels still served as the Recorder of Halifax for the last nine years of his life. He was also the High Sheriff of Gloucester from 1945 to 1946, but he never held government office.

HARRY DAY 1880–1939

Over the years there has been a fair amount of barnstorming in parliament. Few MPs have been able to observe the masters of the craft as well as Colonel Harry Day, who in his youth had sold tickets for Barnum and Bailey circus shows. In later life he owned a number of music halls and married the beautiful Kitty Colyer, a famous music hall artiste. He was also at one time the manager of the great escapologist, Harry Houdini.

Where Day found the interest to stand as a Labour candidate for Southwark in 1924 is obscure, as his true occupation was the production of revues, a form of entertainment which has sadly almost disappeared. Certainly, as the *Jewish Chronicle* reported in its 1924 election coverage, 'Colonel Day takes no part in communal affairs'. Where the rank of Colonel came from is also unknown. Day held Southwark for seven years and was famous in the House for the number of questions he asked ministers. In some sessions he asked more than any other MP. As with all the Jewish Labour MPs, he lost his seat in 1931. But he regained it in 1935 and was still in harness when he died in 1939 at the age of 59, in Canada.

SAM FINBURGH 1867–1935

Sam Finburgh was a Manchester cotton manufacturer and, unlike many of the Jewish MPs who won seats in 1924, he was deeply committed to the Jewish community. He was president of the Manchester Shechita Board and of the Higher Broughton Synagogue and was also a member of the Board of Deputies. Finburgh was president of the North Salford Conservative Association and won the seat from the prominent socialist, Ben Tillett, with a slim majority of 1,186. His success was the first for a Jew in Manchester. He was the son of a rabbi and wouldn't campaign on the Sabbath. When he died in 1935, the *Jewish Chronicle* wrote, 'He was a rugged and honest personality, with a high sense of duty, both to his own co-religionists and to the State and his whole life was one of sterling and unselfish service as citizen and Jew'. His courage was praised: 'a courage not too conspicuously shared by some of his fellow Jewish members of parliament'. This last accolade probably referred to the efforts that Finburgh and Sir Isidore Salmon successfully made on their own to block a Private Member's Bill to outlaw the Jewish ritual slaughter of animals. During his brief years in the Commons, he organized the Parliamentary Palestine Committee to counterbalance the Zionist influence in the House and he would have done more if his health had not let him down. He had to retire in 1929 and died a few years later.

ROBERT GEE 1876–1960

The most distinguished Jewish ex-soldier in the British army in the First World War was Robert Gee, VC and MC, the victorious member for Woolwich East in 1921. Gee had won the Victoria Cross at the age of 41 – a time of life when a stroll down the seventeenth fairway at a leisurely pace might be considered sufficient exercise. Instead Captain Gee found himself on the Western Front. He was in the Royal Fusiliers Brigade Headquarters when it was captured. Gee escaped and organized the brigade staff to attack the enemy. When he found a German machine-gun nest still causing havoc, he took a revolver in each hand and charged. He killed eight of the enemy, silenced the gun and was awarded the highest military honour. During the war, he was wounded three times and mentioned in dispatches four times. He also won the Military Cross.

After the war, Gee decided to go into politics and beat Ramsay Macdonald to win Woolwich East for the Conservatives in a by-election in 1921. As Macdonald had been a pacifist during the war, Gee had at least a head start with the majority of the electorate. Gee lost the seat in 1923 but won Bosworth in 1924, which he served until 1927. At which point he disappeared in what was called the Gee Affair and resurfaced in Australia. As he explained years later: 'I was wounded in the head and had half my stomach shot away. I couldn't stand it so I went'. In Australia, he worked for the government and only returned to England in 1956 for a review by the Queen of surviving VCs. He was the oldest in the parade. He died at 84 in 1960.

FRANK MEYER 1886–1935

Jews have been in the diamond industry for hundreds of years; the stones were easily transportable if you were expelled from a country and easy to hide. Making jewellery requires great skill and diamonds are popular in any part of the world. Jews had been involved in the Indian diamond trade during the eighteenth century and the South African trade at the end of the nineteenth century. One family so engaged were the Meyers and Frank Meyer's father, Carl, was deputy chairman of De Beers Consolidated Mines. The father was keenly interested in the arts and in 1909 gave £70,000 (£5 million today) towards construction of the first Shakespeare Memorial Theatre at Stratford. Frank, his only son, was educated at Eton where he was the Captain of the Oppidans, boys who distinguished themselves academically. He went on to New College, Oxford where he graduated in 1908. He was called to the Bar in 1910. During the First World War he served as a captain in the Essex Yeomanry and was mentioned in dispatches.

He was elected as Conservative MP for Great Yarmouth in 1924 and served until 1929. He would have stood again but was made deputy chairman of de Beers, as his father had been, and felt the demands of that office had to take precedence. He played little part in the House in his time, except to appeal for the remnants of the wartime Defence of the Realm Act to be abolished as the conflict had been over for several years. In 1935 he died in a riding accident when his horse stumbled over a rabbit hole. He was only 49.

ISIDORE SALMON 1876–1941

Among the Jewish MPs who won for the first time in 1924 was Isidore Salmon. Salmon had served on the LCC for eighteen years from 1907 to 1925 and as vice-chairman from 1924 to 1925. He was elected for Harrow as its Conservative MP in 1924. He succeeded Oswald Mosley who had decided to join the Labour Party. Salmon was a prime example of the Jewish passion for coming in on the ground floor when a new industry is created. The Salmons and Glucksteins were originally cigar makers, but wondered if catering to the public at exhibitions – which, after the Great Exhibition of 1851, were now being held in various parts of the country – would be a profitable venture. In case it wasn't, the new company was called after one of their obliging friends – and that was how Lyons came into existence. By 1924 it was a major catering company noted for some massive hotels in London, but particularly for its teashops. The smart service of the waitresses made the 'Nippies' famous throughout the country.

Salmon sat in the House for seventeen years until he died in 1941 at 65. It couldn't be said that he achieved a great deal for his industry as an MP because the power of the brewers was far greater than that of hoteliers and caterers. For example, bills introduced to divorce hotels from pubs in terms of taxation and licensing laws were unsuccessful. So, incidentally, was the effort of the Labour governments in his time to get waiters paid a salary instead of having to live off their tips. He did sterling work, however, as the chairman of the London War Pensions Committee and was chairman of the Home Office Committee on the Employment of Prisoners. He was also very keen on decimalization, like Samuel Montagu before him, but in this he was again ahead of his time.

What Salmon should be remembered for most was the improvement of catering in the armed forces during the Second World War. It was he who was called in by the government and created the Royal Army Catering Corps. Salmon was another rarity among the Jewish MPs of his time in that he was a stalwart of the Orthodox community. He served as treasurer and vice-president of the United Synagogue and was also vice-president of the Board of Deputies. He was a major in the First World War and received a knighthood.

MICHAEL MARCUS 1894–1960

Michael Marcus flitted briefly across the parliamentary stage when he became MP for Dundee for Labour in 1929 and then lost his seat in 1931. He was never elected again, losing in 1931 and 1935. He had come a long way from the board school where he started his education. He went on to George Heriot's and Edinburgh University before being called to the Bar, where he became a member of the Middle Temple. He was also a solicitor, a member of the Edinburgh Town Council in 1926 and honorary solicitor to the Edinburgh Trades and Labour Council from 1926 to 1930. In the Commons, he was Parliamentary Private Secretary to the Under-Secretary of State for Scotland in the short-lived Labour government of 1929. Marcus was an ardent Zionist and was honorary secretary to the Palestine Parliamentary Committee, and served on the Council of the Jewish Agency. A former treasurer of the Edinburgh Zionist Association, he wrote extensively throughout his life and died in 1960 aged 66.

HARRY NATHAN 1889–1963

Harry Nathan packed an enormous amount of work into his 74 years. He was educated at St Paul's School and at 17 he canvassed for Rufus Isaacs. This inspired him to become a politician, just as the legal work of Isaacs prompted him to become a solicitor in 1913. From the early age of 19, Nathan became involved in Jewish communal work. He was the secretary of the Jewish Brady Boys Club in the East End of London which helped poor young Jews to find a purpose in life and to get on. He was the founder of the Jewish Athletics Association and served on the Board of Deputies from 1925 till the end of his life.

Nathan was one of the original officers in the Territorial Army and was wounded in action in the Great War. In 1929 he won Bethnal Green North West for the Liberals but switched to the Labour Party in 1934 and was elected for Wandsworth in 1937. He was made a peer in 1940. In the Attlee government, he was the Parliamentary Under-Secretary of State for War in 1945, vice-president of the Army Council and was made a Privy Councillor in 1946. In that year he became Minister of Civil Aviation.

He involved himself in a host of charitable activities. He was chairman of the Westminster Hospital and of the British Empire Cancer Campaign. He was on the General Medical Council and president of the Old Paulines. In 1958 he was appointed president of the Royal

Geographic Society and in freemasonry he reached the very high office of Past Grand Warden. He was also chairman of Gestetner. In 1953 he raised £110,000 (over £2 million today) to plant the Queen Elizabeth Coronation Forest in Israel. There was universal regret at his passing in 1963.

MARION PHILLIPS 1881–1932

Marion Phillips was the first Jewish woman MP, sitting for Sunderland from 1929 to 1931. Like all the other Jewish Labour MPs she lost her seat at the 1931 election and she died of stomach cancer in 1932 at the early age of 51. Phillips was a remarkable woman. She came from a prosperous Jewish family in Melbourne, Australia and went to Melbourne University. In 1904 she came to London on a research scholarship at the London School of Economics, which was a major achievement for a woman in her time. Between 1906 and 1910 she worked for Beatrice Webb on a committee investigating the Poor Laws. Her work led her to try to get far more women involved in the Labour Party but she never became a suffragette. She did become secretary of the Women's Labour League in 1912 and between 1917 and 1932 she was secretary of the Standing Joint Committee of Industrial Women's Organisations.

Through her efforts, Dr Phillips got hundreds of thousands of women involved in areas where we now take their presence for granted, but which were new avenues for them at the time – school meals, clinics and play areas for children, a more safety-conscious approach to the design of homes, and equality for women in the workplace. In these issues and many others Phillips was a pioneer and, although she never married, she certainly acted very much like a Jewish mother. In Phillips' day a vast number of homes had no indoor bath and inadequate toilet facilities. Phillips made her beliefs absolutely clear: 'If Labour councillors will not support us on the demand, we shall have to cry a halt on all municipal housing until we have replaced all Labour men by Labour women'. Phillips became the Chief Woman Officer of the Labour Party and it remains indebted to her memory as one of the true founders of the movement.

JIMMY DE ROTHSCHILD 1878–1957

In many ways, James Armand de Rothschild was a typical scion of his international family. A member of the French branch, he went to Cambridge University. Like Muffy Rothschild, he loved racing and in

1909 his horse, Bomba, won the Ascot Gold Cup at a handsome 33–1. He was a member of both the Jockey Club and the Turf Club. In 1913 at the age of 35, he married the 17-year-old Dorothy Mathilde Pinto, and they lived happily ever after for forty-three years. He remained French until 1919, so he joined the French army as a private at the outbreak of the First World War. He ended it in the British army as a major in Palestine in the 39th (Jewish) Battalion. This was part of the Royal Fusiliers and Rothschild was awarded the Distinguished Conduct Medal.

In 1922 he inherited Waddesdon, which his great uncle, Ferdinand de Rothschild, the Liberal MP from 1895 to 1898, had built in the Aylesbury countryside. He entered parliament as the Liberal member for the Isle of Ely in 1929 and stayed till 1945. During the Second World War he served as Parliamentary Secretary to the Ministry of Supply from 1940 to 1945 and he was Deputy Lieutenant for the County of London. A typical wealthy playboy far divorced from the common people? Not according to Henry (Chips) Channon, whose diaries throw fascinating light on the period. He wrote in 1942:

> Jimmy de Rothschild rose, and with immense dignity, and his voice vibrating with emotion, spoke for five minutes in moving tones on the plight of these peoples. (The victims of the Holocaust.) There were tears in his eyes, and I feared that he might break down; the House caught his spirit and was deeply moved. Somebody suggested that we stand in silence to pay our respects to those suffering peoples and the House as a whole rose and stood for a few frozen seconds. It was a fine moment, and my back tingled.

Rothschild didn't forget his roots; when the State of Israel was founded, he gave £6 million to help build the Knesset (the parliament building). When he died in 1957 at nearly 80, he left Waddesdon to the National Trust.

GEORGE STRAUSS 1901–1993

Strauss's father, Arthur, had served thirteen years in the House between 1895 and 1918; George managed forty-seven years. He was elected for Lambeth North in 1929 and for other Lambeth divisions and Vauxhall from 1934 to 1979 when he retired to the Lords. He had been the Father of the House since 1974. Strauss was both a convinced socialist and extremely wealthy. The family business in Germany had been metal broking, and they were very good at it.

Strauss went to Rugby School and fought Lambeth North in 1924, when he was only 23, losing it by just twenty-nine votes. He was on the LCC from 1925 to 1946 and served as Stafford Cripps's Parliamentary Private Secretary before the war. Influenced by Cripps, he supported the proposed National Front against Nazism, which he felt should include the Communists. For this he was temporarily expelled from the party, but he was soon readmitted when Russia became one of the Allies in the Second World War. He was on the Gestapo's list of people for execution, if Britain was defeated.

Winning the war depended on having sufficient aircraft; Strauss was Minister of Aircraft Production from 1942 to 1945. Recovering from the war meant using the available supplies to their best advantage; Strauss was the Minister of Supply from 1947 to 1951. The Labour Party believed that nationalizing major industries was the best way forward; Strauss introduced the Iron and Steel Nationalisation Act in 1949. Free speech is vital in a democracy; Strauss introduced the bill to abolish stage censorship in 1968. He was a very safe pair of hands. He died at the age of 92.

5 1931–1945: Slump, War, Holocaust and Survival

Two events dominated the 1930s: the Slump and the growth of National Socialism. It was clear to many that Hitler's rise to power would have dreadful consequences for the Jews in Germany. Initially, the worldwide effort which would be needed to rescue the community and the costs involved were massively underestimated, but international Jewry coped as the demands became greater. What they could not do, of course, was anticipate the Final Solution as it was inflicted on most Jews in Continental Europe by the Nazis in the Second World War. The impact of the Holocaust would leave an indelible scar on the whole Jewish community in Britain for very many years.

The 1931 National Government included Herbert Samuel and Rufus Isaacs. After 1933, it showed typical British concern for Jewish victims in Germany. It accepted the promise of the Board of Deputies that refugees granted immigrant visas would not become a burden on the state. The Jewish community undertook to support them all financially if necessary. Between 1933 and 1939, the government allowed 50,000 Jewish refugees to come into Britain even though, owing to the Slump, there was severe unemployment in the country. The Jewish community for its part donated £3 million (£144 million today) to help their brethren. World Jewry enabled 85 per cent of German Jews to emigrate before the war broke out.

The Home Office was extremely helpful. On one occasion, dealing with a request for 500 visas for synagogue officials in Germany, they asked what special skills the migrants could bring with them which the UK couldn't obtain otherwise. A *Tsitsis* is a Jewish religious garment which has fringes with knots that must be tied in a particular way. The Home Office was assured that the migrants could make *Tsitsit* knots, and they agreed to provide the 500 visas. In fact, after *Kristallnacht* in 1938, the Home Office issued thousands more visas than were taken up. A mixture of false hopes of better times to come and bureaucratic inefficiency left Jews stranded who could have used the visas to save their lives.

At the end of the decade, the imperative need to placate the Arab world in the event of a major war led to another White Paper which did effectively stop Jewish migration to Palestine. Those who opposed it in parliament were completely outnumbered. The Arabs had the oil and, if war broke out, adequate oil supplies would be absolutely vital. Those Jewish MPs who were Zionists did what they could but to little avail. When the war started many Jewish MPs joined the colours; one was lost when Dudley Joel died at sea in 1941.

The Labour Party in opposition to the National Government found it easy to support the ideal of the National Home. They didn't have to cope with the difficulties which plagued the mandatory power in Palestine. In both the Labour Party conferences and the Trades Union Congresses from 1936 onwards, motions supporting the National Home were regularly passed. These were vote winners among the Jewish community. When Labour eventually won power after the war, the situation would be different and more difficult. As Stanley Baldwin, the Conservative Prime Minister, quipped to an opponent, 'Power without responsibility has been the prerogative of the harlot throughout the ages'.

As the full horror of the Holocaust became known during the war, the Church of England determined to stretch out the hand of friendship to the Jewish community. Where formerly there had been a concentration on the desirability of converting the Jews to Christianity, now there would be the Council of Christian and Jews, devoted to a better understanding between the two faiths. As the popularity of belief started to wane in both camps after the war, the supporters of religion found themselves fighting the same opposition.

There were fifty Jewish candidates in the 1935 election, and about 40 per cent won their seats. Jewish MPs elected to the Parliaments of 1931 and 1935 and in by-elections were:

1931   Leopold Amery (Conservative), **Alfred Chotzner** (Conservative), **Louis Gluckstein** (Conservative), **Albert Goodman** (Conservative), Percy Harris (Liberal), Leslie Hore-Belisha (National Liberal), **Barnett Janner** (Liberal), **Dudley Joel** (Conservative), **Thomas Levy** (Conservative), **Abraham Lyons** (Conservative), Harry Nathan (Liberal), Marion Phillips (Labour), Jimmy Rothschild (Liberal), Isidore Salmon (Conservative), Arthur Samuel (Conservative), Herbert Samuel (Liberal), Sam Samuel (Conservative), Philip Sassoon (Conservative), Edward Strauss (Liberal)

1934 George Strauss (Liberal), **Marcus Samuel** (Conservative)
1935 Leopold Amery (Conservative), Harry Day (Labour), **Dan Frankel** (Labour), Louis Gluckstein (Conservative), Albert Goodman (Conservative), Percy Harris (Liberal), Leslie Hore-Belisha (National Liberal), Dudley Joel (Conservative), Thomas Levy (Conservative), Abraham Lyons (Conservative), Jimmy Rothschild (Liberal), Isidore Salmon (Conservative), Arthur Samuel (Conservative), Marcus Samuel (Conservative), Philip Sassoon (Conservative), Manny Shinwell (Labour), **Sidney Silverman** (Labour), Edward Strauss (Liberal)
1936 **Lewis Silkin** (Labour)
1937 Leslie Haden-Guest (Labour), **Daniel Lipson** (Independent), Harry Nathan (Liberal)
1942 **John Mack** (Labour)

ALFRED CHOTZNER 1873–1958

Chotzner won West Ham for the Conservatives in 1931 but his life, up to that time, had been spent mostly in India where he was a civil servant in the service of the Raj. After Harrow and St John's College, Cambridge, he successfully sat the Indian Civil Service exams in 1895. He spent the next thirty-three years working his way up the ladder. He passed his Law exams in 1910 and in 1924 he was appointed a Puisne Judge of the High Court of Judicature in Calcutta, serving in that capacity until 1928. For light relief he was also a Steward of the Royal Calcutta Turf Club in 1926 and 1927.

The streets of West Ham must have presented a stark contrast to the racecourse in Calcutta, but Chotzner won the seat and served his constituents faithfully. With his illustrious education and career, it might be expected that his roots were laid deep in the Cousinhood. Not a bit of it. His father had taught at Harrow and was for many years the eminent rabbi of the synagogue in Belfast. Alfred Chotzner only served as an MP for three years. In 1934 he applied for the Manor of Northstead, an ancient way of resigning from the Commons. The explanation was ill health, though he lived another twenty-four years, to die aged 85 in 1958.

LOUIS GLUCKSTEIN 1897–1979

When Louis Gluckstein won Ely for the Conservatives in 1931, he was the tallest MP ever to serve in the Commons. He was over 6' 7" and, like Isidore Salmon, came from one of the families that ran Lyons, the caterers, hoteliers and food manufacturers. He was a barrister, educated at St Paul's School and Lincoln College, Oxford, and took silk in 1945. Gluckstein fought in the two world wars and was mentioned in dispatches in both. He always worked hard and was duly rewarded for his endeavours. He was colonel of the 5th Suffolk Regiment of the Territorial Army and in 1970 was elected treasurer of Lincoln's Inn. He also served as president of the Royal Albert Hall and was for many years a director of British Transport Hotels. He was knighted in the Coronation Honours list in 1953. In his communal life, Gluckstein was a vice-president of the Liberal Synagogue. Gluckstein won the constituency of East Nottingham in 1935 but he lost his seat in 1945 and failed to regain it in 1950. But he did manage to gain a seat on the GLC from 1964 to 1967 and he was an alderman from 1967 to 1973. He was a keen golfer who also liked shooting. He died at the age of 82.

ALBERT GOODMAN 1880–1937

Albert Goodman's father was an Australian and Albert was educated in Melbourne. By the age of 24 he was in India and didn't come to England until 1924 when he became an estate agent. He took a keen interest in the Territorial Army and was honorary colonel of the 27th (London) AA 5/2 Battalion of the Royal Engineers (TA). He took the title of colonel from that point and first stood for election for Bow and Bromley in East London in 1929 where he was well beaten by George Lansbury, who went on to become Leader of the Labour Party. When Labour did so badly in the 1931 election Goodman was able to win Islington North as a Conservative, holding the seat in 1935. He died in 1937 at the age of 57.

BARNETT JANNER 1892–1982

Barnett Janner, usually known as Barney, was a prominent parliamentarian, a Jewish leader and Zionist and an indefatigable defender of the rights of ordinary citizens. His parents came from Lithuania and he grew up in Barry in South Wales where he won scholarships at the County School and at the University of Wales. His first communal office was as chairman of the University of Wales Jewish Students Union. As a soldier in the Great War, he survived being gassed in the trenches and returned to Cardiff where he qualified as a solicitor and built up a successful practice. In 1931 Janner was elected in a by-election as Liberal member for Whitechapel and St Georges. He was a leader of those who opposed Mosley and his Blackshirts. He lost his seat in 1935 but changed his political allegiance and won Leicester West for Labour in 1945. He remained a Leicester MP until he retired in 1970 when he was made a peer.

Strongly supportive of Israel and always in the forefront of protests against the Communist bloc's treatment of its Jewish communities, he was elected president of the Jewish Board of Deputies from 1955 to 1964. When he was knighted in 1961 it was the first time the award had been given for services to the Board of Deputies in their nearly 200-year history. It was Janner who was chosen to respond to the speech of the Duke of Edinburgh at the Tercentenary Dinner in 1956.

In 1952, Janner was British Jewry's appointed delegate to the Conference on British Claims against Germany. He guided several bills through parliament including an important one on leasehold reform. His longest battle was to get Britain to ratify the Genocide

Convention. He was so persistent that the measure became known in the House as the 'Jannercide' Convention. He finally succeeded in 1969. Janner was decorated by both Belgium and Holland. He was associated in one capacity or another with almost every Jewish organization of any significance, and, among his many successes, he arranged for the Jews in Aden to have the right to settle in Britain after the colony achieved independence. Janner died in 1982 in his ninetieth year.

DUDLEY JOEL 1904–1941

In 1931, the scion of a fabulously wealthy Jewish family, Dudley Jack Barnato Joel won Dudley – an odd coincidence – for the Conservatives. Joel's ancestors had made a fortune in South Africa at the end of the nineteenth century in precious metals and diamonds. The best known was probably Barney Barnato, after whom Dudley was named. Yet if Joel had been born with a jewel-encrusted spoon in his mouth, he still grew up to work hard and effectively. After King's College, Cambridge he took up another of the family's interests – horse racing. His father, Lieutenant Colonel Solomon Joel, had a fine stable up the road in Newmarket and Dudley took over control of it when he was only 28. His official occupation as an insurance underwriter would have helped with the overheads.

Even with such a patrician background, Joel still found time to serve on the committee of the Jewish Brady Boys Club in the East End of London. Brady opened its doors in 1897 and its founders encouraged rich and educated young Jews to work at the Club as volunteers to help and advise their poorer brethren about how to get on in life. Joel was re-elected in 1935, and in 1939 he joined the Royal Naval Volunteer Reserve. His wife died that year and Joel was killed in 1941 when his ship was bombed by enemy aircraft off Cape Cornwall. He was 37 years old. In his will he left over £1 million (the equivalent of at least £44 million today). There were legacies of a year's wages for anybody who had worked for him for five years, and six months' if they had been with him for two years. He was buried in the family plot at Willesden cemetery, alongside Barney Barnato.

THOMAS LEVY 1874–1953

Thomas Levy went to the City of London School which has nurtured a large number of Jewish boys since its foundation, and which received a great deal of support from Marcus Samuel, the founder of

Shell, when it started. Levy played his part in the First World War by becoming the Executive Officer for Food Control in Bournemouth from 1914 to 1918. During the General Strike he was in charge of transport.

Levy won the constituency of Elland in 1931, sitting as a Conservative until 1945. During his time in the Commons he introduced a Private Member's Bill which was taken up by the government, becoming the Firearms Act 1934. Apart from tightening up a number of regulations about the possession of handguns, the bill raised the age at which you could hire or own a handgun from 14 to 17! Levy also served in the House as chairman of the Parliamentary Textiles Committee from 1932 to 1935, and from 1935 to 1939 he was chairman of the Parliamentary Tariff Policy Committee. From 1939 to 1940 he was chairman of the British Wool Advisory Committee and he sat on the Board of British Celanese. He died in 1953 when he was nearly 80.

ABRAHAM LYONS 1894–1961

Abraham Lyons went to the Collegiate School in Grimsby and the Old Clee Grammar School. By 1922, he was a barrister, taking silk in 1933. He was Recorder of Grimsby from 1936 to 1961 and was the Leader of the Midland Circuit. During the First World War Lyons served as a lieutenant in the Durham Light Infantry from 1914 to 1916, and as a major in the Second World War, liaising with the French forces. Lyons's political career in the Commons started when he was elected for Leicester East as a Conservative in 1931, holding the seat until he was defeated in 1945. In 1959 he was made Master of the Worshipful Company of Pattern Makers. Lyons was an Orthodox Jew and highly regarded. At the end of his life he was asked by the Chief Rabbi to chair a committee enquiring into the prices of kosher meat, but he died at the age of 67 before the work could be completed.

MARCUS SAMUEL 1873–1942

Marcus Samuel followed a profession favoured by the Jews since at least the tenth century – he was an East India man. He traded with Asia and there are records from that distant time of Sephardi Jews trading with China from Europe. Samuel was educated at University College School and abroad. He was a cousin of the Marcus Samuel who founded Shell and a nephew of Sam Samuel who helped him to do so. When Sam Samuel died, Marcus Samuel won the subsequent by-election for Putney in November 1934 standing as a Conservative, and was elected again in 1935. Samuel was very much anti-socialist and wrote a good deal about protection. Sir Oswald Mosley wrote a book titled *Revolution by Reason*, so Samuel composed a rebuttal, *Revolution by Miscalculation*. Another of his efforts was *Socialism in Theory and Practice in Russia*, from which the Communist regime did not emerge unscathed. Samuel died in 1942 at the age of 68, still in harness at the Commons.

SYDNEY SILVERMAN 1895–1968

The Jews have survived partly because of a steely determination to do so. All his life, Sydney Silverman typified this Jewish trait. He fought against the odds, refusing to accept defeat, no matter how rough the going. Silverman was born to a refugee family from Romania who managed to scratch a living in Liverpool. There was no money to pay for an expensive schooling, so he won scholarships to the Liverpool Institute and Liverpool University, where he read English Literature. When the First World War broke out, Silverman was already a socialist and hated the carnage that he knew would inevitably take place. He believed that capitalists were sacrificing the workers on the battlefields for their own ends, and so he became a member of a despised minority – the conscientious objectors, just like Ramsay Macdonald. Silverman was arrested and spent over two years in prison because he refused to be any part of the war effort, going on hunger strike for long periods.

After the war, Silverman couldn't get a decent job in Britain so he went to Helsinki University where he taught as an English lecturer from 1921 to 1924. Then he decided to return home and become a solicitor. He passed with first-class Honours in 1927, and so could now devote himself to his true interest, protecting and defending workers in compensation claims and landlord and tenant cases. He built his reputation on battling for the poor and was elected to Liverpool City Council from 1932 to 1938.

During this period members of the Nelson and Colne constituency Labour Party got to hear of his reputation and recognized a promising candidate for the 1935 election. They offered Silverman the opportunity and he won in spite of encountering a good deal of anti-Semitism on the hustings. Silverman would represent the constituency for the next thirty-three years and his support for the working classes was unwavering. During the Second World War he successfully defended striking workers, even though striking was illegal in wartime.

When Attlee won the 1945 election, Silverman was regarded as a left-winger and not offered a post in government. Indeed, he was expelled from the party for a time because he supported nuclear disarmament – in 1959 he was one of the founders of the Campaign for Nuclear Disarmament. Even so, Silverman served as a member of the Labour Party's National Executive from 1956 to 1968.

On the other side of the pacifism coin is a hatred of capital punishment, and Silverman's 1956 Private Member's Bill to abolish hanging was passed by the Commons but killed in the Lords. It would be another ten years before capital punishment was finally ended. Communally, Silverman was a keen Zionist. He was president of the Zionist Central Council and a provincial member of the executive of the Zionist Federation of Great Britain. He was elected in 1940 as the first chairman of the British section of the World Jewish Congress and fought for the survivors of the Holocaust to be allowed to emigrate to Israel.

It was unusual for MPs to sport beards. When Silverman grew one it was said that Attlee commented, 'I move the previous face'. Silverman died in 1968 at the age of 73. Just before he passed away he said, 'The only memorial I would value is that I have given a lifetime of service in the Labour Party's continuing effort to establish a secular society under a Labour government in this country'.

DAN FRANKEL 1900–1988

Dan Frankel won Mile End for Labour in 1935 and held the seat for ten years. In 1945, he was beaten by another Jewish MP, the Communist, Phil Piratin. Frankel's life was devoted to the Labour Party and the trade union movement. He was a tailor and cutter by profession and his political career had been based in Stepney where he had been chosen as Mayor in 1928 to 1929 when he was only 28. He represented Stepney on the LCC from 1931 to 1945 and was vice-chairman of the LCC Medical Services Committee. Within the Jewish community, Frankel took most interest in the Jewish Friendly Societies, for which he worked very hard. He lived to be 88 but didn't serve in the House again. Frankel was one of the foot soldiers in the Labour Party and, like many other Jewish MPs, part of the backbone of the movement.

LEWIS SILKIN 1889–1972

Lewis Silkin went to London University and started his own solicitor's practice in 1920. His path to parliament was via the LCC where he became a member in 1925. He chaired the Town Planning and Housing and Public Health Committees. Elected for Peckham for Labour at a by-election in 1936 he retained the seat until 1950 when he was made a peer. He served as Deputy Leader of the Opposition in the House of Lords. In Attlee's government, Silkin was appointed Minister of Town and Country Planning from 1945 to 1950. It was one of the most important ministerial posts because of the enormous amount of damage caused by enemy bombing during the war. It was while Silkin was in office that a bill was passed to create the new towns like Milton Keynes. In the House of Lords, Silkin was ahead of his time in trying to extend defamation to attacks on whole sects and not just individuals. In this he was unsuccessful, but the marker was laid down for the future.

Communally, Silkin was extremely active. In 1951 he founded the British Technion Society to help the institution in Israel and he gave a great deal of time to such Jewish charitable organizations as the Jewish National Fund and ORT (now an educational charity, the name derives from the Russian acronym for 'The Society for Trades and Agricultural Labour', founded 1886). He was also a strong supporter of the Jewish Secondary School Movement. Silkin was made a Companion of Honour in 1965 and died in 1972, aged 83.

DANIEL LIPSON 1886–1963

In 1937 Cheltenham was one of the safest Conservative seats in the country. Any Tory candidate was likely to win hands down. So when the sitting member, Sir Walter Preston, retired the logical and eminently safe candidate was Daniel Lipson, who had been the Mayor of the town for the last two years. He was a Cambridge-educated school teacher who had worked as a house master at Cheltenham College from 1923 to 1935. The only problem for the Cheltenham Conservative Party was that Lipson was a Jew. So they refused to endorse him. For many candidates that would have been the end of the road, but Lipson was made of sterner stuff. He decided to stand as an Independent and was triumphantly elected. He went on to serve as the only Independent in the House of Commons for the next thirteen years. In 1945, when Conservative candidates were going down like ninepins and not a single Conservative Jewish candidate won a seat, Lipson skated home.

In 1950, at the age of 64, he was unwise enough to stand again but this time the official Conservative candidate beat him easily. He remained an alderman of the Gloucester City Council until his death in 1963. It was, and remains, almost impossible for a lone Independent to have any major effect in the Commons on national politics, but Lipson was a popular member and his views were always listened to with courtesy. By his very presence, he showed that British electorates were perfectly capable of being more tolerant than selection committees. He died in 1963 at the age of 77.

JOHN MACK 1899–1957

John Mack began to try for a seat in parliament in 1929 and again in 1931, but it wasn't until 1942 that he won Newcastle-under-Lyme for Labour, unopposed in a by-election. He retained the seat in 1945 and 1950 but he stood down in 1951. By profession, Mack was a life insurance agent, which demands many of the same skills as an MP – fluency, logical argument, attention to detail and a thorough mastery of the subject. He was a member of the National Amalgamated Union of Life Assurance Workers and became a Liverpool City Councillor in 1928. He served on the council for the next eighteen years and lectured at the National Council of Labour Colleges.

Communally, he was a member of the Liverpool branch of Poale Zion ('The Workers of Zion', founded circa 1900) and in 1943 he joined the Committee for a Jewish Army. He became its vice-chairman and in 1944 a Jewish brigade was founded. In 1946 he discussed with the Romanian government the condition of Jews in the country and what could be done to ameliorate their condition and to combat the anti-Semitism which still existed in Romania, even after the Holocaust. He died in 1957, at the age of 58.

It had been ten years since the 1935 election and the world had changed. The National Government, largely Conservative, was widely blamed for not preventing the war. The country was looking for scapegoats for the immense losses that the war had brought and no section of the community was more angry at the carnage than the Jews, who had lost so many of their co-religionists in the Holocaust. A large number of them had friends and relatives on the continent who had not survived, so they had personal tragedies to contend with, often on a horrific scale. Whole families wiped out and murdered in the most appalling way. Six million dead.

The country's own main concern was that it wanted greater equality between rich and poor, and in 1942 Manny Shinwell wrote the original manifesto for the Labour Party which was most likely to bring this about. One of its major planks was the nationalization of key industries. The result of the 1945 election was a massive victory for Clement Attlee who took over from Winston Churchill. There were twenty-nine Jews elected to that parliament, by far the largest number ever. The 1935 Conservative and Liberal Jewish MPs disappeared completely. Dan Lipson won Cheltenham again and was a Conservative in everything except his nomination papers. Otherwise there were no survivors. Seven of the former Jewish MPs were defeated – Amery, Frankel, Gluckstein, Harris, Hore-Belisha, Levy and Rothschild. Nine were dead – Day, Goodman, Joel, Lyons, Salmon, Arthur and Marcus Samuel, Sassoon, and Edward Strauss. Harry Nathan was in the Lords and four Labour MPs had survived both the war and the election – Mack, Shinwell, Silkin and Silverman.

So the class of Jewish MPs in 1945 was cast in a new mould. It has to be said, though, that if the trade unions were on the march, the elected Jewish MPs would have had some difficulty in presenting themselves as horny-handed sons of toil. Of the thirty elected, only three were genuinely working-class – Herschell Austin, Ian Mikardo

and Manny Shinwell. The others included six barristers, three solicitors, four doctors, a chartered accountant, a university professor and
a company secretary. Five had been to Oxford and one to Cambridge.

Some of the Jewish Labour MPs were Orthodox, some were not,
but what they had in common was that they all believed in the socialist cause. They were all genuinely left-wing and some were on the
left-wing of the left-wing. One reason why so many Jews have been
labelled revolutionaries in the past has been because the government
they were trying to overthrow had discriminated against them. Even
in Britain, by his very presence in the House, the Independent member, Daniel Lipson, still demonstrated an open and unacceptable level
of anti-Semitism among a number of Conservative Associations.

After the war, Labour constituencies in urban seats were less likely to turn away a well-qualified Jewish candidate; they knew they
needed intelligent professionals to represent them in parliament.
Many local Labour leaders recognized they would be totally out of
their depth if they themselves tried to act on the national stage. It
wasn't necessarily true, but a barrister from Balliol, an officer and a
gentleman, like Major Lyall Wilkes, ex-secretary of the Oxford
Union, could be perceived by Labour voters to have a better chance
of representing the electorate of Newcastle Central effectively than
the average welder from the shipyards.

The team of Jewish Labour MPs who won in 1945, when Labour
enjoyed a landslide victory, almost all retained their seats after the
1950 election when Labour's lead was reduced to single figures.
Lipson lost his seat, as did Phil Piratin for the Communists, but otherwise only Austin, Comyns, Levy, Segal, Silkin and Solley were
defeated. Twenty-one Jewish Labour MPs lived to fight the good fight
in the Commons for another day.

The period immediately after the war saw the relations between
the Jews and the British government strained as never before. As the
mandatory power, Britain had to keep the peace in Palestine and be
seen to be even-handed. The Jews in Palestine were, naturally, determined to get the survivors of the Holocaust into the country some-
how. No humanitarian cause could have a stronger case, but the pre-
war regulations were still in force and the British Foreign Secretary,
Ernest Bevin, was intent on maintaining them. In Palestine there was
considerable violence between Arab and Jewish militias between
1945 and 1948 and the British forces, trying to keep the peace, were
dragged into the melee.

Jewish extremists murdered many British soldiers, and there were
particularly heavy casualties when the King David Hotel in Jerusalem

was blown up. The stoicism of the British reaction at the time was similar to the treatment of the Irish in Britain during the IRA troubles in the 1970s and after; there was little or no attempt to take revenge locally. Jewish MPs still tried to get the government to relax its immigration quotas but to no avail. There were heart-rending scenes as, for example, unseaworthy hulks of ships which had limped into Palestine transporting Holocaust survivors were sent back to Europe and the camps.

When Britain gave up the Mandate in 1948, the War of Independence began. Five Arab nations sent armies to destroy the fledgling Jewish state – Egypt, Iraq, Jordan the Lebanon and Syria. Volunteers came from Saudi Arabia, Libya and the Yemen. The Jews, fighting for their lives yet again in their history, beat them all. This was in spite of an international arms embargo against providing arms to either side which in fact favoured the Arab nations, who already had what they needed. Only an airlift from the armaments factories in Czechoslovakia enabled the Jews to face their enemies on anything like equal terms. Architect of the airlift was a former member of British Intelligence, a Czech by birth and who had worked with them during the war. He had changed his name to Robert Maxwell.

A large proportion of the Arab inhabitants of Palestine fled and were placed in refugee camps by the neighbouring Arab nations. There was no attempt to integrate them into the countries where they sought safety, as refugees have been for centuries, and their sufferings were used for propaganda purposes. Neither would the Arab nations admit defeat. The best that could be arranged was an armistice and this did not prevent further wars and bloodshed over the next sixty years.

The Jewish community in Britain was in an impossible situation; they could not turn their backs on the only country in the world which could guarantee a safe refuge for Jews because it was a state governed by the Jews. At the same time, the vast majority didn't want to live in that country and considered Britain their home and nation. As Israel almost immediately lined up with the western powers, the country could at least be regarded as an ally, which was not the case as far as the Russian Jews were concerned. As Israel turned from the neo-communism of the kibbutz movement to a strong alliance with the Americans, the treatment of Jews in Russia deteriorated.

In Britain, support for Israel by the Jewish community was almost universal but, as Israel became stronger over the years, that support came to be regarded less as a helping hand for the underdog. Israel introduced National Service for all their youngsters of both sexes.

They had little option if they wanted to survive. Arab nations continued to condemn the existence of the Israeli state and swore to destroy it. They tried to do so on other occasions and lost each war. They tried economic sanctions and those had only very limited success. The core fact remained, as far as the Jewish community in Britain was concerned, that Israel remained at war with Iraq, Syria and the Lebanon – peace treaties would be signed with Egypt and Jordan in later years – and they held the country as the spoils of war.

That the Holy Land was immensely precious to almost all Jews was not in doubt, but it would be difficult to justify a claim by the Italians to rule Britain because the Romans had done so centuries before, or for China to rule half of Asia because Genghis Khan had managed it. The Jews recovered Israel because they fought for it successfully. As the strongest military power in the Middle East today, they hold it for the same reason.

That this support could be forthcoming from the Zionist Federation of Great Britain created no problems. The difficulty arose for the Board of Deputies, which had been split down the middle on the issue of the National Home way back in 1917. It was perfectly possible that, in private, Board members might disagree with aspects of Israeli policy, but to say so publicly would be to give ammunition to Israel's enemies who wouldn't hesitate to quote them. To this day, the Board doesn't publicly criticize the Israeli government. Not all the Jewish MPs would take the same view. There would be harsh Jewish critics of Israel's more contentious policies. At the end of the day, though, the major criticism would come from the countries with which Israel was at war – not because it wanted to be in conflict, but because the Arab nations involved wouldn't agree to a peace treaty.

Successive British governments would do their best to bring the conflict to an end. The Foreign Office, recognizing the economic needs of Britain, gave full recognition to the Arab grievances. When the Arab League introduced their boycott of companies doing business with Israel, the British government wouldn't make it illegal, as the Americans did. Efforts by Jewish MPs to achieve such a result were unsuccessful. As the former mandatory power, the relations between Britain and Israel were always sensitive, but in the Cold War they had Russia as a common enemy which helped to cement good relations.

Attlee's administration made revolutionary changes to the structure of the country and many of the Jewish MPs had a part to play in the government. The following Jewish men were successful in the elections between 1945 and 1955, but there were no Jewish women to follow in the footstep of Marion Philips.

1945 **Herschel Austin** (Labour), **Louis Comyns** (Labour), **John Diamond** (Labour), **Maurice Edelman** (Labour), **Mont Follick** (Labour), Barnett Janner (Labour), **George Jeger** (Labour), Santo Jeger (Labour), Harold Lever (Labour), **Benn Levy** (Labour), **John Lewis** (Labour), Daniel Lipson (Independent), **Marcus Lipton** (Labour), John Mack (Labour), **Ian Mikardo** (Labour), **Harry Morris** (Labour), **Maurice Orbach** (Labour), **Phil Piratin** (Communist), **Sam Segal** (Labour), Manny Shinwell (Labour), Lewis Silkin (Labour), **Julius Silverman** (Labour), Sidney Silverman (Labour), **Leslie Solley** (Labour Independent), George Strauss (Labour), **Barnett Stross** (Labour), Moss Turner-Samuels (Labour), **David Weizman** (Labour), **Lyall Wilkes** (Labour)

1948 **Austen Albu** (Labour)

1950 Austen Albu (Labour), John Diamond (Labour), Maurice Edelman (Labour), Mont Follick (Labour), Barnett Janner (Labour), George Jeger (Labour), Santo Jeger (Labour), Harold Lever (Labour), **Leslie Lever** (Labour), John Lewis (Labour), Marcus Lipton (Labour), John Mack (Labour), Ian Mikardo (Labour), Harry Morris (Labour), **Gerald Nabarro** (Conservative), Maurice Orbach (Labour), Manny Shinwell (Labour), Julius Silverman (Labour), Sidney Silverman (Labour), George Strauss (Labour), Barnett Stross (Labour), Moss Turner-Samuels (Labour), David Weizman (Labour), Lyall Wilkes (Labour)

1951 Austen Albu (Labour), Maurice Edelman (Labour), Barnett Janner (Labour), George Jeger (Labour), Santo Jeger (Labour), Harold Lever (Labour), Leslie Lever (Labour), Marcus Lipton (Labour), Ian Mikardo (Labour), Harry Morris (Labour), Gerald Nabarro (Conservative), Maurice Orbach (Labour), Manny Shinwell (Labour), Julius Silverman (Labour), Sidney Silverman (Labour), George Strauss (Labour), Barnett Stross (Labour), Moss Turner-Samuels (Labour), David Weizman (Labour)

1952 **Lord Mancroft** (Conservative)

HERSCHEL LEWIS AUSTIN 1911–1974

Herschel Lewis Austin as listed in yearbooks and quoted in the press was always 'H.L. Austin'. He was a Lancashire man, educated in an elementary school until he left at 11 to become a carpenter. He rose to be works manager and then moved on to be a director of an aircraft factory. He joined the navy in 1943 and ended the war as a sub lieutenant. He was selected for Stretford in the 1945 election, won easily and served five years in the House before losing the seat just as easily, in 1950. He was a keen Zionist and a member of the Anglo-Palestinian Club. After 1950, the trail goes cold until he died in Brighton in 1974 at the age of 63, mourned by his wife, children, brothers and sisters.

It would be easy to dismiss Austin as 'division fodder'. He did serve on Labour Committees for Defence and the Armed Services but never rose high in parliamentary ranks. Yet a study of Hansard shows how hard he worked on behalf of his constituents and how much interest he took in the work of the Commons. In a two-month period in 1949 he asked eight questions and made two speeches, apart from his constituency work. The breadth of his questions was considerable. They ranged from footballers getting tax-free benefit matches to repairing council housing in London, and from encouraging good relations with the Chinese to the most effective proportions in mixing cod liver oil. He spoke at some length on housing and in the debate on the Finance Bill he made a major speech on the problems of the spinning industry in Lancashire. His contributions were erudite, clear and comprehensive. Austin may have started at the bottom but he still became a respected MP.

LOUIS COMYNS 1904–1962

Louis Comyns was a good Scottish doctor, one of those who had left his native land to help the English run theirs. He was a man who cared about contributing to society; at Glasgow University he had been secretary of the Labour Club. When he was just qualified, he worked on committees for the local Jewish Lads Brigade, the Hebrew Benevolent Loan Society and the Glasgow Jewish Institute. When he transferred to London in 1932, apart from his thirteen years as a local GP, he worked for Jewish charities in his new home town.

Being a doctor in the Blitz was a hazardous occupation and on one occasion Comyns was wounded as he went to help casualties during the regular bombing of the docks. He was elected as Labour member for West Ham Silvertown in 1945 and was particularly annoyed at the slow progress in rebuilding the East End. In harassing the government on this issue, he was allied with Phil Piratin, the Jewish Communist member for nearby Mile End. Looking at the devastation the Blitz had caused throughout the area, it was no wonder that he considered new housing one of the main priorities.

In 1950, his constituency was abolished and he didn't bother to find a new one, serving instead on the West Ham Executive Council from 1948 to 1962. He may well have thought he could do more good there than he had as part of a 1945 parliament dominated by an immense Labour majority. During the same period he was also chairman of the West Ham Hospital Management Committee. A dapper man, with large horn-rim spectacles and carefully brushed hair, Comyns was the perfect image of a family doctor. As such he was a good choice for chair of the South West Essex Orphan Aid Society and the Ilford Joint Palestine Appeal. He died in 1962 at the age of 58.

JOHN DIAMOND 1907–2004

John Diamond was originally a Leeds accountant with his own practice. Educated at Leeds Grammar School, he became one of the successful Jewish candidates in the 1945 election. Diamond had an up-and-down career in the Commons, losing his Blackley seat in 1950 and winning Gloucester in a by-election in 1957. He succeeded one Jewish MP – Moss Turner-Samuels – and was eventually beaten by another, the Conservative Sally Oppenheim. Three Jewish MPs in succession, with very few Jews living in Gloucester.

Diamond's ability was never in doubt. He was Parliamentary Private Secretary to the Minister of Works in the Attlee Government and Chief Secretary to the Treasury in the 1964 Wilson Government. He was appointed a Privy Councillor in 1965 and sat in the Cabinet from 1968 to 1970. Diamond lost his seat in 1970 and was made a peer that year as Baron Diamond of Gloucester. So he didn't completely sever his links with the city but he did leave the Labour Party in 1981 when he joined the newly formed Social Democratic Party. He led the SDP group in the House of Lords from 1982 to 1988 but didn't like the idea of its joining with the Liberals. So he left the SDP in their turn and in 1995 was welcomed back into the Labour Party. Diamond was an honorary secretary of the Fabian Society and chairman of the Royal Commission on the Distribution of Income and Wealth from 1974 to 1979. He lived to the remarkable age of 96 and died in 2004.

MAURICE EDELMAN 1911–1975

Maurice Edelman was one of that dedicated group of Jewish Labour MPs who first entered parliament in 1945. He had been a war correspondent in North Africa and at the landings in Normandy. He had also worked at Supreme Headquarters Allied Expeditionary Forces (SHAEF) with the American army. Dodging bullets on Normandy beaches was a long way from his birth in Wales, the son of a Jewish family from Eastern Europe. He was a second-generation refugee and was one of many at that time who took advantage of the far greater opportunities Britain offered. From Cardiff High School he won a place at Trinity College, Cambridge. Those were the days when Cambridge produced a string of socialists and Communists, the youngsters choosing the left wing as the most likely way of successfully opposing Fascism. Edelman even wrote two books on Russia, which he had visited in his youth. For ten years after leaving Cambridge he researched plastic materials for aircraft production, helping as a back-room boy to improve the technical standard of fighters and bombers, which had such a major effect in enabling Britain to win the war.

In 1945, Edelman won Coventry West and in 1950, Coventry North. In 1974 it became Coventry North West and by the time he died in 1975 Edelman had won ten elections in a row. He was vice-chairman of the British Council from 1957 to 1967 and as chairman of the Franco-British Parliamentary Relations Committee, awarded the Legion d'Honneur. He was also president of the Anglo-Jewish Association.

MONT FOLLICK 1887–1958

Mont Follick did not consider himself Jewish, which was a bit difficult to justify, as he was from an old-established Jewish family in Cardiff and was bar mitzvah in the local synagogue in 1900. Follick spoke fourteen languages and was educated at the Sorbonne and the Universities of Halle and at Padua, one of the few Italian universities which had been prepared to take Jewish students from the eighteenth century onwards. He was Professor of English at Madrid University for four years and founded the Regent School of Languages in London. During his lifetime, he was secretary to the Prime Minister of Queensland, the Aga Khan and the Sultan of Morocco – Jewish merchants were responsible for Moroccan overseas trade throughout the eighteenth century, so he was following a familiar path. Follick

1, Lionel de Rothschild (© Rothschild Archive)

2, Sir David Salomon (© *The Jewish Chronicle*)

3, Sir Francis Goldsmid (© *The Jewish Chronicle*)

4, Sir George Jessel (© *The Jewish Chronicle*)

5, Samuel Montagu

6, Rufus Isaacs (© *The Jewish Chronicle*)

7, Herbert Samuel (© *The Jewish Chronicle*)

8, Sir Philip Magnus (© *The Jewish Chronicle*)

9, Alfred Mond (© *The Jewish Chronicle*)

10, Walter Rothschild (© Rothschild Archive)

11, Manny Shinwell (© Photoshot)

12, Robert Gee (© jewish Military Museum)

13, Leslie Hore-Belisha (© *The Jewish Chronicle*)

14, Marion Phillips (© *The Jewish Chronicle*)

15, Barnett Janner

16, Leo Abse

17, James de Rothschild (© Rothschild Archive)

18, Sir Ivan Lawrence

19, Phil Piratin (© Sam Harris)

20, Joel Barnett (© *The Jewish Chronicle*)

21, Harold Lever (© *The Jewish Chronicle*)   22, Sir Henry d'Avigdor-Goldsmid
(© *The Jewish Chronicle*)

23, Sir Keith Joseph (© *The Jewish Chronicle*)   24, Sheila Faith

25, Leon Brittan

26, Nigel Lawson (© Photoshot)

27, Helen Hayman

28, Malcolm Rifkind

29, Michael Howard

30, Oona King

31, David Miliband

32, Ed Miliband

was Labour MP for Loughborough from 1945 to 1951 but he didn't stand in 1955 and died in 1958 at the age of 70. While in the Commons he advocated the causes of spelling reform and decimal currency.

GEORGE JEGER 1903–1971

Winchester had been the capital of England long before London, and until 1945 it had never elected a Labour MP. George Jeger broke that tradition when he won the seat, but he decided that he wouldn't try his luck twice. In 1950 he switched to Goole and served there until he died in 1971. So Jeger won eight elections in a row – impressive indeed. His brother, Santo, was also an MP. Jeger was one of those men without whom the country seizes up. He was prepared to put in the hours, go through the fine detail and serve Britain and his constituents in every way he could. He was a company secretary by profession and a committed socialist from his youth. He was even made a Knight Commander of the Order of Liberation of the Spanish Government in 1960 while that government was still in exile, after Franco had won the Spanish Civil War in 1939. Jeger had worked hard for the Spanish government during that war, setting up hospitals in Spain as secretary of the Spanish Medical Aid Committee. He continued to oppose Franco when he was elected an MP.

Jeger was born in London and educated at an elementary school from which he successfully moved to the London School of Economics. From the age of 23 to 35 he served as a member of the Shoreditch Borough Council and he was the Mayor from 1937 to 1938. He chaired numerous committees – Finance, Air Raid Precautions, Jubilee and Coronation Celebrations, the Law and Parliamentary Committee, and the one for Libraries. When you needed a safe pair of hands in Shoreditch you turned to Jeger.

During the war he was attached to the Canadian forces fighting in north-west Europe where he finished up as a captain, and was mentioned in dispatches. After the war, he was chairman of the Refugee Committee of the Council of Europe in 1956. He was also chairman of the Anglo-Austrian Parliamentary Group. When you consider the responsibilities that Jeger shouldered in public life, he might not have seemed the obvious choice for general manager, company secretary and a director of the firm which owned the Whitehall Theatre from 1945 to 1964. After the war the Whitehall began to present farces, famously starring Brian (now Lord) Rix, in the classic British tradition of broad comedy where the hero loses his trousers at some point in the proceedings. The most successful was *Reluctant Heroes,* which ran to over 1,600 performances. Jeger held all three offices in the company, so he didn't have to rely entirely on his salary as a backbench MP. He died at the age of 68 in 1971.

SANTO JEGER 1898–1953

Santo Jeger was a dedicated socialist and a doctor. After graduating at University College, Cardiff, he completed his medical training at the London Hospital and St Mary's. He was early into politics, elected to the Shoreditch Borough Council when he was only 27. By the time he was 30 he was the Mayor. Santo Jeger laboured in Shoreditch long before the creation of the National Health Service. He worked hard for his poorer constituents, establishing clinics for them in the borough. He founded the Socialist Medical Association and was elected to the LCC in 1931, serving on the Council for fifteen years. During the Spanish Civil War Jeger worked on the side of the Republicans, taking charge of an ambulance unit.

After the war ended, Jeger won St Pancras South East for Labour in 1945 and held the seat until he died in 1953 at the age of 55. He advocated Palestine becoming a British dominion and, while acknowledging that he had never been a Zionist, he still attacked anti-Jewish comment about the Jewish position in the Holy Land. Jeger's work was carried on by his widow, Linda Jeger, who won his seat at the by-election and who is now Baroness Jeger. Santo's younger brother, George, was also elected for Labour in 1945 and they sat in the House together for eight years.

HAROLD LEVER 1914–1995

One of the new batch of Labour MPs after the war was Norman Harold Lever, a barrister from Manchester Grammar School and Manchester University. He was from an Orthodox family and it was typical of Lever's brilliance that he was disqualified from sitting the university exams because of his poor attendance record, yet he was still called to the Bar at the age of 21. Lever was Manchester through and through and served as one of the city's MPs for the next 24 years. He was then promoted to the House of Lords in 1979 in Prime Minister Callaghan's dissolution list and worked hard there until he died in 1995.

Lever was very rich, first through his involvement in property flotations and then after his third marriage to the daughter of a

Lebanese banker. He lived in a palatial home in Belgravia, and he wasn't a typical Labour MP in other ways either. He supported Eden over Suez and opposed Labour's initial objections to joining the Common Market. He was capable of the grand gesture, once filibustering for two and a half hours to defeat a bill which would have given the British film industry finance he felt would be wasted.

Harold Lever, as he was always known, was part of the economic brain of the Labour Party. He was Financial Secretary to the Treasury from 1967 to 1969 and solved a major financial crisis through his successful negotiations with the International Monetary Fund in 1968. In the 1974 government, he served as Chancellor of the Duchy of Lancaster. A dapper man, Lever moved up to be the best bridge player in the House of Commons after Ian McLeod died and when he went to the Lords, it was the Upper House which usually won the annual Lords-v-Commons bridge match. In 1972, Lever suffered a serious stroke which paralysed one side, but he simply used a stand to hold his bridge cards and played on with one hand. It did however cost him his chance of being appointed Chancellor.

Shakespeare wrote of the dead that 'the good is oft interr'd in their graves', so Lever is unlikely to be remembered as the chairman who arbitrated the 1980 Steel Strike, one of the longest in the UK's troubled industrial history. He was also made responsible for negotiating with a number of American oil companies over their involvement in North Sea oil. One of his major contributions was that, when he was already over 70, he co-wrote a book advocating that the debt burden of the developing world should be written off, as it was crippling their chances of building sustainable economies. That recommendation was finally adopted by the G7 nations in 2005.

With so much emphasis today on freedom of information and the right to privacy, it was Lever who produced the Private Member's Bill which led to the 1952 Defamation Act. This made it possible to apologize for unintentional libel without incurring financial penalties and it also changed the law on justification. It would now be possible to avoid being found guilty of libel if the majority of what was alleged was true.

Communally, Lever was chairman of the Anglo-Jewish Association, a member of Poale Zion for 40 years, and chairman of the Research Board of the Institute of Jewish Affairs. Although he was treasurer of the Socialist International from 1971 to 1973 and a governor of the London School of Economics in 1971, Lever was probably more comfortable on the boards of a number of banks after he became a peer. He was also a trustee of the Royal Opera House from

1974 to 1982. Lord Lever was the acceptable face of Champagne Socialism. He died at 81.

BENN LEVY 1900–1973

Amongst all the professional Jewish MPs who were elected for Labour in 1945 there was the singular figure of the playwright, Benn Levy. He represented Eton and Slough but eventually decided at the end of the parliament that he had had enough of political life. He stood down in 1950, having played a full part in the Attlee government. Levy was educated at Repton School and University College, Oxford. He served in both world wars, being one of the early members of the RFC in 1918 and a naval lieutenant in the Second World War. In 1944 he was wounded and decorated in action in the Adriatic. He was married for forty years to the famous film star, Constance Cummings.

A committed Zionist, he attacked the government's foreign policy on Palestine and later on Israel. He was to the left of his party and a keen supporter of the Campaign for Nuclear Disarmament. His efforts to abolish stage censorship were unsuccessful but he paved the way for this measure to be passed fifteen years later as he was the main author of the Earl of Longford's report opposing censorship. Communally, he spoke for British ORT and the Friends of the Hebrew University. After he left the Commons, Levy served on the Arts Council from 1953 to 1961 and wrote twenty-one books. He also became a farmer and died in 1973, aged 73.

JOHN LEWIS 1912–1969

John Lewis was a rubber technologist creating, for example, fire-resistant multiple belting for the National Coal Board. He also controlled the delivery of belting as a steward of the British Boxing Board of Control. He was educated at the Grocers' School which had been taking Jewish boys for many years and encouraging them to practise their religion. This was unusual at the time, when Jewish pupils at public schools were often not allowed to be absent on Jewish festivals and had to attend school chapel services. He went on to the City of London College.

Afterwards, Lewis joined the family business and in 1927 the Labour Party. He was elected for Bolton in 1945 and retained the seat in 1950. During his time in the House, he was a member of the Sports Television Advisory Committee and chairman of the Empire Games

Appeals Committee. Communally, Lewis was vice-chairman of British Technion, which supports the Israel Institute of Technology. When Lewis lost his seat in 1951, he went back to running the family business as chairman and managing director. He died in 1969, aged 57.

MARCUS LIPTON 1900–1978

Marcus Lipton started his education at the Hudson Road council school in Sunderland, going on to Bede Grammar and then to Merton College, Oxford on a scholarship. He was called to the Bar in 1926 and ran a free legal advice surgery in Brixton from 1933. He was elected to the Stepney Borough Council in 1934 and became a Lambeth Council alderman in 1937, serving on the Council until 1959. As a young man, Lipton had joined as a private in the territorial army and when the Second World War broke out he was commissioned in the RAEC, ending the war as a lieutenant colonel. He was elected for Brixton as the Labour member from 1945 to 1974 and for Lambeth Central from 1974 to 1978, when he died in harness at the age of 78.

Lipton remained a backbencher throughout his parliamentary career but was notable for suggesting, using parliamentary privilege, that Kim Philby was a Russian spy. He had to withdraw his comments as Philby strongly denied the accusations, though in fact they were true. He was also chairman of the Anglo-Bulgarian, Anglo-Nepalese and Anglo-Haitian Parliamentary Groups. When asked his favourite recreation, Lipton said it was giving advice. Communally, Lipton was president of the London branch of the Association of Jewish Ex-Servicemen (AJEX) and a member of the Board of Deputies.

IAN MIKARDO 1908–1993

The Mikardo family were refugees from the Russian empire just before the Aliens Act of 1905 substantially cut access to Britain. They were tailors and earned their living repairing uniforms for the navy in Portsmouth. The Jewish community in Portsmouth had started in the early eighteenth century and refugees strengthened its Orthodoxy. Young Mikardo not only went to a secular school but also to a rabbinical seminary. He grew up to be a strong socialist and had a number of jobs between the wars in London. He eventually became a management consultant and during the Second World War worked on increasing efficiency in aircraft production, an absolutely vital area for the war effort.

Settling in Reading after the war, Mikardo beat both James Callaghan and Austen Albu for selection as Labour's candidate in the 1945 election. It was a long time since Reading had been the Liberal seat of Sir Francis Goldsmid and Rufus Isaacs. Mikardo won for Labour and served till 1959. He then lost to a fellow trade unionist, but won Poplar in 1964 and Tower Hamlets in 1974, where he remained as the MP until 1987.

Mikardo spent thirty-seven years in the Commons but always as a backbencher. He was too far to the left of the party to win favour, supporting Aneuran Bevan in the 1950s and then as a member the Tribune group with Michael Foot and Richard Crossman. He was also a strong Zionist all his life. Within the Labour Party, Ian Mikardo was always extremely popular. He epitomized the beliefs of 'Old Labour' and was elected to the National Executive from 1950 to 1959 and 1960 to 1978. He was chairman of the party from 1970 to 1971 and chairman of the International Committee from 1973 to 1978. From 1966 to 1970 he also chaired the Parliamentary Committee on Nationalized Industries. Mikardo was pugnacious, but it was a forcefulness that was always available to help the poor. He died at 85, in 1993.

HARRY MORRIS 1894–1954

In 1952, a couple of years before his death, Harry Morris – by then Lord Morris of Kenwood – summed up his approach to life when he said, 'I have never been able to find anything incompatible between a deep patriotism as a British citizen and a moral and spiritual affinity with Israel – between being a good citizen of the country and being a good Jew at the same time'. That was certainly the way Morris had lived. He was born and died in Sheffield. He became a solicitor in 1920 and a barrister in 1936. From 1920 he served on the Sheffield City Council, initially as the representative of discharged soldiers. He stayed until 1926 and was elected again from 1929 to 1937.

His progress in life was interrupted by both world wars. In the first he joined up as a private and finished as a captain; in the second he joined as a sergeant and ended the war as a lieutenant colonel. Morris won Sheffield Central for Labour in 1945 and found himself with over twenty other Jewish MPs, some of whom had little interest in their faith. Morris was scathing. He said there were three kinds of Jewish MP – overt, discreet and deniers. It was his experience that deniers were always held in contempt by the House.

Morris was always loyal to his party but he didn't hesitate to be critical if he thought it appropriate. In his maiden speech, he attacked the government for changing its mind on what to do with Palestine after the war. Within the Jewish community, Morris was very active. He served as president of the Jewish Ex-Servicemen's Association, a vice-president of the Joint Palestine Appeal, as warden of the Sheffield Orthodox Synagogue, and in senior roles in the Zionist Federation.

Although Labour's majority was slashed to only six in 1950, Morris won Sheffield Neepsend by a good margin. As some key figures in the Labour Party had been defeated and there was a need to find a safe seat for the Solicitor General, Sir Frank Soskice, Morris agreed to go to the House of Lords as a hereditary peer in order to create the necessary by-election. Sadly, he died of heart disease in July 1954 at the age of 60. Both the Union Jack and the Israeli flag were flown at his funeral.

MAURICE ORBACH 1902–1979

In one of Maurice Orbach's election campaigns he was described by two canvassers for his opponents as a German Jew. He was in fact born in Cardiff and Orbach is a Welsh name. He went to technical college in Wales but completed his education as an extra-mural student in New York. He became an engineer but he was strongly attracted to politics and cut his teeth while losing elections in 1935 and 1938. At the time he actively opposed fascism, for which he was praised by the Board of Deputies. He was elected to the LCC from 1937 to 1946, but he resigned from the Anti-Nazi League because of its anti-Zionist stance.

In 1940 he founded the Jewish Trades Advisory Council which aimed to remove causes of friction affecting Jews in industry, remaining its secretary until 1978. One of the main tasks of the Council for many years was to combat the Arab Boycott of Israel and a vast amount of work was done in private to help achieve this. In 1945 he won Willesden East for Labour and served until eventually defeated in 1959. He found a new seat in Stockport South in 1964 and remained in the House until he died shortly before the 1979 election.

Orbach was a lifelong member of Poale Zion and a member of the British branch of the World Jewish Congress. He also served on the executive board of the international WJC. On their behalf, he went to Egypt in 1954 to try to save the lives of Jews who had been arrested for spying for Israel. He also tried to create a modus vivendi between Egypt and Israel, but he came to be condemned by Nasser as a British spy. Orbach's mission was misinterpreted and Ian Mikardo later said at his memorial service that he lost his Willesden seat at the next election because of 'the politically illiterate hysteria of the Jewish press'. Orbach was chairman of the National Council against Racial and Religious Discrimination and fought successfully to get the Race Relations Act on the statute book. He also did sterling work as chairman of the Central Middlesex Group Hospital Management Committee.

PHIL PIRATIN 1907–1995

Phil Piratin was elected as a Communist MP in 1945 and as a Communist he constituted a rare exception in that he was a successful candidate for a seat in the Commons from the far left. The far right has never been successful in this way; no one standing as a Fascist has ever been elected to parliament. There have only been two Communists, both elected in 1945, when the repute of our Russian ally in the war was still very high. The other successful Communist candidate was Willie Gallacher.

Jewish families who retain their faith are accustomed to being in a small minority. Piratin would not have felt out of place in that role. He was Jewish, Communist, anti-fascist and a stout defender of tenants' rights against landlords. He was not popular with the powers-that-be. He opposed Oswald Mosley's marches through the East End of London before the war, was elected to the Stepney Borough Council in 1937 and became chair of the Borough's Communist Party. During the war, he led 100 people to an underground station to take shelter during the Blitz. It was typical Piratin. He felt it was his job in life to stand up for the poor and disadvantaged and this was a case where he triumphantly succeeded. Sleeping in safety on Underground platforms had not been approved before his exploit, but the practice soon became widespread.

When Piratin was elected for Mile End in 1945 he succeeded Dan Frankel, another Jewish MP. There wasn't much left of the East End after the bombing and Piratin set out to do his very best for his constituents. He joined forces with a number of other Labour MPs to form the Labour Independent Group. This was, again, not at all pleasing to the hierarchy and some of the members were expelled from the party for allegedly being crypto-Communists.

Unfortunately for Piratin, there were sweeping changes to the Mile End constituency boundaries in 1950 and he lost the Stepney seat in 1950. Willie Gallacher also lost and no other Communists have been elected to the Commons since then. After leaving the House, Piratin became the circulation manager of the main Communist newspaper, the *Daily Worker*, from 1954 to 1956. He then went into business and he died in 1995, aged 88.

JULIUS SILVERMAN 1905–1996

It isn't the best training for speaking in the Commons to be brought up in a family which conversed solely in Russian and Yiddish. But then Silverman came from among the poverty-stricken Jewish refugees who eked out a living in Leeds at the turn of the twentieth century. He fought all his adult life for the poor and underprivileged because he had been there and done that. Silverman went to Leeds Central High School but left at 16 to become a warehouseman. You had to show talent to stay on until 16 and after Silverman had studied at night school, he was accepted at Gray's Inn as a pupil when he was 23, becoming a member of the Bar at 26.

While practising in Birmingham, Silverman won election to the City Council and served for eleven years. He lost Birmingham Moseley in the 1935 election, but he won Birmingham Erdington in the 1945 Labour landslide and served as a Birmingham MP for the next thirty-eight years. Always on the extreme left of the party, he focused his efforts on Russia and India. There was a substantial Indian community in Birmingham and he looked after their interests. Israel he regarded as the model Democratic Socialist state but he was far more committed to his work as vice-chairman of the All-Party British-Soviet Parliamentary Committee. Silverman was the best chess player in the Commons for many years and even got a draw from the Russian Grand Master, Mikhail Botvinnik. He retired in 1983 and died at the age of 90.

LESLIE SOLLEY 1905–1968

Leslie Solley was another son of immigrants who dragged himself up by his boot straps. He went to Davenant Foundation School, an elementary school, but was clever and hardworking enough to gain a place at London University. He changed career from being a research scientist to become a barrister in 1934, when he was the Profumo Prizeman and won the Yarborough-Anderson Scholarship. His new persona sported a bow-tie, not a hair out of place and an appearance much like Arthur Askey, the famous Jewish comedian.

In 1945, Solley won Thurrock for Labour but he did not find it easy to follow the party line. Against Labour Party policy, he publicly supported the Italian socialists who were extremely left-wing and militant, and received a warning from the Whips. He then campaigned against the North Atlantic Treaty, advocating instead a United Europe long before the Common Market was more than a gleam in the founders' eyes. This time he was expelled from the party, together with Konni Zilliacus, in 1949. He sat out the parliament as an Independent but lost his seat at the 1950 election, to the official Labour candidate.

Solley went back to the law and became vice-president of the Songwriters Guild of Great Britain and Ireland. He worked on the TV programme, *The Adventures of Twizzle*, writing the 'Twizzle Song' and his best-known work, the 'Dance of the Blue Marionettes'. He was eventually readmitted to the Labour Party and died in 1968 at the age of 63.

BARNETT STROSS 1899–1967

The Stross family came to Britain from Poland at the end of the First World War and Barnett then went to Leeds University to study medicine. Either his English teacher in Poland had been excellent or he learned languages with great ease because he qualified in 1926. Stross set up practice in the Potteries where the industrial disease of pneumoconiosis was prevalent. He fought for compensation on behalf of the workers who had succumbed to the condition and successive governments did take action because of his campaigns.

He joined the Labour Party in 1930 and became an active member of the Socialist Medical Association, founded by Santo Jeger. He was a Stoke councillor from 1937 to 1952 and in 1945 won Stoke-on-Trent, Hanley for Labour. He served as a Stoke MP for the next twenty-one years. During his time in the Commons, he remained a backbencher until 1964 when he was appointed Parliamentary Secretary to the Ministry of Health, but many MPs had Stross to thank for medical attention when they fell ill, in both the Lords and Commons. He was particularly in demand when sick MPs had to be brought to the House to help the government win crucial votes. Stross was deeply affected by the fate of Lidice, a Czech town wiped out in a Nazi reprisal in 1942. He led a campaign to rebuild the town and became chairman of the British-Czechoslovakia Society. Stross died at 68, in 1967.

DAVID WEIZMAN 1898–1987

When David Weizman was elected yet again in 1974, he became the last MP in the House to be born in the nineteenth century and the oldest member of the Commons. He had first tried to win a seat way back in 1935 when he lost Stoke Newington, but he eventually won it ten years later. He continued to represent the constituency for nearly thirty years. Weizman was born in Blackburn into an Orthodox family and educated at Hutcheson's Grammar School and Manchester University. Between school and university he spent three years as a private in the Manchester Regiment during the First World War. At university he gained a First in History and went on to study for the Bar to which he was admitted in 1922. He joined the Labour Party in 1923.

He didn't find it easy to earn a living, teaching in elementary schools during the day and lecturing at night. He also worked as the Poor Man's Lawyer at the Jewish Centre in the East End of London. As an MP, Weizman concentrated on looking after his electorate. He took silk in 1951 but still found time to keep a wary eye on Ridley Road, which was in his bailiwick, famous for the battles between the Communists and the Fascists before the Second World War. Weizman became a QC in 1951 and was delighted when his son, David, also took silk. As an MP, he retained his connection with the Jewish community through his membership of the Board of Deputies. Weizman died at 88 in 1987.

LYALL WILKES 1914–1991

Lyall Wilkes achieved a lot in his life, from getting into Balliol and becoming secretary of the Oxford Union in 1937, to being mentioned in dispatches as a major in the Second World War. He was also a County Court judge and MP for Labour for Newcastle Central from 1945 to 1951. A good author, he covered a wide range of subjects from the biography of a famous landscape gardener to vignettes about notable people on Tyneside. As a barrister, he was a member of Broad Chore, one of the most distinguished chambers on the North East circuit, which could also boast Lord Taylor, the future Jewish Lord Chief Justice. Wilkes died at the age of 77 in 1991.

AUSTEN ALBU 1903–1994

Austen Albu went to Tonbridge School but his highest academic qualification was a City and Guilds Certificate. At 27 he became a manager at Aladdin Industries and worked there from 1930 to 1946, so he gained a lot of experience with trade unions. During the war it was vital to keep up the production of essential equipment and services and those involved in this work were not called up for military service. From 1946 to 1947, Albu was deputy president of the Governmental Sub-Commission of the Control Commission in Germany. He went on to become deputy director of the British Institute of Management and in a by-election in 1948 he won Edmonton for Labour.

Although Britain had an enviable record for inventing new products in the nineteenth and twentieth centuries, the status of engineers was never as high as the profession warranted. Albu was always very keen that more professional engineers should be trained in university. Recognizing his contribution through this work, he was made a Fellow of the Imperial College of Science and Technology. Albu held Edmonton for twenty-six years and became Minister of State at the Department of Economic Affairs from 1965 to 1967. He retired in 1974 when he was over 70 years old, and died in 1994 at the ripe old age of 91.

LESLIE LEVER 1905–1977

Leslie Lever was Harold Lever's older brother and together they became peers. They both went to Manchester Grammar School but Leslie went on to Leeds University and became a solicitor. He was a lawyer who represented the poor and if the case was lost, he often paid the bills himself. Before Legal Aid was introduced in 1948, it was only through lawyers like Lever that the impoverished could get justice. Four of Lever's siblings were lawyers.

In 1950, he was elected Labour MP for Manchester Ardwick and served the constituency for twenty years. He was also a Manchester City Councillor and in his year of office as Mayor, he fulfilled 2,700 engagements – that's seven a day, seven days a week. In the House, Lever worked very hard to obtain better pensions for war widows and severely wounded ex-servicemen. He was also greatly interested in denominational education. Unusually for a Jew, he was knighted by two Popes – John XXIII and Paul VI – and by the Queen in 1970. He didn't hold government office. When Lever retired in 1970, he went to the Lords and died in 1977 at the age of 72.

GERALD NABARRO 1913–1973

Gerald David Nunes Nabarro was never included in the list of Jewish MPs in his lifetime, but the Nabarro family have been distinguished members of the Sephardi community for very many years so he belongs in this book, even though he converted to Christianity.

Nabarro in his public life fostered an aristocratic image, sporting a large handlebar moustache. The truth was that his father was a failure in business and young Nabarro left his council school at 16 and joined the army; seven years later, he was a sergeant. When he left the army he became a works manager, though he remained a member of the Royal Artillery Territorials and was in the Royal Ordinance Territorials from 1943 until his death.

Kidderminster was his constituency from 1950 to 1966. He allied himself to the image and policies of the old Tory Party. He was against the Common Market, supported the death penalty and agreed with Enoch Powell's views on commonwealth immigration. On the plus side, he had notable success with a Private Member's Bill on pollution and smog, which became the Clean Air Act in 1956. He regularly mocked the anomalies in Purchase Tax regulations until the system was abolished. He also worked hard for electricity to be brought to remote villages. He was knighted in 1963. Nabarro was too ill to fight the 1964 election but recovered to win South Worcestershire in 1966. He retained the seat in 1970. In 1971, he was accused of a traffic offence and suffered two strokes during a retrial. He was acquitted but died a few months later in 1973, at the age of 60. It was ironic that from 1951 to 1955 he had been president of the Road Passengers and Transport Association.

LORD MANCROFT 1914–1987

Lord Mancroft was in the Churchill, Eden and Macmillan governments, but was, obviously, never elected as an MP. You will find all about him in Appendix A, listing the Jewish non-elected members of government.

Many of the Jews who were first elected to the Commons in 1945 had settled in to serve their party for the long haul – MPs like Joel Barnett, Harold Lever, Manny Shinwell and Sidney Silverman would represent their constituencies for many years. Their ranks were swelled by other Jewish MPs, destined to stay for similar or even greater periods of time – Leo Abse, Robert Sheldon, Renée Short and the Silkins. The ranks of the Jewish Conservative MPs remained thin in the extreme until 1970, when Ted Heath brought in the first Conservative administration for six years. There was a balance of the parties in power between 1945 and 1970 – Labour governments for twelve years and Conservative for thirteen. In the next twenty-seven years the situation would change dramatically – Conservative governments for twenty-two years and Labour governments for only five. Which meant that if you were a Jewish Labour politician at the time, the likelihood of government office was very small.

From 1955 to 1970, the number of Jewish MPs increased – from nineteen in 1955 to twenty-three in 1959, thirty-nine in 1964 and forty-two in 1966. Harold Wilson made full use of them. John Diamond was Chief Secretary to the Treasury and Edmund Dell Minister of State for Trade. John Silkin was Deputy Leader and Harold Lever Financial Secretary to the Treasury. Jews also occupied a number of minor government posts.

The period began with the nationalization of the Suez Canal by Gamal Abdul Nasser and the subsequent invasion of Egypt by British, French and Israeli forces. The Conservatives were in power and the policy of Hugh Gaitskill and the Labour Party was to oppose the invasion, on the grounds that a satisfactory legal case had not been made for the attack. All the Jewish Labour MPs toed the party line and voted against the invasion, except Manny Shinwell and Harold Lever. Shinwell went on the record and declared, 'Israel was right. I have the utmost contempt for those Jews, including British MPs, who, though professed Zionists, claim to see in Israel's action an offence against international law. They ought to be ashamed.' It was perfectly true that Israel only broke an armistice, rather than committed an act of unprovoked war and there had been constant incursions by Egyptian forces into Israel from the Gaza Strip over the years, also breaking the armistice, and which had resulted in a considerable number of fatalities.

The Labour Party's position caused a breach in its relationship with the community. It wasn't helped when the Labour leader, Hugh Gaitskill, said the Conservative Party's action was like a policeman who decided 'to go in and help the burglar shoot the householder'. In 1957, the Labour Friends of Israel was founded to try to improve the Labour Party's image. But for the first time for many years, the Conservative Party started to offer a more sympathetic home for a larger proportion of the votes of the community.

After 1956, the main effort of the Arab nations was focused on stopping trade between their countries in the Middle East and any company which traded with Israel. The Americans made giving in to such demands an offence for United States companies. In England, it wasn't tackled in that way and Lord Mancroft, for one, had to resign a directorship to enable a company he represented, the Norwich Union, to continue trading with Arab countries.

While the problems of Israel were always likely to have Jewish MPs agonizing over what line to take, it is important to remember that the whole topic of Israel and the Middle East didn't concern the Commons very often. On every other subject, the Jewish MPs had no difficulty in supporting their parties, although there are always occasional instances where any MP may find the interests of his constituents at variance with those of the majority of other members.

The concentration of Jewish voters changed after the Second World War as their economic position improved. The importance of the Jewish vote in the East End of London was no longer a major consideration and was replaced by its effect on North London seats, particularly in the borough of Barnet. The small Jewish provincial communities would continue to decay, as their congregations in the major centres of Manchester and Leeds, Bournemouth and Brighton increased in size. What remained constant was that there were very few constituencies where the Jewish vote made any difference at all. Normally, only in marginals could it swing a result if the total Jewish electorate was of a mind to sink its political differences, which it usually wasn't.

Where MPs had a substantial Jewish electorate in their constituencies, what they had to recognize now was that a considerable proportion of the Jewish community had a phobia in common; the community feared, quite irrationally, that anti-Semitism could become a serious threat in the United Kingdom. There was no justification for this. British fascists were hardly likely to be well supported after the war. In election after election, both for parliament and local councils, their votes would be derisory. In general elections their candidates invariably lost their deposits.

The core problem was that the phobia had been justified – and was still justified – in many parts of the world. To the immigrants giving their children first-hand accounts of Eastern European pogroms in the nineteenth century had been added the German Jewish refugees who had suffered under Nazism before they were able to flee to the UK before the war. Now there were new witnesses to the destructive force of anti-Semitic bigotry – refugees from the Middle East communities who had been driven from their ancestral homes in the aftermath of the 1948 Arab–Israel war. Jewish communities had lived in the Middle East since biblical times but now they were dispersed again and many came to England. There was even a substantial Indian Jewish community, who could recount the appalling effects of partition on India when the British granted independence in 1947. The hundreds of thousands who died as Hindus and Muslims slaughtered each other in the name of religion were a terrible example of the effects of religious prejudice.

There was another reason for the warnings that came from the immigrants. The vast majority of them loved their native countries. They respected the cultures in which they had been reared and they took pride in the achievements of their famous fellow citizens. Now they were no longer a part of those cultures, their government had turned on them, and they had had to run for their lives. In England, these immigrants mixed with people who had no such problems, whose cultural norms and rule of law were clearly far superior to those of the kind of dictatorships from which they themselves had fled. To honour the historical reputation of their native lands, there was only one possible excuse to be advanced – 'it could happen here'.

A substantial proportion of the community did believe it was feasible that something similar could happen in Britain. This was nonsense, and there were 300 years of history to prove that it was nonsense, but then the Final Solution had been unimaginable before it actually happened. 'It could happen here' remained the frightened refrain and the community armed itself with organizations and committees to protest if the slightest sign of prejudice appeared. MPs had to be aware of these sensitivities and, while there was understanding and sympathy for the ordeals of Jewish communities around the world, it was sometimes difficult to foresee the offence that quite innocent off-the-cuff comments might give. Many MPs felt that the Jews tended to be over-sensitive, but they also realized that they hadn't had their relatives murdered for no other reason than that they were members of the Church of England.

In the 1960s a new factor emerged – the arrival in Britain of substantial numbers of non-white immigrants. The spotlight on racialism became far more intense as parliament grappled with colour prejudice. There is no doubt that it was widespread; 90 per cent of London hotels would not accept black guests in the 1960s. The West Indian cricketer, Lord Constantine, at that time Leary Constantine, had been refused accommodation during the war. Many landlords from every background wouldn't let their properties to black applicants. Jewish MPs were active in seeking legislation which would outlaw racialism, even though a few members of their own community might even go so far as to join the fascist National Front because they agreed with their anti-coloured immigration policies.

If colour prejudice was widespread, one consequence was that the Jewish community was now perceived in a different light. They were no longer seen as the archetypal outsiders because, like the overwhelming majority of the population, the Jews were white. The focus of prejudice, where it did exist, shifted from the Jews to the non-white immigrants. This would remain the situation for many years until the public became more tolerant of the newcomers. Then, for the tiny minority of bigots, some of the old anti-Semitic attitudes would re-emerge.

Jewish MPs elected between 1955 and 1970 were:

1955 Austen Albu (Labour), **Frank Allaun** (Labour), **Henry d'Avigdor Goldsmid** (Conservative), Maurice Edelman (Labour), Barnett Janner (Labour), George Jeger (Labour), Harold Lever (Labour), Leslie Lever (Labour), Marcus Lipton (Labour), Ian Mikardo (Labour), Gerald Nabarro (Conservative), Maurice Orbach (Labour), Manny Shinwell (Labour), Julius Silverman (Labour), Sidney Silverman (Labour), George Strauss (Labour), Barnett Stross (Labour), Moss Turner-Samuels (Labour), David Weizman (Labour)

1956 **Keith Joseph** (Conservative)

1957 John Diamond (Labour)

1958 **Leo Abse** (Labour), **Michael Cliffe** (Labour)

1959 Leo Abse (Labour), Austen Albu (Labour), Frank Allaun (Labour), Henry d'Avigdor Goldsmid (Conservative), Michael

Cliffe (Labour), John Diamond (Labour), Maurice Edelman (Labour), **Myer Galpern** (Labour), **David Ginsburg** (Labour), Barnett Janne (Labour), George Jeger (Labour), Keith Joseph (Conservative), Harold Lever (Labour), Leslie Lever (Labour), Marcus Lipton (Labour), **John Mendelson** (Labour), Manny Shinwell (Labour), Gerald Nabarro (Conservative), Julius Silverman (Labour), Sidney Silverman (Labour), George Strauss (Labour), Barnett Stross (Labour), Moss Turner-Samuels (Labour), David Weizman, (Labour)

1963 **John Silkin** (Labour)

1964 Leo Abse (Labour), Austen Albu (Labour), Frank Allaun (Labour), Henry d'Avigdor Goldsmid (Conservative), **Joel Barnett** (Labour), **Edmund Dell** (Labour), John Diamond (Labour), **Jack Dunnett** (Labour), Maurice Edelman (Labour), **Reg Freeson** (Labour), Myer Galpern (Labour), David Ginsburg (Labour), Barnett Janner (Labour), George Jeger (Labour), Keith Joseph (Conservative), **David Kerr** (Labour), Harold Lever (Labour), Leslie Lever (Labour), Marcus Lipton (Labour), **Robert Maxwell** (Labour), John Mendelson (Labour), Ian Mikardo (Labour), **Maurice Miller** (Labour), Gerald Nabarro (Conservative), Maurice Orbach (Labour), **Paul Rose** (Labour), **Arnold Shaw** (Labour), **Robert Sheldon** (Labour), Manny Shinwell (Labour), **Renée Short** (Labour), John Silkin (Labour), **Sam Silkin** (Labour), Julius Silverman (Labour), Sidney Silverman (Labour), Henry Solomons (Labour), George Strauss (Labour), Barnett Stross (Labour), **Raphael Tuck** (Labour), David Weizman (Labour)

1966 In the 1966 election all the Jewish MPs who were in the Commons in 1964 were re-elected except Henry Solomons and Barnett Stross. There were five new Jewish Labour MPs: **Arthur Davidson, Stanley Henig, Edward Lyons, Eric Moonman** and **David Winnick**

FRANK ALLAUN 1913–2002

Frank Allaun was a prime mover in the Campaign for Nuclear Disarmament. In 1958 he organized the first of many annual protest marches to the nuclear plant at Aldermaston. As a boy, Allaun had won a scholarship to Manchester Grammar School and he went on to become a chartered accountant. Although over forty of the Jewish MPs have been either solicitors or barristers, few have been accountants. Perhaps, as far as the hourly pay rate of MPs is concerned, they decided the figures didn't add up! But it was the profession which didn't appeal to Allaun and he left it to become a journalist on the *Manchester Evening News* before joining the Labour Party's main supporter in Fleet Street, the *Daily Herald.*

In 1955, Allaun won Salford East for Labour and represented the constituency for the next twenty-eight years. When he finally stood down at the age of 70 he was still the vice-president of the Council for Nuclear Disarmament. He continued writing until the end of his life and died at 89 in 2002.

As a youngster, Allaun was a Communist and he was never less than a strong socialist. The Jewish hatred of the Czarist regime always made the communist and extreme left-wing opposition attractive as a rallying point, and Allaun represented a constituency with more than its share of poverty. He made his maiden speech on the appalling housing conditions in Salford where homes without an inside toilet, hot water and bath were commonplace. He spoke in the House about a constituent, an aged, bedridden widow, whose roof collapsed. Five minutes later, her rent collector was back to collect the 50p owing from a member of the family. Allaun was horrified.

In 1955, an MP only earned £25 a week and out of it had to pay for his accommodation in London, his food, secretary, postage and stationery. Not surprisingly, Allaun found it hard to make both ends meet. Allaun's devotion to his parliamentary work inevitably led to him neglecting his family. He was particularly torn between the needs of his constituents and those of his sick wife. He still found time though, to become vice-president of the Association of Public Health Inspectors and he was a member of three trade unions. It was typical of Allaun that he never accepted a paid role outside parliament as he felt the hours spent on it would deprive his constituents of his time. There was an obvious connection in Allaun's mind between social conditions and the defence of the country. As he said, 'The choice is between bathrooms and bombers, between houses and H bombs. If they were given the choice, there is little doubt what most people would plump for.'

In 1978, Allaun was elected chairman of the Labour Party, still strongly on its left wing, alongside other Jewish socialist stalwarts such as Harry Cohen and Ian Mikardo. The Conservatives denounced him as 'one of the Soviet Union's foremost apologists in this country', so the member for Salford did not fit easily into government. He did become Parliamentary Private Secretary to the Secretary of State for the Colonies in 1964 but that only lasted a few months before he resigned in protest against the government's attitude to the Vietnam war. In Salford, Allaun served large Catholic and Jewish communities but he found little time for Jewish life.

HENRY D'AVIGDOR GOLDSMID 1989–1976

The last of the Goldsmids to serve in the House of Commons was Henry, known as Harry. He wasn't an observant Jew like his forebears, but he still strongly supported the community. As his fellow Conservative Jewish MP, Sir Keith Joseph, said, 'On two occasions, he effectively demolished efforts to outlaw the Jewish ritual method of slaughter'. And that was in spite of the fact that the way the animal was killed didn't matter to him personally at all. It was suggested at the time that the rationale for leaving the situation unchanged was that Jews and Muslims had more votes than cows and sheep, but that is to discount the view, supported by so many eminent veterinarians, that Schechita is the most humane method of slaughter.

As a youngster he went to Harrow School and Balliol College, Oxford. He served in the Royal West Kents and the Royal Artillery Corps and was at Dunkirk and on the Normandy beaches. He was mentioned twice in dispatches, and was awarded the DSO and MC. He ended his military career as a major general. Like his ancestors, d'Avigdor Goldsmid was a bullion broker and he achieved high office in Kent where he was a JP, Deputy Lieutenant and High Sheriff. In commerce, from 1961 he was chairman of the Anglo-Israel Bank and from 1969 to 1971 of Pergamon Press. He inherited the baronetcy from his father.

In the House he never became a minister but Ted Heath made him chairman of the Select Committee on Nationalized Industries and of the Committee studying Parliamentary Expenditure. Unlike most MPs, he had first-hand experience and an excellent track record in senior positions in commerce. He represented Walsall South as a Conservative from 1955 until he stood down in 1974. For many years, he and Sir Keith Joseph were the only Jewish Conservative MPs. Henry d'Avigdor Goldsmid died in 1976 at 66.

KEITH JOSEPH 1918–1994

Keith Joseph was one of only two Jewish MPs representing Conservative constituencies for many years between 1945 and 1974. He always denied that this reflected for a moment any anti-Semitism within the party but did muse on one occasion that 'To be a Jew in the Tory party you have to fire on all cylinders'. Joseph fired on all cylinders throughout his life. He was the son of the founder of Bovis, the construction company. His father had been Lord Mayor of London in 1942/3. Keith Joseph went to Harrow School and Magdalene College, Oxford, where he gained a First in Jurisprudence. Afterwards he became a Fellow of All Souls, which is a major academic distinction.

In the Second World War he was wounded in Italy and mentioned in dispatches. He left the army as a captain in the Royal Artillery and was called to the Bar. He became chairman of Bovis in 1958 and was also an underwriter at Lloyds. The record of many MPs in commercial life has not been outstanding but Joseph was a man who could have earned a handsome living in many fields of endeavour. If the Cousinhood had still existed, Joseph would have been a distinguished member.

Joseph lost narrowly in 1955 but was elected MP for Leeds North East at a by-election in 1956. He represented the constituency for the next thirty-one years. He was first appointed to the Cabinet in 1962 as Minister for Housing and Local Government, after Macmillan's 'night of the long knives'. Joseph immediately announced plans to build 400,000 houses by 1965. When Wilson took office in 1964, Joseph became one of the Conservative's most prominent policy developers. He was Secretary of State for Social Services in the Heath government and, in opposition again in 1974, he was instrumental in setting up the Conservative Centre for Policy Studies. Joseph was attracted by Milton Friedman's monetarist theories in America and Margaret Thatcher came to accept the same philosophy. When Joseph supported her for the leadership of the party, she gave him overall responsibility for policy and research. From this came the privatization of nationalized industries which marked Thatcher's years in office. Thatcherism owed a great deal to Joseph's thinking. Joseph left the Commons in 1987 and was made a peer. He died seven years later at the age of 76.

LEO ABSE 1917–

Leo Abse, a solicitor, was for thirty years the colourful MP for Pontypool, and his exotic clothes often matched the originality of his parliamentary contribution. Born in 1917, the grandson of immigrants from the Pale, he joined the Labour Party at 17 and, after taking his degree at the London School of Economics, he served during the war in the Middle East. After the war, Abse went into local politics in Cardiff and in 1953, while chairman of the City Labour Party, he created and chaired the Poale Zion branch in Wales. Winning Pontypool in a by-election five years later, Abse became one of the few Jewish MPs representing a Welsh constituency.

Responsible for more private member's Acts than almost any other member – including those radically altering the laws relating to divorce, homosexuality and adoption – he has attributed his legislative success to the happy coincidence of being born a Jew and a Welshman, always an outsider. As he says, he was 'able to be critical of the stale conventions of the compact majority' . In his 1994 book, *Wotan, My Enemy*, which won the *Jewish Quarterly* Wingate Prize, he vigorously asserted the benefits of his Jewish heritage. He celebrated his 90th birthday in 2007.

MICHAEL CLIFFE 1904–1964

Michael Cliffe was a tailor, like so many other Jews from refugee families who emigrated to Britain from Russia. He was an under-presser and he became an active member of the National Union of Tailors and Garment Workers. He was born in Sheffield but came to London and in 1949 was elected to the Finsbury Borough Council. In 1956/7, he was Mayor of the borough. When a by-election occurred in 1958, it was Cliffe who was selected to contest the Shoreditch and Finsbury seat for Labour. He won with a comfortable majority. In the House, Cliffe seldom spoke, but he worked hard for his constituents. He was also a prominent opponent of nuclear testing. Communally, he was a member of the Jewish Labour Committee for Israel and always attended memorial gatherings for the victims of the tragic 1943 Warsaw Ghetto uprising. At the time he was elected, Cliffe's health was poor. He died in 1964 at the age of 60.

MYER GALPERN 1903–1993

Myer Galpern was Glasgow through and through. He was born when his city was the second largest in Britain and famous for everything from its shipbuilding to its municipal art galleries and museums. After graduating from Glasgow University, Galpern started a furniture shop, which was a popular occupation for Jews at the time, as hire purchase was making it possible for more people to furnish their homes properly 'on the never-never'. Slowly but surely, Galpern also moved up the ranks of the local Labour Party, becoming Lord Provost in 1958. By this time, Glasgow was experiencing difficulties with many of its traditional economic foundations. It was time for Galpern to move on to the national stage and he stood for parliament in 1959. Although Harold Macmillan still retained power with the Conservatives, Galpern won the Glasgow Shettleston seat and held it for twenty years. He was 76 when he retired and he was rewarded with a peerage.

Galpern was always a very safe pair of hands. He was not a Scottish radical like Manny Shinwell and the Clydesiders. During the Wilson/Callaghan years he was a Deputy Speaker in the Commons. He was the president of the Jewish Old Age Home for Scotland and would have easily qualified as a resident by the time he died in 1993 at the age of 90.

DAVID GINSBURG 1921–1994

David Ginsburg's parents came to Britain after the Russian Revolution. He was another Jewish alumnus of University College School who became an MP. He graduated from Balliol College, Oxford and was commissioned in the Oxfordshire and Buckinghamshire Light Infantry in 1941, after which he spent the war as a captain in military intelligence. He was an economist by training and became a Senior Research Officer on the government's Social Security Survey from 1946 to 1952. Then he became secretary of the Labour Party Research Department, for the next seven years.

In 1959, Ginsburg was chosen as the Labour candidate for Dewsbury where Sir John Simon had preceded him almost 100 years before. He served the constituency until 1981 when he defected to the Social Democrats. He stood again for Dewsbury in 1983 but split the left-wing vote, enabling the Conservative to win. Ginsburg got 25 per cent of the votes cast. After he left the Commons, Ginsburg continued to act as an economics, marketing and market research consultant and one of his accounts was Saatchi & Saatchi, the famous advertising agency. In 1990, he accepted the chairmanship of Ajax Health Care. He died on his seventy-third birthday in 1994. In Judaism, it is considered a mark of merit to die on your birthday.

JOHN MENDELSON 1917–1978

It is not always necessary to hold office in government to be influential; John Mendelson was an example of this. Born of Polish parents and speaking fluent French and German, Mendelson went to London University. He worked in factories in the north of England and, when the war broke out, rose through the ranks to be a captain. After the war, he became a political science lecturer at Sheffield University. He was vice-president of the Sheffield Trade and Labour Council. Mendelson's ability as an intellectual thinker was recognized on the left of the Labour Party and he became a strong supporter of Bevan and the Tribune movement. When Gaitskill died, Wilson hesitated to put himself forward as his successor. It was Mendelson who spoke for a delegation asking him to do so and Wilson agreed.

In 1959, he was elected for Peniston and remained its MP until 1978. Mendelson was a stubborn debater and often criticized, even-handedly, both Communism and the American involvement in the Vietnam War. He remained at the intellectual heart of the party but his views eventually became too right wing for its left wing, as the party grew more extreme during the 1970s. He considered this a generation gap problem but was severely put out when he wasn't nominated for the National Executive. He remained a backbencher throughout his political career, though he served on the Parliamentary Public Accounts Committee. From 1973 to 1977, he was a member of the Consultative Assembly of the Council of Europe. John Mendelson died in 1978 at the age of 61.

JOHN SILKIN 1923–1987

John Silkin was the son of Lewis and the brother of Sam Silkin – three members of a family of politicians who each held senior government office. John was the younger brother and went to Dulwich College, the University of Wales and Trinity Hall, Cambridge. During the war, he was a lieutenant commander in naval intelligence from 1942 to 1946. He served primarily in the Pacific on battleships. After the war, he returned to Cambridge and then in 1950 joined his father's law practice as a solicitor in London. He tried to get elected to the Commons in 1950 and 1959 and managed at last to win Deptford in 1963. Deptford became Lewisham Deptford and Silkin remained in the Commons until his death twenty-four years later.

In parliament, Silkin had a very good career. He was made a Privy Councillor in 1966, then Chief Whip until 1969 and Deputy Leader of the Commons from 1969 to 1970. In Callaghan's government, he was Minister of Planning from 1974 to 1976 and Minister of Agriculture and Fisheries from 1976 to 1979, but he did not enjoy the arguments with the EC in Brussels on the subject. He sat in the

Cabinet with his brother, Sam: the first time that two brothers had ever sat in the Cabinet together. Silkin stood for the Deputy Leadership of the party after Callaghan resigned but came fifth out of six nominations. He served in opposition as a shadow spokesman on a number of areas. He was married for nearly thirty years to the fine British actress, Rosamund John, whom he had met in 1950 when canvassing for the strongly Conservative seat of Marylebone. He died in 1987 at the age of 64.

JOEL BARNETT 1923–

Denis Healey has been described as the best Prime Minister Labour never had. As Chancellor in the Callaghan government, Healey's right-hand man was Joel Barnett, Chief Secretary to the Treasury. Barnett is a Manchester man, educated at the Derby Street Jewish School and then at the Central High School, leaving to become an accountant. He served in the Royal Army Service Corps during the war and ended it in the military government in Germany. At 34 he was on Prestwich Borough Council and in 1964 he was elected for Labour for Heywood and Royton with a majority of only 863, but he retained the seat until 1983 when it was abolished through boundary changes.

Public spending in England, Scotland, Wales and Northern Ireland needed reforming when Barnett was at the Treasury and the result is known as the Barnett Formula. He was in the Cabinet from 1977 to 1979 and chairman of the Public Accounts Committee from 1979 to 1983. When he left the Commons he was elevated to the House of Lords. He went on to be a Trustee of the Victoria and Albert Museum, vice-chairman of the BBC from 1986 to 1993 and a Trustee of the Open University in 1995. Without ever changing his political views, Barnett was considered to the right of the party during the Callaghan government and is now to the left of the Brown government. Communally, he has always taken a great interest in the Maccabi Jewish sports organization and the Association of Jewish Ex-Servicemen.

EDMUND DELL 1921–1999

If a broad highway stretched before you to the boardroom of Imperial Chemical Industries, would you choose to turn off and become the MP for Birkenhead instead? It shows Dell's commitment to the Labour Party that he said goodbye to a fine career with one of the largest British companies of its time to enter parliament. Edmund Dell was the son of the veteran Zionist, Reuben Dell. The lad got a First in History at Oxford and from 1941 to 1945 was a lieutenant in an anti-tank unit. He had been a colleague of Denis Healey in the Oxford Communist Party but after a stint as a lecturer at Oxford from 1947 to 1949, he became an overseas sales manager for ICI. He also served seven years on the Manchester City Council, but failed to win a parliamentary seat in the 1955 general election.

The balancing act between his career and his political life did not endear itself to his company, who persuaded him not to stand in 1959, but in 1964 he couldn't resist the offer of a safe seat at Birkenhead and was comfortably elected. He was successively Parliamentary Private Secretary to three ministers and was promoted to Minister of State for Trade in 1968, and for Employment in 1969 and he was made a Privy Councillor in 1970. In 1971 Dell voted with sixty-eight other Labour rebels in favour of entry to the Common Market. He performed several ministerial roles in the Wilson and Callaghan governments but resigned his seat in 1979 when tipped for the Chancellor's job. He felt that his party was drifting too far to the left and he didn't want to go with them. So he joined the SDP and, after 1988, he became a Liberal Democrat. He never sat in Parliament again but seats in prestigious boardrooms he occupied in plenty. Chairman of Guinness Peat, the investment holding company, a director of Shell Trading and the creator and first chairman of Channel 4 television were just three of his appointments. Dell wrote two important political histories at the end of his life and died in 1999 at the age of 78.

JACK DUNNETT 1922–

There have been some great Jewish sportsmen: Harold Abrahams, winner of the 100 metres at the 1924 Olympics; Daniel Mendoza, British Heavyweight Champion; Mark Spitz, the American swimmer, and Vic Seixas, the tennis champion who won Wimbledon in 1953, were just four of them. But Jews are more often to be found organizing sports clubs and Jack Dunnett comes into this category. Dunnett went to Whitgift Middle School, Croydon and Downing College, Cambridge. He was a captain in the Cheshire Regiment during the Second World War, serving in Italy for three years. He qualified as a solicitor in 1949. From 1958 to 1963 he served on Enfield Borough Council, on Middlesex County Council from 1958 to 1961 and on the Greater London Council from 1964 to 1967. He was selected as Labour candidate for Nottingham Central and won the seat in 1964.

He went on to Nottingham East in 1974, retired from parliament in 1983 but has worked in local politics since.

It was in the world of football that Dunnett was most visible. He was at one time chairman of Brentford and then of Notts County for nineteen years. He was elected president of the Football League on three occasions and was also vice-president of the Football Association Council three times. If you obey the laws of Judaism, it is very difficult to attend football matches, as you're not allowed to drive a car or ride on the Sabbath. Still, there is a great deal of Jewish support for football and it is only if there's a match on Yom Kippur that you find most of the Jewish season-ticket seats empty. Jack Dunnett is now 85. We follow the Jewish custom in inviting him to be strong and of good courage and in hoping that he will live to be 120.

REG FREESON 1926–2006

Reg Freeson was Old Labour and labelled 'a notorious left winger' by as good a judge as Richard Crossman. He was born Reginald Yarnitzy Freeson and his grandparents were refugees from the pogroms in Poland. His paternal grandfather was a mason and worked on the Anglican cathedral in Liverpool. Freeson was born in London in 1926 but he remembered the family's origins and became chair of the Warsaw Memorial Committee from 1964 to 1971 and also chair of Poale Zion. Freeson was orphaned young and spent his childhood from 5 to 14 in the Jewish Orphanage in West Norwood. Norwood was then and remains a very caring organization, but when Freeson left he had to grow up very quickly. At 17, he volunteered for the RAF but was posted to the Rifle Brigade and then the Royal Engineers in Egypt, where he served in highly dangerous bomb disposal work.

When he was demobilized, Freeson became a journalist, working primarily for left-wing periodicals and newspapers. He was elected an alderman of Willesden Borough Council when he was only 29. By 32, he was Leader of the Council and he became chair of the new Council of Brent. He remained a Brent Councillor until he lost his seat five months before he died, at the age of 80. By narrowly winning Willesden from the Conservatives in the 1964 election, he helped the Wilson government finish up with a majority of five in the Commons.

Freeson served as Parliamentary Private Secretary to the Minister of Transport and then to the Minister of Power. Then he became Minister of State for Housing and Urban Affairs. Freeson's had been a slow rise, by sheer hard work, from a very low base in the grassroots. It was a typical Jewish progression in the Labour government. After 1979 internecine warfare broke out in the Brent Council and in 1987 Ken Livingstone ousted Freeson from the parliamentary seat. He died in 2002 at the age of 80.

DAVID KERR 1923–

David Kerr went to Whitgift School. He trained to be a doctor at the Middlesex Hospital from 1941 to 1946 and was Macloghlin Scholar at the Royal College of Surgeons in 1941. He then practised as a family doctor and was one of the founders of the College of General Practitioners. He represented Wandsworth on the London County Council and was chairman of the Wandsworth Health Committee and vice-president of the Socialist Medical Association. He was elected Labour MP for Wandsworth Central, from 1964 to 1970, but then stood down.

Kerr served as a governor of the British Film Institute from 1966 to 1971 and director of the charity, War on Want, from 1970 to 1977. He left his medical practice in 1983 and was then chief executive of the Manor House Hospital for six years. He worked part-time as a locum GP in Hertfordshire in the 1990s. He also served as a councillor on Hertfordshire County Council. In 2008, at the age of 85, he wrote: 'my sight is poor, my hearing is worse but my enthusiasm for living is undiminished'. Long may that continue.

ROBERT MAXWELL 1923–1991

Maxwell was born Jan Hoch, in Czechoslovakia, and escaped from France to England in 1940 at the age of 17. He joined the army, landed on the beaches of Normandy in 1944 and fought his way to Berlin. From his enlistment as a private, he ended the war as a captain and won the Military Cross. His knowledge of Czech made him a natural contact with the post-war Czech government and when war broke out in Palestine in 1948, he played a vital part in arranging an airlift of weapons from Czechoslovakia to the Jewish forces. For that, even after his shameful handling of the *Daily Mirror* pension funds in later life, the Israeli government gave him what was almost a state funeral.

Maxwell went into publishing after the war, notably of academic papers, and in 1964 he was elected Labour MP for Buckingham. He held the seat in the 1966 election, only to lose it in 1970. His business career should have ended at the time when a DTI report into a take-over bid concluded that 'he is not, in our experience, a person who can be relied on to exercise proper stewardship of a publicly quoted company'.

Instead he carried on in publishing and in 1984 bought Mirror Group Newspapers who published the largest circulation pro-Labour paper in the country. He was immensely helpful to those who were trying to rescue the remnants of Jewish communities from Communist countries in Eastern Europe and obtaining visas to Israel. As the 1980s wore on, Maxwell's financial affairs worsened and in 1991 he died after falling overboard from his yacht. Subsequent investigation found that hundreds of millions of pounds had been lost by the pension funds of his companies. Israel's Prime Minister Shamir said at his funeral, 'He has done more for Israel than can today be said'. During his lifetime, Maxwell also received decorations from Sweden, Belgium, Finland, France, Poland and Sweden. But this gives little comfort to the members of his companies whose pensions Maxwell destroyed.

MAURICE MILLER 1920–2001

Maurice Miller was the son of a teacher and went to school and university in Glasgow. He became a doctor and during the war served as a Squadron Medical Officer. After the war, he started Glasgow's first health centre and became scoutmaster of the first Jewish scout group in the city. He was elected to Glasgow Corporation in 1950 and he was Bailie from 1954 to 1957. In 1964, he won Glasgow Kelvingrove for Labour, held it for ten years and then won East Kilbride where he stayed until 1987. Miller remained a backbench MP except for a period as an assistant Government Whip from 1968 to 1969. He was, however, consulted by many MPs who had problems with their health and always advised or tried to help them. He retired in 1987 and died in 2001, at the age of 81. Communally, Miller was chairman of Poale Zion from 1970 to 1973, secretary of the Labour Friends of Israel, and vice-chairman of the Zionist Federation in 1994.

PAUL ROSE 1935–

Paul Rose went to Bury Grammar School and Manchester University. He has always said that his fascination with politics was inspired by Richmal Crompton, who wrote the *Just William* books. In one of them, William was trying to become Prime Minister and Rose thought this an excellent career path. He was called to the Bar in 1957 and became a lecturer in the Department of Liberal Studies at the Royal College of Advanced Technology in Salford.

He joined the Labour Party in 1952, and in 1964, when he was only 29, he won Blackley and held the seat until 1979. He worked very hard in the House and was Parliamentary Private Secretary to Barbara Castle from 1966 to 1968, when she was at her peak as a minister. He was vice-chairman of the Labour Committee for Europe from 1974 to 1977 and a member of the Labour Friends of Israel and of the Committee on Electoral Reform. Rose resigned his seat in 1979, concerned about what he saw as the impotence and ineffectiveness of parliament.

ARNOLD SHAW 1909–1984

Arnold Shaw was a stalwart of the Ilford Labour Party – a man who devoted many years to public works. There is a large Jewish population in Ilford and he reflected the community at its best. Shaw was educated at the Coopers' Company School and at University College, Southampton where he read Modern History. By the time he was 25 he had joined the Labour Party and was on the Stepney Borough Council, where he sat from 1934 to 1949. He was a teacher by profession and after the war he moved to Ilford. He served on its Borough Council from 1952 to 1964. In all, Shaw stood for parliament for Ilford six times and won twice, from 1966 to 1970 and from 1974 to 1979. In the Commons, he was Parliamentary Private Secretary to Reg Freeson, the then Minister of Housing. Communally, Shaw was secretary of the Barking and Becontree Hebrew congregation, and served as co-chairman of Poale Zion. He died in 1984 at the age of 75.

ROBERT SHELDON 1923–

Robert Sheldon is a further representative of the Manchester Jewish community's contribution to national life. He went to technical college and then to London University, becoming a director of a textile exporting firm. He was by profession an engineer. In 1964, he won Ashton under Lyne in Greater Manchester for Labour and retained the seat until 2001, when he became a peer; thirty-seven years in a single constituency is a remarkable record. Sheldon was Financial Secretary to the Treasury from 1975 to 1979 and chairman of the Public Accounts Committee of the Commons from 1983 to 1997. For several of the Labour Party's years in opposition – twenty-two of his thirty-seven years as an MP – he was pressed into service by the party as their spokesman on Treasury and economic affairs. He was made a peer in 2001. In the Lords, Sheldon has been present for more than half the votes in House. He has not always agreed with the views of his party and has voted against its declared position on 34 out of 532 occasions. He has always been and remains an independent and respected spirit.

RENÉE SHORT 1919–2003

Renée Short lost her mother when she was very young and was brought up by her paternal grandparents, who were strict Anglicans, but she always considered herself Jewish and remained close to the community. She was educated at Nottingham County Grammar School and Manchester University. By profession, she was a journalist and in her latter years was always credited as 'Parliamentary Adviser' to a Yorkshire Television sitcom called *The New Statesman*.

Short started her political career when she was elected to the Hertfordshire County Council in 1952 and served on it till 1967. She was also on the Watford Rural District Council, from 1952 to 1956. She won Wolverhampton North East for Labour in 1964, after failing on two previous occasions in other parts of the country. She was sponsored by the Transport and General Workers Union and her views often clashed with those of the MP for the neighbouring constituency, Enoch Powell. Indeed, she was labelled a red-headed Labour firebrand. Once Short was in the Commons, she held on to her seat until 1987, in spite of the strength of the Conservatives under Margaret Thatcher. She just scraped in at the 1983 election, by 214 votes.

Short's main interests in the House were women's rights, prison reform and nursery education. She was on the left wing of the party and sat on the Labour National Executive from 1970 to 1981 and from 1983 to 1988. She remained a backbencher throughout her parliamentary career, although she made no secret of the fact that she'd like government office. She served as the national president of the Nursery Schools Association and was the author of a book on *The Care of Long-Term Prisoners*. Communally, she was head of the Rapid Response Unit set up by the Commonwealth Jewish Council to counteract anti-Semitism and anti-Zionism in remoter parts of the world. Renée Short died at the age of 84 in 2003.

SAM SILKIN 1918–1988

Sam Silkin was the second son of Lewis Silkin. He went to Dulwich and Trinity Hall, Cambridge and was called to the Bar in 1941. During the war, he reached the rank of lieutenant colonel and was mentioned in dispatches. Unusually for a British Jew, Sam Silkin was a very good cricketer and played one match for Cambridge and one for Glamorgan. Like the rest of the family, Silkin was strongly Labour and chaired the Society of Labour Lawyers. He was a Camberwell Councillor from 1953 to 1959 and became a QC in 1963.

In 1964, Silkin won Dulwich and remained its member until he retired in 1983. From 1966 to 1970, he was chairman of the Labour Party Group on Common Market and European Affairs and from 1966 to 1971, he served as Recorder of Bradford. In the Wilson and Callaghan governments, he served as Attorney General from 1974 to 1979 when he also became a Privy Councillor. In 1985, he was created a peer. From 1981 until his death in 1988, he was chairman of Waterlows, who make money by making money. Silkin was a member of the Athenaeum Club.

RAPHAEL TUCK 1910–1982

In the Jewish community, the name of Tuck is associated with the printing firm who invented the Christmas card in the nineteenth century; Raphael Tuck was a great-grandson of the founder. He was educated at St Paul's School, the LSE, Trinity Hall, Cambridge and Harvard where he obtained a Law degree. At the LSE he joined the Labour Party and remained a loyal member all his life. Tuck became a political scientist and a legal expert, working initially for the Canadian government. From 1941 to 1945, he was Professor of Law at Saskatchewan and Professor of Political Science at McGill. He was a Professor at Tulane University in the USA from 1947 to 1949, leaving to return to England and be admitted to the Bar in 1951. At the age of 54 Tuck decided on a new career and in 1964 was elected for Labour as the member for Watford. He served the constituency very actively for the next fifteen years. He took a particular interest in the disabled and was vice-president of the National Association of Swimming Clubs for the Handicapped. He was knighted in 1979 and he died soon after leaving the Commons at the age of 72.

ARTHUR DAVIDSON 1928–

Arthur Davidson went to the King George V School in Southport, Liverpool College and then on to Trinity College, Cambridge, where he was a member of the University athletics team and edited *Granta* magazine. He did his National Service with the Merchant Navy and was called to the Bar in 1953. Only two years later, he became a parliamentary candidate. He lost in 1955 and 1959 but was successful in 1966, when he won Accrington for Labour. He served the constituency for seventeen years and then in 1983 was beaten by only twenty-one votes.

Professionally, Davidson was the legal director of a national newspaper group and legal adviser to media organisations. He became a

QC in 1978. In the Commons, he was Chairman of the Jazz Club. From 1973 to 1983, he was on the Council of the National Youth Jazz Orchestra. He was a minister in the Law Offices department from 1976 to 1979 and in opposition he was Shadow Army Minister, followed by Shadow Attorney General. He sat on a variety of working groups, including such diverse subjects as colour prejudice in education, the role of the Board of Visitors in Penal Policy and on Consumer Affairs. Outside parliament, he was on the Council of the Consumer Association.

STANLEY HENIG 1939–

One of the most effective local politicians in Britain in the mid-twentieth century was Leicester's Sir Mark Henig. It was with that quality and example before him that his son, Stanley, undertook an academic and political career, notably as Professor of European Politics at the University of Lancaster and as MP for Lancaster from 1966 to 1970. Henig went to Wyggeston Grammar School and Corpus Christi and Nuffield Colleges, Oxford. In 1964, he was one of the founders of the Department of Politics at Lancaster when it was a very young university. He went on to the University of Warwick, the Civil Service College and the University of Central Lancashire. He is now a Senior Research Fellow at the Federal Trust.

After he lost his seat, Henig didn't stand for parliament again, but in the 1990s he was Leader of Lancaster City Council. His former wife, Ruth Henig, was made a peer in 2004. Henig is now Deputy Pro-Chancellor of Lancaster University and has been chairman of the Royal Northern College of Music and a governor of the British Institute of Recorded Sound. He is managing director of Historic Masters Ltd and secretary of the Historic Singers Trust. Henig has always been deeply committed both to his local Jewish community and to looking after the interests of Jewish students at the universities with which he has been connected.

EDWARD LYONS 1926–

Edward Lyons was a Labour MP who became a founder member of the new Social Democratic Party in 1981, which ended his political career. He had served as MP for Bradford East from 1966 to 1974 and for Bradford West from 1974 to 1983. Despite his gaining 13,000 votes as an SDP candidate, Labour retained the seat in 1983. Lyons is the son of a tailor and was educated at Roundhay High School and

Leeds University. He joined the Royal Artillery in 1944, studied Russian at Cambridge and after the war, served with the Allied Control Commission in Germany from 1946 to 1948, as a Russian interpreter. Demobilized in 1948, he became a barrister and was called to the Bar in 1952, taking silk in 1974. From 1972 to 1998 he served as a Crown Court Recorder. In 1983 he was elected a Bencher of Lincoln's Inn.

In the Commons, Lyons took a great interest in the fate of Russian dissidents and the plight of Soviet Jewry. His fluent Russian was often helpful when receiving Communist visitors in the Commons. On one occasion in 1967, he was showing Mongolian visitors round the House and entertained them in the Strangers' Dining Room by singing Russian love songs, which was much appreciated by the visitors. Bradford has substantial ethnic minorities and Lyons was always very popular with them because of the hard work he put in on their behalf. When he joined the SDP, he served on its National Council from 1984 to 1989. In 2003, aged 77, he obtained an Honours degree in European Studies at Leeds University.

ERIC MOONMAN 1929–

Eric Moonman is a senior academic who has always taken a keen interest in the affairs of the Jewish community. As the member of a Reform congregation, he was opposed by the Orthodox section of the community for the top position of president of the Board of Deputies but became senior vice-president in 1985. Moonman was born in Liverpool, attended the Rathbone School and Christ Church School in Southport. He went on to both Liverpool and Manchester Universities and became a Senior Research Fellow in the Department of Management Science at Manchester. In 1956, he moved to London to become an adviser to the British Institute of Management and started his political career on Stepney Borough Council. He became the Council Leader in 1965.

In 1966, Moonman won Billericay for Labour, losing the seat in 1970. He was back in the House in 1974 as member for Basildon until 1979. He returned to the world of universities and has been both the Professor of Management at City University and a Senior Fellow at the University of Liverpool. He was awarded the OBE in 1992. Communally, he remains the energetic and highly regarded president of the Zionist Federation of Great Britain. In 2003, he became a founder member of the Parliamentary Association of Former Members and is now an executive officer. He is an adviser to ITN on terrorism.

DAVID WINNICK 1933–

David Winnick is Old Labour, devoted throughout his life to the trade union movement, human rights and getting a better deal for the poorer parts of the population. He was a branch chairman of the Clerical and Administrative Workers Union and in later life, vice-president of APEX (Association of Professional Executive, Clerical and Computer Staff) from 1983 to 1988. By the time he was 25, he was on the Willesden Borough Council and was elected MP for Croydon South in 1966. He lost the seat in 1970 and returned to the House as the member for Walsall in 1979. He remains the energetic and vocal MP for that constituency.

Winnick served on the Select Committee on Race Relations and Immigration in Harold Wilson's second administration and, from 1984, was chairman of the UK Immigrants Advisory Service. His commitment to human rights made him an opponent of the American intervention in Vietnam and of apartheid in South Africa. Later he advocated the war to overthrow Saddam Hussein and he also supports British intervention in Afghanistan against the Taliban.

Winnick has always been an influential backbencher. It was, for example, his amendment to the bill proposing detention without trial for a maximum of ninety days that resulted in the Blair government's first defeat in nine years. Winnick proposed a maximum of twenty-eight days and this passed by a narrow majority. He remains critical of Israel's post-1967 occupation of territories won in the war of that year, which he considers unacceptable and doomed to failure.

The 1970s were very difficult years, dominated by the quadrupling of the oil price in the aftermath of the Yom Kippur War and massive inflation in Britain – in some years more than 20 per cent. Both the Conservative and Labour Parties were in power for parts of the decade which ended with the election of a government led by a woman Prime Minister for the first time in Britain. The decade also marked the high point in the number of Jewish MPs elected to the Commons. There were forty-six elected in 1974, an increase on the forty-two of 1970. The increase over the 1966 intake was, of course, largely due to the number of Jewish MPs who now came from the ranks of the Conservative Party. Where there had only been three for many years, now there were thirteen. Among the new intake were some of the future stars of Margaret Thatcher's Cabinet – men like Leon Brittan, Nigel Lawson and Malcolm Rifkind.

Within the Labour Party, many of the Jewish MPs who came in after the war were still in service twenty-five years later. They included Maurice Edelman, Harold Lever, Marcus Lipton, Ian Mikardo, Maurice Orbach, Manny Shinwell, Julius Silverman, George Strauss and David Weizman. Through all the Conservative administrations from 1951 to 1964, they had been re-elected time and again. In addition, the next generation started to emerge as Sam and John Silkin followed in their father Lewis's footsteps, and Greville Janner won Barnett Janner's Leicester seat.

As the immediate cause of the oil price rise was the Yom Kippur War, the resulting economic chaos could be put down to the inability of the Jews and Arabs to make and keep peace in the Middle East. But on this occasion, the war had been started by Egypt, which left the Israelis in the position of the victims, rather than the aggressors. This did not prevent the government from placing an arms embargo on both sides in the conflict. This was now partially posturing, because the Israelis looked to the United States for most of their weaponry, but it certainly wasn't helpful to their cause. Only two of the nine Conservative Jewish MPs elected in 1970 voted for the government arms embargo. A number of the other nine non-Jewish rebels sat for marginal constituencies where the Jewish vote could sway the balance. Indeed, the MPs for Ilford South and Middleton and Prestwich both lost their seats in the 1974 election. It worked the other way as well. The MP for Hendon South, who wasn't Jewish, had voted against the government and the 1974 swing to Labour in his constituency was much smaller than the London average.

During the 1974 election campaign, the Zionist Federation issued a list of every MP who had voted with the government on the arms embargo with the headline 'Why did they ignore Israel?' In 1974, Michael Fidler formed the Conservative Friends of Israel, Anthony Eden agreed to act as patron and the Duke of Devonshire was the first president. It was a very strong Tory line-up.

While the majority of the Jewish community would support Israel, the community never had any real influence on the Israeli government. While they had benefited from the sympathy which resulted from the Holocaust, they would suffer in future from the changing perception of Israel, no longer seen as a small country fighting for its life but one which was now the dominant military power in the region. Not all Jews supported Israel in any case; a large number of the mainly Orthodox British Jewish community were very concerned about the increasingly secular position of the Israeli government. They had looked to Israel to be 'a light unto the nations' as they considered this was a God-given responsibility. In their commitment to democracy and the rule of law, the equal rights of women and the ethics and morality to be found in the Bible, the Israeli governments did their job, but they were less concerned with religious observances. The importance of oil would, reasonably enough, continue to dominate Western thinking, as issues of realpolitik had to be set alongside the fact that Israel was the only real democracy in the Middle East and firmly in the Western camp.

The Jewish UK community was now beginning to decline in numbers, primarily through intermarriage, and elected Jewish MPs were less frequently pillars of Jewish communal life. What remained was the number who had emerged from migrant backgrounds, and the price of taking in the Jewish refugees from Germany during the 1930s was repaid many times over by the contribution they and their children subsequently made to British public life.

Jewish MPs elected from 1970 to 1979 were:

1970   Leo Abse (Labour), **Robert Adley** (Conservative), Austen Albu (Labour), Frank Allaun (Labour), Henry d'Avigdor Goldsmid (Conservative), **James d'Avigdor Goldsmid** (Conservative), Joel Barnett (Labour), **Stanley Clinton-Davies** (Labour), Arthur Davidson (Labour), Edmund Dell (Labour), Jack Dunnett (Labour), Maurice Edelman (Labour), **Michael Fidler** (Conservative), **Geoffrey Finsburg** (Conservative), Reg Freeson (Labour), Myer Galpern (Labour), **David Ginsburg** (Labour), Stanley Henig (Labour), **Greville Janner** (Labour), George Jeger (Labour), **Toby Jessel** (Conservative), Keith Joseph (Conservative), **Gerald Kaufman** (Labour), Harold Lever (Labour), Marcus Lipton (Labour), Edward Lyons (Labour), John Mendelson (Labour), Ian Mikardo (Labour), Maurice Miller (Labour), Gerald Nabarro (Conservative), **Sally Oppenheim** (Conservative), Maurice Orbach (Labour), Paul Rose (Labour), Robert Sheldon (Labour), Renée Short (Labour), John Silkin (Labour), Sam Silkin (Labour), Sidney Silverman (Labour), **Harold Soref** (Conservative), George Strauss (Labour), Raphael Tuck (Labour), David Weizman (Labour)

1971   **Neville Sandelson** (Labour)

1973   **Clement Freud** (Liberal)

Feb.'74 Leo Abse (Labour), Robert Adley (Conservative), James d'Avigdor Goldsmid (Conservative), Frank Allaun (Labour), Joel Barnett (Labour), **Leon Brittan** (Conservative), Stanley Clinton-Davies (Labour), Arthur Davidson (Labour), Edmund Dell (Labour), Jack Dunnett (Labour), Maurice Edelman (Labour), Michael Fidler (Conservative), Geoffrey Finsberg (Conservative), Reg Freeson (Labour), Clement Freud (Liberal), Myer Galpern (Labour), David Ginsburg (Labour), Greville Janner (Labour), Toby Jessel (Conservative), Keith Joseph (Conservative), Gerald Kaufman (Labour), **Ivan Lawrence** (Conservative), **Nigel Lawson** (Conservative), Harold Lever (Labour), Marcus Lipton (Labour), Edward Lyons (Labour), John Mendelson (Labour), Ian Mikardo (Labour), Maurice Miller (Labour), Eric Moonman (Labour), Sally Oppenheim (Conservative) Maurice Orbach (Labour), **Malcolm Rifkind** (Conservative), Paul Rose (Labour), Neville Sandelson (Labour), **Harry Selby** (Labour), Arnold Shaw (Labour), Robert Sheldon (Labour), Manny Shinwell (Labour), Renée Short (Labour), John Silkin (Labour), Sam Silkin (Labour), Julius Silverman (Labour), **Anthony Steen**

(Conservative), George Strauss (Labour), Raphael Tuck (Labour), David Weizman (Labour)

Oct. '74 All the Jewish MPs elected in February 1974 retained their seats in the October 1974 election except James d'Avigdor Goldsmid and Michael Fidler. There were two new Jewish MPs, both Labour – **Helen Middleweek** who married while in the Commons and was later known by her married name, Helene Hayman, or as she now is, Baroness Hayman. The other was **Millie Miller** who was highly regarded but died young.

ROBERT ADLEY 1935–1993

Robert Adley was a marketing man, the member of a family which practically created cinema advertising. Adley started his political career as a Slough Borough Councillor in 1965. It was somewhat different from his day job as sales director of the impressively luxurious May Fair Hotel, off Berkeley Square. He stood as a Conservative for Birkenhead in 1966 but lost. He won election for Bristol North East in 1970. Adley's decision to leave the burgeoning hotel industry for a political life could have been influenced by the passing of the Gaming Act. His chairman could spot a pot of commercial gold better than most and immediately closed the hotel's ballroom to turn it into a casino. The only problem? There were about 200 contracted bookings for the room over the next year and Adley had to get the company, Grand Metropolitan, out of them without ending up in court or paying out vast sums in compensation. He managed it very well but when the job was done, the problems of an MP must have seemed attractive by comparison.

In parliament, Adley became the secretary of the Parliamentary Tourism Committee and also treasurer of the Parliamentary Hovercraft Group. Despite his efforts, successive governments paid little attention to the potential of tourism. Adley's wasn't a particularly distinguished political career but he did serve twenty-three years as an MP and was well-known as a great railway enthusiast. Representing constituencies in the west country, he was one of the hordes who still considered that the Great Western Railway (the GWR) before nationalization fully deserved its alternative soubriquet of God's Wonderful Railway. Soon after he was elected to the Commons, Adley informed the *Jewish Chronicle* that he no longer wished to be listed among the Jewish MPs.

JACK D'AVIGDOR GOLDSMID 1912–1987

There have never been many very senior Jewish officers in the British Army, even if you include General Monash from the First World War, whose military brilliance was recognized, but then he was a New Zealander. Before the army reforms of the nineteenth century, Jews weren't even allowed to be commissioned, though Wellington did have one Jewish general on his staff. So Major General James Arthur d'Avigdor Goldsmid was a notable exception to the general rule as was his brother, Henry, who was an MP for many more years.

D'Avigdor Goldsmid went to Harrow School and Sandhurst. He

was in the army for thirty-five years and from 1963 was colonel of his old regiment, the 4th/7th Royal Dragoon Guards. He had been a second lieutenant in the regiment in 1932 and from 1939 to 1945 he served in France and was wounded, fighting his way through Germany. He won the MC in 1944. After the war, he commanded the 4th/7th from 1950 to 1953 and the 20th Armoured Brigade Group from 1958 to 1961. He finished up as director of the Royal Armoured Corps. From 1972 to 1978, he was the commander of the Royal Hospital, Chelsea and, naturally, he was a member of the Cavalry, Turf and Jockey Clubs. Indeed, when he finally left the army, he went on to the Jockey Club and served as a steward on many courses. This is definitely not a typical Jewish CV, but it explains why, when Ted Heath surprisingly won the 1970 election, d'Avigdor Goldsmid won the seat for Lichfield and Tamworth as a Conservative. He lost the seat in the second general election of 1974 and died at 75, in 1987.

STANLEY CLINTON-DAVIS 1928–

Stanley Clinton-Davis, now Lord Clinton-Davis, has come a long way from Hackney Downs School and later Mercers' School in the City. He then attended King's College London and became an LL.B in 1953, qualifying as a solicitor in 1953. He fought Portsmouth and Yarmouth and finally won Hackney Central for Labour in 1970 and held the seat for the next thirteen years. Appointed a Minister for Trade, he served in both the Wilson and Callaghan governments. When he left the Commons in 1983, he became the EC Commissioner in Brussels responsible for Transport, Environment and Nuclear Safety.

Outside the Commons, Clinton-Davis has long done a tremendous amount of work for a wide range of organizations. He is still president of the British Airline Pilots Association. He has fellowships from King's and Queen Mary's Colleges in London, an Honorary Doctorate from the Technical University of Budapest and holds the Grand Cross of the Order of King Leopold II of the Belgians for services to the European Union. When Labour regained office in 1997, Clinton-Davis had been made a peer seven years before, but he was still pressed into service as a Minister at the Department of Trade and Industry. He was made a Privy Councillor in 1998. Communally, Clinton-Davis was chairman of the Refugee Council from 1989 to 1997, an executive member of the Institute for Jewish Affairs from 1993 to 1997, a member of the Board of Deputies and president of the Jewish Labour Movement.

MICHAEL FIDLER 1916–1989

Michael Fidler only served in the Commons from 1970 to 1974. He was Conservative MP for Bury and Radcliffe. It was the biggest organization he ever belonged to, but one of very many. Particularly within the Jewish community, Fidler was absolutely indefatigable and took a major part in many Jewish organizations in Manchester. Michael Fidler was an Orthodox Jew. He went to Salford Grammar School and the Royal Technical College. By profession, he was a textile consultant, working in an industry which had always been a favourite with Jewish entrepreneurs. From an early age, Fidler loved to help run organizations, and he served his own community and the wider one. From 1951 to 1955, he was director of the Manchester Chamber of Commerce; in 1957/8 he was Mayor of Prestwich and he was on the Jewish Board of Deputies for twenty-five years before becoming its president from 1967 to 1973. In 1974, after he left the House, he founded the Conservative Friends of Israel and was its first director.

Fidler was happily married for over fifty years but he was a public man. A lukewarm Zionist before 1948, he finished up as president of the Zionist Organisation of Great Britain and vice-president of the Zionist Federation. At the same time, he was deeply rooted in the Orthodox Holy Law South Broughton Synagogue, which he served as president, as had his father before him. Fidler devoted his life to trying to help the causes which mattered to him; not by talking about the problems over dinner but by getting involved and working hard. He underwent open heart surgery and died peacefully some years later in 1989 at the age of 73.

GEOFFREY FINSBURG 1926–1996

If you didn't go into the forces while there was National Service during and after the war, you might have been sent down the mines. These were the 'Bevin Boys' and among them was Geoffrey Finsburg, from 1945 to 1947. Finsburg had been educated at the City of London School, and when he came back to the surface in 1947 he was elected a Borough Councillor for Hampstead, at the age of 22. The contrast could hardly have been starker as Finsburg was a Conservative and stayed in Borough politics until he was elected for Hampstead in the 1970 general election. He was vice-president of the Association of Municipal Corporations from 1971 to 1974 and president of the Parliamentary Assembly of the Council of Europe over the same period. Finsburg was an MP for twenty-two years. During the Wilson and Callaghan governments he was the Opposition spokesman on Greater London. When the Conservatives regained power in 1979 he was appointed Under-Secretary of State at the Department of Education and also held other posts in Health and Social Security. Outside parliament, Finsburg had a senior position in the Personnel Department of Great Universal Stores from 1968 to 1979. He was also joint honorary secretary of the Council of Christians and Jews and a patron of the Maccabi Association. Finsburg did a great deal of other public work as well and only stood down from parliament when he was 66 and made a peer. He died a few years later in 1996 at the age of 70.

GREVILLE JANNER 1928–

Born in Cardiff, Janner came to London when he was 3 years old. His father, Barnett Janner, became Liberal MP for Whitechapel and St Georges. His home was filled with politics and politicians, some British, some Zionist, and many both. In 1940, his father was warned that he was on Hitler's death list. Greville, with his sister, Ruth, was sent to Canada where he became a boarder at the famous and very upper-crust Bishop's College School. The level of anti-Semitism was constant and virulent, 'the worst I ever suffered in my life', he says.

Back home in 1944, he went on to St Paul's School, founding their Athletic Club, and in 1946, won the Southern Counties 100 yards Junior Championship and an Exhibition to Trinity Hall, Cambridge. He did his National Service in the British Army of the Rhine (BAOR) in Germany. He learned to speak German and joined the British War Crimes Group, where he worked in the Search Section, hunting down and arresting Nazi murderers. Janner was deeply moved by visiting the former Bergen-Belsen concentration camp, which was next to the only Jewish Displaced Persons (DP) Camp in the British zone of Germany. Most weekends for the next eighteen months he returned to work with the children in the Kinderheim and in the school.

At Cambridge, he was elected chairman of the Labour Club and president of the Union. He went on to Harvard Law School and in 1953 qualified as a barrister. His father had been elected MP for part of Leicester, but when ill health forced him to retire in 1970, Janner was selected as Labour candidate, won the seat and remained an active MP until 1997, when he left the Commons because of his wife's serious illness. He was appointed a Life Peer later that year.

In the Commons, Janner was chairman of the Employment Committee and founder secretary of the All-Party War Crimes Group.

He served as an officer of the Committee for Homeless and Rootless People, the Campaign for the Release of Soviet Jewry and the British/Israel and the British/India Parliamentary Groups. He was founder and remains president of the Commonwealth Jewish Council and Trust, a vice-president of the World Jewish Congress, and was founder and remains chairman of the Holocaust Educational Trust. He was a director of Ladbrokes plc from 1986 to 1995. Greville Janner speaks nine languages, including Hebrew, and is joint president of the Muslim-Jewish parliamentary organization, the Coexistence Trust, together with Prince Hassan of Jordan. He formed the JSB company, which teaches public speaking and promotional skills. He is a member of the Magic Circle and has written sixty-seven books, mainly on law and public speaking.

TOBY JESSEL 1934–

The Cousinhood lived on in Toby Jessel as his mother was a granddaughter of the founder of Shell, Lord Bearsted, who was the brother of Sam Samuel MP. On his father's side was another great-great uncle, Sir George Jessel MP. Jessel's own background was naval. His father, an ace destroyer captain, was the most decorated Jewish naval officer in the Second World War. Toby Jessel was educated at the Royal Naval College, Dartmouth and Balliol College, Oxford. He represented Richmond on the Greater London Council from 1967 to 1973, and he was elected Conservative MP for Twickenham seven times running from 1970 to 1997. His twenty-seven years constituted the longest continuous service of any of the Jewish Conservative MPs elected in 1970 and 1974. A legendary constituency MP, Jessel would concentrate on obtaining reprieves for local institutions after decisions had been taken to close them, like the Royal Military School of Music, Kneller Hall and the Teddington Memorial Hospital.

An arch Euro-sceptic, in 1993 he voted forty-two times against the party whip to stop the Maastricht Treaty, even though he had been on the Council of Europe from 1976 to 1992. Jessel was chairman of the Indo-British Parliamentary Group from 1991 to 1997 and of the Conservative Backbench Arts Committee from 1983 to 1997. The best pianist in the Commons, in 1993 he raised £30,000 for the NSPCC and £40,000 in 1995. For twenty-four years he competed in the annual parliamentary race at Davos for the Lords and Commons Ski Club against the Swiss parliament.

GERALD KAUFMAN 1930–

Gerald Kaufman is a Leeds man, educated at Leeds Grammar School before taking PPE at Queen's College, Oxford. By the time he was 25 he was a first-class political journalist on the socialist *Daily Mirror* and he remained in journalism until he became a Labour Party press officer and close to Harold Wilson. In 1970, he won Manchester Ardwick and switched to Manchester Gorton in 1983. He has been in the Commons for nearly forty years. He was made a Privy Councillor in 1978.

Kaufman held junior positions in the Wilson and Callaghan governments but then took on greater responsibilities in opposition. He was Shadow Environment Secretary from 1980 to 1983; Shadow Home Secretary from 1983 to 1987; and Shadow Foreign Secretary from 1987 to 1992. He was also on the Labour National Executive from 1991 to 1992. In the next parliament he returned to the back benches and became chairman of the Culture, Media and Sport Select Committee. In this role he has been particularly effective in trying to ensure that the people involved are efficient and within budget. Behind the public man is a very good writer, good enough to have written scripts for the TV satire show, *That Was The Week That Was*. Communally, Kaufman is a member of the Jewish Labour Movement but he has been highly critical of Israeli governments. His constituency contains a considerable number of Muslim voters and there have been efforts to deselect him. He still won in 2005 and was knighted in 2004.

SALLY OPPENHEIM 1930–

Oppenheim was the surname of one of the most famous families in the South African diamond industry, which Jews had done so much to develop during the nineteenth century. Sally Oppenheim once worked as a diamond cutter, although she was originally trained as an actress at RADA. When she first stood for election as Conservative candidate for Gloucester in 1970, it was ironic that she defeated another Jewish MP, John Diamond, who was the only Cabinet Minister to lose his seat in that election.

Oppenheim won five elections in all and was made a Privy Councillor in 1979. She was Minister of State for Consumer Affairs in Margaret Thatcher's first government, from 1979 to 1982. In 1983 she had the pleasure of seeing her son, Philip, join her in the Commons as member for the Amber Valley; this may have been the only occasion when mother and son have served together in the House. In 1989, when she lost her seat, she was promoted to the House of Lords and is now Baroness Oppenheim-Barnes.

She has served as the national vice-president of the Townswomen's Guild and also on the board of Boots. Communally, she was born Orthodox but became a member of the Reform synagogue; she is not in favour of many Orthodox practices. But then, as she once said, 'Jewishness is a race rather than a religion', so strict observance of its laws was never likely to be attractive to her. During her years in the House, Oppenheim gave the lie to any suggestion that Jewish MPs voted as a single group. She went on record as saying, 'Jewish Labour MPs make me ashamed. There is no kinship whatever with them. None at all. I believe in right and wrong.'

HAROLD SOREF 1916–1993

As a white supremacist, Harold Soref was an embarrassment to the vast majority of the Jewish community. From a family of Romanian refugees, he was educated at the Hall School and St Paul's School in London and Queen's College, Oxford where he read History. Before the war, he joined Mosley's fascists though he did report what was going on to the *Jewish Chronicle* when he saw the anti-Semitic nature of the party. During the war, he served as a private in the Royal Scots and the Intelligence Corps from 1940 to 1946.

Soref went into the family export business and became its managing director in 1959. In 1963 he joined the Conservative Monday Club – a powerful pressure group – and was on its Executive Council for a time. Soref's interests included Africa, immigration and terrorism. He had been a delegate to the first All-British African Conference in Rhodesia as early as 1937, when he was 21. He was deeply involved in both the Anglo-Rhodesian and Anglo-Zanzibar Societies.

In 1970, Soref became the Conservative MP for Ormskirk but lost the seat in February 1974. During his four years in the Commons he was notable for attacking the level of immigration into Britain from which his parents had benefited. He also attacked the terrorism of the IRA; the policies of Idi Amin in Uganda; the People's Republic of China in general, and voted against joining the Common Market. He was a warm supporter of Ian Smith in Zimbabwe and of Enoch Powell and was against allowing Indian refugees to enter the country from Uganda. Speaking out against terrorism does takes courage. It is highly likely that the IRA tried to assassinate Soref in 1974 but killed the wrong man in a similar car.

Communally he was a member of the Liberal synagogue and served on the Board of Deputies and the Anglo-Jewish Association, editing its magazine, *Jewish Monthly*, from 1947 to 1951. He attacked the community for not replacing the Cousinhood with people equally strongly committed to its service. In 1981, the *Jewish Chronicle* denounced his views on racial issues and he left the Board of Deputies in 1984 after more disagreements. Soref died in 1993 at the age of 77.

NEVILLE SANDELSON 1923–2002

Neville Sandelson was a Labour MP who gave the party whips more sleepless nights than most. He came from a Jewish business family in Leeds and was educated at Westminster School and Trinity College, Cambridge. He was president of the Union and was called to the Bar after he had graduated. All highly respectable. He decided not to practise, made TV documentaries and became a publisher. In the twenty years from 1950 onwards he stood for parliament eight times and lost every time. He was finally elected for Labour in a 1971 by-election in Hayes and Harlington and served the constituency until 1983. During his period in parliament, Sandelson voted for Britain's entry into the Common Market, which was against party policy. He became well known for shouting out 'Rubbish' and 'Nonsense', but usually when his own side were speaking. In 1979, he said he would vote with the Conservatives on defence issues because he was against nuclear disarmament, which was, again, contrary to his party's policy at the time. Worst of all, he conspired with some other right-wing Labour MPs to work for Michael Foot to be elected leader rather than Denis Healey. This, he later said, was not out of admiration for Mr Foot; Sandelson intended to defect to the SDP and thought that Healey would be a harder opponent to overcome for leadership of the left. Not surprisingly, there were two attempts to deselect him when he was sitting as a Labour MP, but Sandelson fought them off. He finally defected to the SDP in 1981.

Sandelson found time to be secretary of the British-Greek Parliamentary Group and vice-chairman of the SDP Friends of Israel – from which he resigned over the bombing of Beirut in 1982. He was also vice-chairman of the Afghanistan Support Committee. He stood for the SDP in 1983 but lost his seat and went back to law. Discouraged by the policies of the SDP he defected again and was allowed to rejoin the Labour Party in 1996 – magnanimity on a munificent scale. He died in 2002, when nearly 80.

CLEMENT FREUD 1924–

Clement Freud is the grandson of Sigmund Freud, the father of psychoanalysis. When his family came to Britain before the Second World War, Freud was sent to St Paul's School. During the war, he served in the Royal Ulster Rifles and was later an aide to Field Marshal Montgomery. He finished his army career as British liaison officer at the Nuremberg trials. He got on well with his superiors.

Freud made his name with his journalism, his wit and his many appearances on TV and radio. He was also the proprietor of a nightclub above the Royal Court Theatre from 1952 to 1962. He was a sports writer for the *Observer* from 1956 to 1964. His career was very different from his illustrious and professional antecedents. His father had been an architect and when Freud was working as a waiter at the Dorchester Hotel in Mayfair, he was fully aware he had chosen a very different road to success and public recognition. Freud took no part in Jewish affairs and sought to be his own man.

This he felt he had achieved when he won the Isle of Ely for the unfashionable Liberals in 1973. It was not according to plan that he was then hailed by the *Jewish Chronicle* as the first Jewish Liberal MP for years – the first, in fact, since Jimmy Rothschild held the constituency from 1929 to 1945. Henry Mond had also represented Ely for the Liberals from 1923 to 1924. Freud served in five parliaments as a member for a minority party. He was knighted when he finally lost the seat in 1987 after fourteen years in parliament.

LEON BRITTAN 1939–

Leon Brittan's family came to the UK in the 1920s, not as refugees but as economic migrants. His father practised medicine in London and Brittan went to Haberdashers' School before going on to Trinity College, Cambridge. He was elected president of the Union, studied English and Law and became a barrister. Brittan cut his political teeth when losing North Kensington in 1966 and 1970 but stood successfully as Conservative for Cleveland and Whitby in February 1974. He moved to the Richmond constituency in Yorkshire in 1983 and left the Commons in 1988, to be succeeded by William Hague, an ex-president of the Oxford Union.

Once Margaret Thatcher took office in 1979, Brittan had a meteoric rise. Minister of State at the Home Office from 1979 to 1981; then in the Cabinet as Chief Secretary to the Treasury until 1983; on to Home Secretary from 1983 to 1985; and then to Trade and

Industry for some months, before he resigned over what became known as the Westland Affair. This was a Cabinet row about whether the British helicopter manufacturer should be sold to the Americans or the Europeans, which got totally out of hand. In 1989, Brittan was appointed one of the UK's two Commissioners in the European Commission and remained in Brussels until 1999 when he was serving as vice-president of the Commission. He was Chancellor of the University of Teeside from 1992 to 2005 and is a non-executive director of Unilever and vice-president of the UBS Investment Bank. He became a QC in 1978 and was awarded a peerage in 2000.

IVAN LAWRENCE 1936–

Ivan Lawrence was educated at Brighton Grammar School and Christ Church, Oxford. He became a barrister in 1962 and specializes in criminal cases. He became a QC in 1981, a Crown Court Recorder in 1983 and Head of his Chambers in 1997. As his website says, he has been involved in seventy murder trials and is also highly experienced in the prosecution of drug trafficking, smuggling, rape, child abuse and large scale commercial frauds. The Kray twins, Denis Nilsen the serial killer, the Brighton 'Babes in the Wood' murders and Brinks Matt are some of the most notorious cases to have come Lawrence's way. He has also defended an alleged Serbian war criminal at The Hague, is involved in international human rights, and remains very much at the top of the legal tree.

He was elected MP for Burton in 1974 and held the seat for the next twenty-three years. Apart from energetic work improving criminal justice as chairman of the Home Affairs Select Committee from 1992 to 1997 and as chairman of the Conservative Parliamentary Legal and Home Affairs Committees for many years, he was also a member of the Foreign Affairs Select Committee from 1983 to 1992. He was chairman of the UK branch of the Commonwealth Parliamentary Association for three years and chairman of the Burton Breweries Charitable Trust for fifteen years. It was Lawrence's Private Member's Bill which led to the creation of the National Lottery. He was knighted for political service in 1992 .

Communally, Lawrence has sat on the Board of Deputies since 1979 and was an officer and chairman of the Conservative Friends of Israel for many years. For over fifteen years he was vice-chairman of the All-Party Parliamentary Committee for Soviet Jewry and was asked by the Russian government to help them in redrafting their exit laws for the benefit of Soviet Jews. Lawrence worked hard to get the

War Crimes Act on to the statute book and has been an officer of many other Jewish organizations.

NIGEL LAWSON 1932–

Nigel Lawson was one of the success stories of Margaret Thatcher's government. He was Chancellor of the Exchequer for more years than anyone since Lloyd George, though Gordon Brown would subsequently serve longer. Lawson went to Westminster School and Christ Church, Oxford, did his national service in the navy, becoming commanding officer of a motor torpedo boat, and then joined the *Financial Times*. He became city editor of the *Sunday Telegraph* in 1961 when he was still under 30 and edited the *Spectator* magazine from 1966 to 1970.

Elected Conservative MP for Blaby in Leicestershire in 1974, he remained the constituency's MP for eighteen years. When Thatcher took office in 1979, Lawson was made Financial Secretary to the Treasury under Geoffrey Howe and was largely responsible for carrying out the abolition of exchange controls. In 1981 Lawson became Secretary of State for Energy and set out to execute the government's privatization policy. He strongly believed that the private sector could do a better job than the government in running industry.

As Chancellor from 1983, until his high-profile resignation in 1989, he instituted the most far-reaching programme of tax reform since the war, simplifying the system and reducing most rates of tax, in particular income tax, while bringing the public finances from deficit to surplus. In 1992, Lawson went to the Lords. Since leaving government he has had a number of business appointments, including a non-executive directorship of Barclays Bank, and he is currently chairman of Oxford Investment Partners.

HARRY SELBY 1913–1984

Harry Selby went to Queen's Park Secondary School in Glasgow and became a barber. He was a private in the Highland Light Infantry in 1940 and moved on to the Corps of Signals in 1941. Selby was a Trotskyite, well to the left of the Labour Party. The idea was for a small number of members to infiltrate the party and win power by working harder than anybody else. When the other delegates had left the meeting or couldn't be bothered to write up the minutes, the Revolutionary Socialists could come into their own. Selby was the leader of the Left Faction and they came to dominate the Glasgow

Govan Labour Party. He also lectured at the National Council of Labour Colleges and served on Glasgow Corporation from 1972 to 1974. He was elected for Glasgow Govan in February 1974 but stood down in 1979 and died in 1984 at the age of 70. Selby was not very involved with the Jewish community.

ANTHONY STEEN 1939–

Educated at Westminster School, the University of London, Gray's Inn and trained as a concert pianist, Anthony Steen has now served thirty-four years in the Commons. He achieved this long and continuous record even though two of his constituencies were abolished in boundary changes. He sat for Liverpool Wavertree from 1974 to 1983, South Hams from 1983 to 1987 and since 1997 has been elected for the Totnes constituency. Steen practised as a barrister, specializing in Landlord and Tenant and Planning Law. He also acted for the National Association of Head Teachers and the Ministry of Defence at court martials.

From 1959 to 1964, Steen worked in a number of Jewish Settlements as a youth leader in East London. He then started a London organization called Task Force which recruited young people to volunteer to help the old and lonely; 15,000 recruits resulted and that prompted former Prime Minister Harold Wilson to invite Steen to establish a national counterpart with government funds. The *Jewish Chronicle* called Steen 'a dynamo from St Johns Wood'. Communally, he is a council member of the Anglo-Jewish Association and on the Council of Christians and Jews. He has contributed to an innumerable number of parliamentary committees and is currently chairman of the All-Party Group on the Trafficking of Women and Children. This has had considerable influence on government action and has played an active part in Commons debates over the two years of its existence. One of Kenneth Clarke's most vociferous supporters for the leadership of the Conservative party, Steen remains a Euro-realist when it comes to the future with Europe.

HELENE HAYMAN (NÉE MIDDLEWEEK) 1949–

Helene Hayman contested her first election in February 1974 when she stood as the Labour candidate in Enoch Powell's constituency, Wolverhampton South West. In October 1974, she stood again and on this occasion was returned as MP for Welwyn and Hatfield. She joined the House of Commons aged 25, the youngest MP in the House and one of only twenty-seven women MPs at the time.

Hayman was educated at Wolverhampton Girls' High School and went on to Newnham College, Cambridge where she read Law and was president of the Union. After graduation, her first job was with the housing charity, Shelter, followed by positions in the Social Services Department of the London Borough of Camden and the National Council for One Parent Families. She married Martin Hayman in 1974; they have four sons, the first of whom was born when she was in parliament, and who had to be brought into the House during crucial votes in 1976. Hayman lost her seat in 1979. She went on to serve as a member of the Royal College of Gynaecologists Ethical Committee (1982 to 1987), the first of numerous roles in the health care sector, including chair of the Whittington Hospital NHS Trust (1992 to 1997) and chair of Cancer Research UK (2001 to 2004). In 1997 Hayman was raised to the peerage and made Opposition Spokesperson for Health. In 1997, when Labour came to power she was made Minister for Roads and subsequently Parliamentary Under-Secretary of State at the Department of Health. In 1999, she was promoted to Minister of State at the Ministry of Agriculture, Fisheries and Food, and in 2001 she was made a Privy Councillor. In July 2006 Hayman became the first elected Lord Speaker of the House of Lords. In her new role she is highly and fondly respected.

MILLIE MILLER 1923–1977

The auburn-haired Millie Miller was a red-blooded socialist devoted to improving the lot of the poorer members of society. She was a social worker and a member of the General and Municipal Workers Union. Miller started her political life as a local government councillor in Stoke Newington where she served as Mayor in 1957/8 when she was only 34. She moved on to Camden, where she was also the Mayor from 1967/8, and from 1971 to 1973 she was the first woman ever to lead a London Borough Council.

Miller lost in the first general election of 1974 by 275 votes but in the second won Ilford North for Labour with a majority of 778. This might well have been one of the very few instances where Jewish voters in a constituency made all the difference to the result. Miller was a Cockney from what she described as a non-synagogue family, but she was the chair of the North London Progressive Synagogue from 1968 to 1972 and took a keen interest in working for Russian Jews to be allowed to emigrate to Israel. She was also prominent in the Labour Friends of Israel. She died in 1977, at the early age of 54.

1979–1997: Conservative Revolution

In the time of Margaret Thatcher, there was a joke doing the rounds in the Commons. Denis Thatcher was the Prime Minister's husband and it was said that he had suggested that if his wife put any more Jews in the Cabinet it might consider moving its meetings to Golders Green! Another comment was that were more Old Estonians in the Cabinet than Old Etonians. It was astonishing that so many gifted Jewish politicians all came into prominence at the same time. Leon Brittan, Michael Howard, Sir Keith Joseph, Nigel Lawson, Malcolm Rifkind and David Young all served in the Cabinet in the Thatcher years. The fairest explanation for their promotion was that they had the necessary talent but it is also true that they were not members of the *old* Conservative establishment. They didn't come from the shires, and they weren't scions of aristocratic families. Nor did Thatcher, and she was intent on creating a meritocracy in government rather than relying on the sources which had, in fairness, stood the Conservative Party in good stead for very many years.

The reaction of some members of the Jewish community to the choice of so many of their co-religionists for high office was muted. If there is anything that many in the community dislike, it is having a high profile. They want to live peacefully and quietly and get on with their lives without arousing negative publicity. This communal sensitivity has no justification in terms of the way they've been treated over the centuries they have lived in Britain. It is just a reaction to the virulence of anti-Semitic attacks in other countries, particularly in Eastern Europe.

Margaret Thatcher didn't just set out to change the economic situation in Britain. She wanted to reduce what she considered over-reliance on the Welfare State. The Church of England was very concerned about how this might affect the underprivileged and produced a paper criticizing the government's performance. They asked the Chief Rabbi, Immanuel Jakobovits, to add his name to the document. To everybody's considerable surprise he said he couldn't. In Judaism, if people are poor, the law is that they should be helped to make themselves better off by being lent start-up money by the richer members of the community. They should not be encouraged simply to rely on charity.

The Prime Minister was delighted, as Jakobovits was echoing her own views. She made him a peer and the Jewish community watched in amazement as the press started to look to Jakobovits as a spokesman on the moral and ethical approach to life. Government ministers would ask his views. One education minister asked about teaching contraception in schools with a specially produced video. Jakobovits said it would be utterly repugnant. The idea was dropped. Jakobovits never gave his own opinion. He simply stated what the law in Judaism had to say on each subject. Whether that was acceptable, popular or fashionable, was utterly unimportant to him. No sitting on the fence, no attempt to see which way the wind was blowing. Just the law.

But there were still causes which would bring the Jewish community to the barricades. In the 1980s, one of these continued to be the treatment of Jews in Russia who wanted to emigrate. The reaction of the Communist regime was most often to refuse their applications and to force them out of their jobs. The British Jewish community, like so many others around the world, protested vigorously. They lobbied parliament; Jewish MPs and their allies denounced the Russian actions and the word 'refusenik' was coined to draw attention those who were affected.

The community also continued to support Israel, and murmured accusations of double loyalties continued to be heard in many quarters. It was difficult for those not involved to understand why a religious community should be deeply concerned about the condition of their co-religionists far away. After all, if there was discrimination against Christian communities in Middle Eastern countries – and there was – you didn't find mass demonstrations by UK Protestants and Catholics. Nationalism might arouse mass protest – the international battle against apartheid in South Africa, for example – but not religion.

In reality, Jews, without a country for 2,000 years, had only survived because of their concern for those of their communities who were in trouble. Every community in the middle ages raised money to ransom Jews kidnapped by pirates in the Mediterranean, to help communities whose synagogues had been destroyed by mobs, or to alleviate poverty in a country where they had been singled out for additional harsh taxation. Jews have always tried to look after each other and the extent of their charity to their poorer co-religionists is at the core of their reputation for being the best fundraisers in the world.

Jewish MPs elected during the eighteen unbroken years of Conservative governments between 1979 and 1997 were:

1979   Thirteen Jewish MPs were out of the Commons after the 1979 election. They were Edmund Dell, Maurice Edelman, Harold Lever, John Mendelson, Helen Middleweek-Hayman, Eric Moonman, Maurice Orbach, Paul Rose, Harry Selby, Arnold Shaw, Manny Shinwell, George Strauss and Raphael Tuck. There were four new Jewish MPs – **Alf Dubs** (Labour), **Sheila Faith** (Conservative), **John Lee** (Conservative) and **Malcolm Rifkind** (Conservative)

1983   Leo Abse (Labour), Robert Adley (Conservative), **Spencer Batiste** (Conservative), **Martin Brandon-Bravo** (Conservative), Leon Brittan (Conservative), **Alex Carlile** (Liberal Democrat), **Harry Cohen** (Labour), **Edwina Currie** (Conservative), Alf Dubs (Labour), Geoffrey Finsberg (Conservative), **Cecil Franks** (Conservative), Reg Freeson (Labour), Clement Freud (Liberal), **Michael Howard** (Conservative), Greville Janner (Labour), Toby Jessel (Conservative), Keith Joseph (Conservative), Gerald Kaufman (Labour), Ivan Lawrence (Conservative), Nigel Lawson (Conservative), John Lee (Conservative), Ian Mikardo (Labour), Maurice Miller (Labour), **Phillip Oppenheim** (Conservative), Sally Oppenheim (Conservative), Malcolm Rifkind (Conservative), Robert Sheldon (Labour), Renée Short (Labour), John Silkin (Labour), Anthony Steen (Conservative), **Michael Stern** (Conservative), **David Sumberg** (Conservative), David Winnick (Labour)

1984   **Lord David Young** (Conservative)

1987   Robert Adley (Conservative), Spencer Batiste (Conservative), Martin Brandon-Bravo (Conservative), Alex Carlile (Liberal Democrat), Harry Cohen (Labour), Edwina Currie (Conservative), Geoffrey Finsberg (Conservative), Cecil Franks (Conservative), **Mildred Gordon** (Labour), Michael Howard (Conservative), Greville Janner (Labour), Toby Jessel (Conservative), Gerald Kaufman (Labour), Ivan Lawrence (Conservative), Nigel Lawson (Conservative), John Lee (Conservative), Phillip Oppenheim (Conservative), **Irvine Patnick** (Conservative), Malcolm Rifkind (Conservative), **David Shaw** (Conservative), Robert Sheldon (Labour), Anthony Steen (Conservative), **Gerry Steinberg** (Labour), Michael Stern (Conservative), David Sumberg (Conservative),

David Winnick (Labour)

1992 Spencer Batiste (Conservative), Alex Carlile (Liberal Democrat), Harry Cohen, (Labour), Edwina Currie (Conservative), **Michael Fabricant** (Conservative), Mildred Gordon (Labour), Michael Howard (Conservative), Greville Janner (Labour), Toby Jessel (Conservative), Gerald Kaufman (Labour), Ivan Lawrence (Conservative), **Peter Mandelson** (Labour), Phillip Oppenheim (Conservative), Irvine Patnick (Conservative), Malcolm Rifkind (Conservative), **Barbara Roche** (Labour), David Shaw (Conservative), Robert Sheldon (Labour), Anthony Steen (Conservative), Gerry Steinberg (Labour), Michael Stern (Conservative), David Sumberg (Conservative), David Winnick (Labour)

1994 **Margaret Hodge** (Labour)

ALF DUBS 1932–

Alf Dubs was another beneficiary of Britain's generous welcome to so many refugees from Nazi persecution before the war. He was born in Czechoslovakia, his father was Jewish, and Alf arrived in England at the age of 6, on a *Kindertransport*. Dubs went to the London School of Economics. He was elected to Westminster City Council and then, in 1979, to parliament as Labour MP for Battersea South. He won the new Battersea seat in 1983 but lost it in 1987. He was appointed to the House of Lords in 1994 and became a Minister in Northern Ireland from 1997 to 1999. He was chair of the Labour Peers from 2001 to 2005.

Between the Commons and the Lords, Dubs was chief executive of the Refugee Council from 1988 to 1995. He has also been deputy chair of the Independent Television Commission and chair of the Broadcasting Standards Commission. He has been chair of the Fabian Society and Liberty, was a trustee of Action Aid, of the Immigration Advisory Service and of the Open University. He is currently chair of the Road Safety Foundation and chairs the Appeal Panel of the Association of Energy Suppliers.

SHEILA FAITH 1928–

Sheila Faith was educated at the Central High School, Newcastle upon Tyne and Durham University, where she qualified as a dental surgeon, going on to practise as a school dental surgeon in Northumberland. In 1972 she became a JP, serving on the bench in Northumberland and later Newcastle Upon Tyne. Of the seventy-seven new Conservative MPs elected in 1979, Faith was the only woman. She was the MP for Belper from 1979 to 1983, serving on the Health and Social Services Parliamentary Select Committee and the Executive Committee of the Conservative Medical Society. As an MP, she took a key interest in dental matters and spoke on behalf of the pharmacists and nurses and on medical affairs in general.

Faith then became the Member of the European Parliament for Cumbria and Lancashire North from 1984 to 1989, after Belper disappeared in boundary changes. She was president of the Cumbria and Lancashire North Conservative European Constituency Council from 1989 to 1994. Faith was appointed a member of the Parole Board of England and Wales from 1991 to 1994. She was the first Jew to serve on the Northumberland County Council and the second Jewish woman Conservative MP. She is a member of the Conservative Friends of Israel.

JOHN LEE 1942–

John Lee was a Conservative when he was in the Commons from 1979 to 1992. He was first elected for Nelson and Colne, Sidney Silverman's long-time Labour seat, from 1979 to 1983, and then sat for Pendle till 1992. He was Parliamentary Under-Secretary of State for Employment in 1986, and from 1987 to 1989 he was the Minister of Tourism and did much good work helping the industry to compete in world markets. Educated at William Holmes Grammar School, he became an account-ant and founded Chancery Consolidated, a firm of investment bankers. Outside the House, John Lee served as chairman of the North West Conciliation Committee of the Race Relations Board. In 2001, Lee defected to the Liberal Democrats and was made a peer in 2006.

MALCOLM RIFKIND 1946–

Malcolm Rifkind came from two small communities: the Jewish con-gregation in Edinburgh and the ranks of Scottish Conservative MPs. He was born in Edinburgh and educated at George Watson's College and Edinburgh University. Rifkind may be the only MP to have appeared on University Challenge. He was called to the Bar in 1970. Rifkind came into the Commons as the member for Edinburgh Pentlands in 1979. From 1986 to 1990 he was Secretary of State for Scotland and gained a reputation as a moderate in Thatcher's Cabinet. He was Secretary of State for Transport from 1990 to 1992 and Secretary of State for Defence from 1992 to 1995. Under John Major, he became Foreign Secretary from 1995 to 1997. When he addressed the United Nations in 1996, it was to call for terrorists to be refused political asylum in any state.

Rifkind was knighted in 1997 after he lost his seat in the House in the general election that year. All the Conservatives in Wales and Scotland were defeated with him. He didn't give up in Scotland, becoming president of the Scottish Conservatives, but losing Pentlands again in 2001. In 2005 he was elected for Kensington and Chelsea, a very safe Tory seat. He served in the Shadow Cabinet but left the Conservative front bench in December 2005. He is associat-ed with a number of commercial companies.

SPENCER BATISTE 1945–

Spencer Batiste is a solicitor who was educated at Carmel College, the only Jewish boarding school of its time. He was much influenced by the charismatic leadership and oratorical skills of the Headmaster, Rabbi Kopul Rosen. Batiste went on to the Sorbonne and to Cambridge where he became involved with debating and politics. He won a number of British Junior Chamber of Commerce national debating and public speaking awards, before being elected as the Conservative member for Elmet in 1983, a seat which he held until 1997. During his time in the House he was in turn Parliamentary Private Secretary to the Ministers of State for Trade and Industry and of Defence Procurement, as well as to Leon Brittan when he was vice-president at the European Commission. Batiste was also a member of the Science and Technology Select Committee. On more than one occasion, Batiste introduced bills to outlaw the Arab boycott of firms trading with Israel. He supported John Major during the challenge to his leadership. He was pro-European and a keen supporter of the Conservative Friends of Israel. Throughout his time in parliament, Batiste maintained his links to the law, and was a founding member of what is now one of the country's largest international law firms. After losing his seat in 1997, he became a judge.

MARTIN BRANDON-BRAVO 1932–

Martin Brandon-Bravo went to Latymer School and after completing two years of National Service took up a trainee management post with a clothing manufacturer. After twenty-five years in the company he became managing director. Brandon-Bravo served on the Nottingham County Council from 1968 to 1970 and from 1976 to 1987. He won Nottingham South for the Conservatives in 1983 and sat in the Commons until he was defeated in 1992. During his time in parliament he was Parliamentary Private Secretary to the Minister of State for Housing, the Home Secretary and, finally, to the Lord Privy Seal and Leader in the Lords. His Private Member's Bill granting lifelong anonymity to innocent young victims of abuse reached the statute book. In 1993, he returned to local politics, winning a seat on the Nottinghamshire County Council which he retains, serving as Deputy Leader of the County Group.

Brandon-Bravo's hobby is rowing and he held an International Umpire's licence until he retired in 1998. He was the principal motivator for the creation of the National Sports Centre at Hulme Pierrepont, and he was elected president of the British Amateur Rowing Association, and rowing is one of our most successful sports as a nation. Brandon-Bravo is now one of the Association's three vice-presidents for life. He was awarded the OBE for services to rowing in 2001.

ALEX CARLILE 1948–

Josef and Johannah Falik came from Przemysl in Poland. Their son, Dr Erwin Falik, left Poland as a medical officer in his unit at the outbreak of the Second World War. His wife and parents perished. Now, seventy years on, his son by a later marriage, Lord Alex Carlile, is the head of one of the leading criminal law Chambers in England. The benefits to Britain of a liberal immigration policy have been proven very many times over the centuries and here is another excellent example.

Carlile was educated at Epsom College and King's College London. He was a QC by the age of 36. From 1980 to 1982, he was chairman of the Welsh Liberals and from 1983 to 1997 he sat as MP for Montgomeryshire. In 1999, he became Lord Carlile of Berriew.

It is difficult to pigeon-hole Carlile. On the one hand, he is in favour of extending the time during which suspects can be held without charge. On the other hand, he is president of the Howard League for Penal Reform and a member of the Council of Justice, the British section of the International Commission of Jurists. In 2001, he was appointed Independent Reviewer of terrorism legislation. In a sensational case, he successfully defended one of Princess Diana's servants against charges of thefts from her estate. Carlile is a member of the Athenaeum and lists Association Football as one of his hobbies. A remarkable man.

HARRY COHEN 1949–

Harry Cohen is a member of the Socialist Campaign Group and cannot be described as New Labour. He is an accountant by profession but was always interested in politics and was elected as a Councillor for Waltham Forest when he was only 23. He is a member of NALGO and in 1983 he won Leyton for Labour. This year, he celebrates twenty-five years in the House. He is deeply involved in his constituency, living and working there. He was chairman of the backbench Defence Select Committee from 1987 to 1992. In 1994, he obtained an MSc from Birkbeck in Politics and Administration. In 2006, he was one of only twelve Labour MPs to vote with Plaid Cymru and the Scottish Nationalists for an enquiry into the Iraq War. He is on the House Work and Pensions Select Committee and is secretary of the All-Party Race and Community Group and chairman of the All-Party Parliamentary Group for Tibet.

Cohen doesn't just concern himself with local issues. He is a strong supporter of the Fair Trade movement which tries to raise wages in third world countries. In 1994. he became chairman of the subcommittee for Economic Co-operation and Convergence with Eastern and Central Europe of the North Atlantic Assembly Economic Committee. He regularly helps asylum seekers, and his forebears would approve of his belief that: 'The crude tabloid press and those obsessed with fear of foreigners have got it wrong. Escaping a life-threatening situation is proper cause, and nastiness to such people is based on ignorance. Once here, refugees add overall to the quality of life.' Which was the Jewish argument against the Aliens Act of 1905 and proved correct, as so many of the refugees and their descendants illustrated.

EDWINA CURRIE 1946–

After studying PPE at Oxford, Edwina Currie took a Masters degree at LSE. From 1975 to 1986 she was a Birmingham City Councillor. In 1983 she became Conservative MP for South Derbyshire and served in Thatcher's government as a Health Minister. Currie was twice re-elected for her constituency. In 1994 she was largely responsible for bringing down the homosexual age of consent from 21 to 18. She lost her seat in 1997 and has since had her own popular radio programme and written ten books, including best-selling novels. Currie was the first woman or MP to appear on the popular TV programme *Have I Got News For You* – which says a lot for the power of her personality. She was described at the time as 'a virtually permanent fixture on the nation's TV screen' and according to an *Economist* poll in 1988, was Britain's best-known MP after Thatcher. Communally, Currie has not played a major part in Jewish affairs but it says much for her innate kindness that she still takes the time regularly to visit one of the major Jewish old-age homes in London and conduct their Book Club. Currie will also be remembered for her relationship with John Major when both were Junior Ministers, revealed many years later. Her ministerial career ended after her controversial warning about food poisoning caused by eggs, at a time when over 500 cases a week were being reported. Currie feels it might have been worse; as she says, she could have kept quiet. She turned down John Major's offer to return to office in 1992.

CECIL FRANKS 1935–

The old borough parliamentary constituency of Barrow-in-Furness had been a Labour stronghold since 1945 but the new county constituency of Barrow and Furness included the peninsula's rural hinterland and the market town of Ulveston. The then sitting Labour MP for the old Barrow constituency, a former Cabinet Minister, was an active member of the Campaign for Nuclear Disarmament, though the main employer in the new constituency remained the Barrow shipyards, building nuclear submarines. The Conservative Party candidate had withdrawn the weekend before the 1983 general election was announced. A crash selection process resulted in Cecil Franks, a solicitor from Manchester who had never been to Barrow until his interview, contesting the seat and, three weeks later, winning it with the largest swing of the election. He held it for the next nine years, until the 1990 Defence Review, following the end of the Cold War, cut the size of the submarine fleet and with it, employment in the shipyards. Franks was educated at Manchester Grammar School and Manchester University. He qualified as a solicitor in 1958 and was the leader of the Conservative group on Manchester City Council from 1975 to 1983. Previously, he had served fourteen years on the Salford City Council from 1960 to 1974. Since losing his seat for Barrow and Furness he has not stood for election again.

MICHAEL HOWARD 1941–

Michael Howard's father was a Romanian shopkeeper called Bernard Hecht who had emigrated to Wales. It was from this unremarkable background that his son emerged as Leader of the Conservative Party in 2003. Howard went to Llanelli Grammar School and Peterhouse, the oldest Cambridge college. He gained a degree in Law and was president of the Cambridge Union in 1962. Howard was called to the Bar in 1964 and specialized in employment and planning law. He became a QC in 1982 and was elected for Folkestone and Hythe in 1983, a constituency he still represents. He was Parliamentary Under-Secretary of State at the Department of Trade and Industry and took the Financial Services Bill through parliament. He then became Minister for Local Government in 1987 and was given the task of introducing what became known as the Poll Tax. This was immensely unpopular but Howard fought hard for it.

In the Cabinet from 1990 to 1997, Howard was successively Secretary of State for Employment, Environment and Home Secretary. After the Conservative defeat in 1997, he became Shadow Foreign Secretary and in 2001 Shadow Chancellor of the Exchequer. In 2003, he was elected unopposed as Leader of the Conservative Party. Communally, he has always identified with the Jewish community but his wife and children are Christian. Every year, however, when the anniversary of his father's death comes round, Howard is to be found in an Orthodox synagogue, expertly leading the evening prayers. 'Honour your father and your mother' is the fifth commandment.

PHILIP OPPENHEIM 1956–

Philip Oppenheim is Sally Oppenheim's son and followed his mother into the Commons in the 1983 election. He won the Amber Valley seat for the Conservatives when he was only 27 years old with the largest swing to the Conservatives in that election. Oppenheim went to Harrow and Oriel College, Oxford. As a youngster, he was involved in the early days of IT and sold the company he created to Reed Elsevier, very profitably. In the Commons, he spent six years as Parliamentary Private Secretary to Kenneth Clarke. He did good work on protecting endangered species and was also an active opponent of fox hunting. As an author, he attacked the US and Europe for protectionist measures against Japan and Third World countries. After he lost his seat in 1997, he wrote for the *Sunday Times*, attacking alleged corruption in the Honours system. He also has close trade links with Cuba.

MICHAEL STERN 1942–

Michael Stern was educated at Christ's College, Finchley, and became an accountant. He was chairman of the Conservative Bow Group from 1977 to 1978. In 1983, he was elected for Bristol North West and retained the seat until 1997, though his majority in 1992 was only forty-five. From 1991 to 1992, he was vice-chairman of the Conservative Party. He acted as a consultant to accountants Cohen Arnold from 1992 to 1998. In 1995, he gave his professional advice to MPs accused of fiddling their expenses. When asked by a national newspaper to comment, he refused to do so on the grounds that he had been consulted professionally and not as an MP. When he was afterwards accused in the paper of helping cover up any falsifications, he took the case to the Press Council and his complaint was upheld.

Stern was one of only two Jewish Conservative MPs in his time who did not join the Conservative Friends of Israel. He said that he wanted to retain his independence and there were occasions when he criticized the actions of the Israel government. Stern has always been teased for being short – he is 5' 5" tall. *The Times* once said that he couldn't be made a minister because he wouldn't be able to see over the Dispatch Box. Stern took it all in good part but kept an eye open for legislation which might act against people who weren't very tall.

In a bill on underage drinking he pointed out that some short people were denied service in pubs because their height was taken as an indication of their age. He was effective in obtaining better pensions for German refugees from the German government and for his work at the time of the Divorce Law Reform Bill. He persuaded the government to include a clause to help Jewish women who had difficulty in getting a divorce from their husbands. His hobby is fell walking and he is a member of the London Mountaineering Club.

DAVID SUMBERG 1941–

David Sumberg was born in Stoke on Trent and educated at Tettenhall College in Wolverhampton and the College of Law in London, becoming a solicitor. In 1983 he was elected Conservative member for Bury South and held the seat until 1997. The constituency is very marginal, with about 10,000 Jews in the 65,000 electorate, the largest percentage outside London. Sumberg once pointed out that his total number of votes went up in each of the four elections he fought, but his majority continually declined. In 1992, it was down to 778. In 1990, he even went to Israel to organize a reunion of Jews who had emigrated from the constituency. As they were likely still to have British passports, they could vote and Sumberg succeeded in getting many of them to register for the Conservatives. During his time in the House, he was Parliamentary Private Secretary to the Attorney General from 1986 to 1990. When the House of Commons was first televised in 1989, Sumberg was one of the first MPs to be seen speaking when he seconded the loyal address following the Queen's Speech.

When he left the Commons, he stood for the European parliament and won one of the North West England seats in 1999, which he retains. With his election to the European parliament, Sumberg became the first Jewish parliamentarian to have served in both the Westminster and European legislatures. Communally, Sumberg was joint secretary of the Conservative Friends of Israel and worked for many other Jewish organizations. In 1994 he rebelled against the proposed doubling of fuel tax because of the effect it could have on fuel bills for the elderly. After leaving the House, Sumberg became director of the Anglo-Israel Association.

DAVID YOUNG 1932–

David Young was drafted into the government by Margaret Thatcher and given a peerage to enable him to take the offices he filled. As he was never elected to the House of Commons, his entry is included in Appendix A.

MILDRED GORDON 1923–

When, in 1987, Ian Mikardo finally left the Commons after thirty-two years, his seat at Bow and Poplar needed a new MP. On the left wing of the party, Mikardo had been an important and popular member and his would be a hard act to follow. The choice of the local party was Mildred Gordon, whose socialist credentials matched Mikardo's own. Her father had been a Labour councillor for Spitalfields East and she had joined the party at the age of 14. Gordon had been married to Trotskyite Sam Gordon, but she soon decided that the Trotskyites' constant hair-splitting was futile and severed connections with them. Nevertheless, when she stood for Bow and Poplar one paper in Fleet Street labelled her 'the biggest red menace this side of the Urals'. In fact, she was a 63-year-old retired teacher whose grandfather had been a founder of the Stepney Jewish Hospital. Of her background, she said, 'I didn't have a religious upbringing but I feel very Jewish. Everyone who's Jewish does.'

Gordon's priorities were to alleviate poverty and suffering. They always had been. She was educated at Raines Foundation School, Pitmans and Forest Teacher Training College. She was a teacher in LCC state schools in the East End from 1945 to 1948 and, after four years in the United States, taught in the East End until 1959. When her son was born in that year she worked part-time as a visiting teacher at Holloway Prison. She went on to teach in Barnet and Brent from 1966 to 1985. She was on the Labour Select Committee on Education from 1991 to 1997, when she retired from the Commons. Mildred Gordon is still deeply interested in the East End. She founded the Tower Hamlets Schools Public Speaking Competition just before she retired and is now active in the pensioners' movement. She is the patron of the Docklands Singers and of the Daneford Trust. She speaks on special occasions and in 1999 was given the Freedom of the Borough of Tower Hamlets.

IRVINE PATNICK 1929–

Irvine Patnick is a product of the Central Technical School and Sheffield Polytechnic. After leaving college he became a builder and was elected a member of Sheffield City council for the Conservatives. He was leader of the South Yorkshire Metropolitan County Council opposition from 1973 to 1986. Patnick won Sheffield Hallam in 1987 and sat for the constituency for ten years. He was 57 years old and expressed the excitement of many MPs when he said, 'It is like the end of a lifetime's dream. I always wanted to be an MP in a Sheffield seat but I thought it had just escaped, and then suddenly came the opportunity. I just can't believe I actually did it.' He served as a Lord Commissioner of the Treasury and deputy chairman of the Channel Tunnel Rail Link Select Committee. He was awarded the OBE in 1980 and was knighted in 1994. Communally, Patnick remains most active in the Sheffield Jewish community and is an executive president of the Sheffield and District Jewish Representative Council. He has been co-chairman of the Council of Christians and Jews since 2005 and vice-president of the Sheffield Jewish Congregation and Centre since 2003. He is also honorary vice-president of Sheffield Maccabi, a former member of the Board of Deputies and former national vice-chairman of Maccabi.

DAVID SHAW 1950–

Shaw was the Conservative MP for Dover from 1987 to 1997 and was notable for being one of the first MPs to use the internet to communicate. He is an accountant by profession and was only 36 when he first entered the Commons. Shaw was formerly chairman of the Conservative Bow Group and had taken a keen interest in politics in Kingston-on-Thames. He warned in the House of the need to be in the forefront of the IT revolution long before it was recognized how important this was going to be. He has also spoken out on the effect of Europe's unfunded pension liabilities on the Euro, which he sees as a major problem. Although Shaw's mother was vice-chair of the Social Issues Committee of the League of Jewish Women, her son is not connected with the community in any way.

GERRY STEINBERG 1945–

Gerry Steinberg was educated at Johnston Grammar School, went on to teacher training at Sheffield College of Education and gained a diploma in special educational needs at Newcastle Polytechnic. He became a teacher, joined the Labour Party and in 1975 was elected to the Durham City Council. In 1979 he became head teacher of Whitworth House Special School with a roll of eighty-five children. A decision to devote your career to helping educationally challenged children is to be much praised.

Steinberg was secretary of the Durham Labour Group from 1981 to 1987 and co-leader of the council from 1983 to 1987. With the North East dominated by Newcastle, Sunderland and Middlesborough, the interests of Durham need promoting with considerable vigour, and Steinberg provided this in full measure. As a result, in 1987 he was elected MP for Durham and remained for seventeen years before he retired in 2005. In the Commons, he was a member of the Education Select Committee and the Public Accounts Committee. In 2005, he was made an Honorary Freeman of the City of Durham. Communally, he is not a member of a synagogue but from the time he entered parliament he announced that he would give his wholehearted support to the campaign to get permission for Russian Jews to emigrate. He promised that he would vociferously support their cause in parliament, and he did.

MICHAEL FABRICANT 1950–

Michael Fabricant's father, Isaac, was a rabbi in Brighton. Fabricant Junior went to Brighton and Hove Grammar School and on to Loughborough University. He then studied at the Universities of Sussex, London, and Southern California where he gained a PhD in economics. Fabricant was director of the International Electronic and Investment Group from 1979 until 1991, which gave him considerable commercial experience overseas. He was also a broadcaster and journalist and advised overseas governments on the establishment of radio stations. He entered parliament in 1992 as Conservative member for Mid Staffordshire and has been an MP ever since, moving to the Lichfield constituency in 1997. In 2001, he was defending a majority of only 238 but increased it to 4,426. He emphasized the necessity to concentrate on local issues if you want to win elections. His Labour opponent felt it only right to praise Fabricant's charm when the results were announced. With a PhD in economics, Fabricant became Parliamentary Private Secretary to the Financial Secretary to the Treasury and later, in opposition, was the Conservative spokesman on economic affairs, in 2003. He became an Opposition Whip in 2005 and remains in that office. He is often asked to contribute to television programmes on news and current affairs. Communally, Fabricant takes an interest in Jewish affairs and keeps well in touch with the community.

PETER MANDELSON 1953–

Peter Mandelson is the son of Tony Mandelson, the much loved advertising director of the *Jewish Chronicle*, and of Mary, daughter of the Labour statesman, Herbert Morrison. Mandelson read PPE at St Catherine's College, Oxford and served three years on the Lambeth Borough Council from 1979 to 1982. He did not seek re-election, as he was dissatisfied with what he considered the ultra-left Labour leadership of the Council. Meanwhile, he worked for London Weekend Television as a current affairs producer and in 1985 was appointed Labour's Director of Campaigns and Communications. There he took on the key task of overhauling the party's image and electoral appeal without sacrificing basic socialist principles. He ushered in the party's 'Red Rose' era.

The 1987 general election was his first major campaign. The party was defeated, in spite of his much admired efforts. In 1992, he was elected MP for Hartlepool, and became a close and trusted ally of Tony Blair. When Labour returned to power in 1997, he was appointed Minister Without Portfolio in the Cabinet Office and later Secretary of State for Trade and Industry. He then became Northern Ireland Secretary and moved the warring factions in that troubled province into the first devolved government that included all parties, following the Good Friday Agreement. Mandelson finally left the government in 2001 after allegations that a government enquiry found to be untrue. In 2004, he was appointed one of Britain's Commissioners in Brussels and became the EU's Commissioner for External Trade. When Mandelson was re-elected in his constituency of Hartlepool in 2001, following his resignation from the government, he said, 'I'm a fighter, not a quitter'. Which he was – and remains.

BARBARA ROCHE 1954–

Barbara Roche was educated at the Jews' Free School in London, where she was head girl. She went on to Lady Margaret Hall, Oxford and trained to be a barrister, being called to the Bar in 1977. In 1992, she won Hornsey and Wood Green for Labour from the Conservatives, with a majority of over 20,000. After the Labour government was elected in 1997, she became a Parliamentary Under-Secretary of State at the Department of Trade and Industry and she was then appointed Financial Secretary to the Treasury in 1999. Later that year, she became Minister of State at the Home Office with special responsibility for immigration. She beat another Jewish candidate, the Liberal Democrat Lynne Featherstone, in 2001 with a majority of over 10,000. She then served in the Cabinet Office and the Office of the Deputy Prime Minister from 2002 to 2003. In the 2005 election, she lost to the Liberal Democrats. A number of other Labour seats were also lost, she felt, due to the Iraq War.

Roche's family comes from both Sephardi and Ashkenazi backgrounds. Some of her family came to the UK at the turn of the century from Eastern Europe as immigrants, so she believed in the importance of migration. In September 2001, she made what became known as the IPPR (Institute for Public Policy Research) speech when she became the first minister to argue that Britain was a country of migrants, that we needed a positive migration policy and that managed migration was good for the UK, economically, socially and culturally. Communally, Roche is a member of the League of Jewish Women and of the Labour Friends of Israel.

MARGARET HODGE 1944–

Eighty-five per cent of the Jews in Germany were successful in leaving the country before 1939. One German banker reached Egypt and his daughter, Margaret Oppenheimer, was born in Cairo. After the war, Egypt wasn't safe for Jews and the Oppenheimers came to England. Margaret went to Bromley High School and later graduated from the London School of Economics. When she was 29 she was elected as an Islington Councillor. The borough was close to the City and likely to attract far more middle-class voters when the financial sector of the economy expanded. In what had previously been a working-class constituency, a coterie of middle-class councillors effectively took over. After defections to the newly formed Social Democrats, Hodge – now her married name – became Leader of the Council.

In 1994, there was a by-election at Barking and Hodge won the seat, holding it ever since. The local Barking council includes twelve members from the British National Party, which is very right wing. Hodge was initially given a number of junior posts, including Children's Minister in 2003, but became Minister of State at the Department of Culture, Media and Sport in 2007. Hodge speaks her mind and must be aware of the effect her statements have in the sections of the media that do not support her views. Nobody can doubt that she has the courage of her convictions, but she is 'good copy' for the newspapers, which means that she is likely to be much in the public eye, and not always to her own advantage. She is married to Sir Henry Hodge, so has the right to call herself Lady Hodge.

10 1997–2008: New Labour

When Labour returned to power in 1997, it was after eighteen years of Conservative government and the battlefields of nationalization, unemployment, entry into the Common Market, trade union power and the redistribution of wealth had fallen silent. Significant ideological differences between the parties had noticeably diminished. Among the Jewish MPs there were also changes. They were half the number they had been at their peak and of the twenty-one elected, the average age of the eleven new MPs was under 40. There were still long-time stalwarts, like Michael Howard, Gerald Kaufman and Anthony Steen, but the majority had their way to make in the Commons. In the House of Lords, on the other hand, there were a number of Jews who had enjoyed distinguished parliamentary careers, and this was a new factor because there had been far fewer similarly qualified men and women in the past.

In terms of Jewish interests, the concerns had also changed. Israel was now the strongest military power in the Middle East and it was difficult to be as alarmed about its image as a country under threat from implacable enemies, though this was still true. The Israeli government's treatment of its Arab citizens and its policy of building settlements in Gaza and on the West Bank were under attack as being unnecessary for the country's national defence. Another of the major examples of discrimination against international Jewry was ended with the fall of communism in Russia. Now at last Russian Jews could leave the country if they wanted to do so and the Campaign for Soviet Jewry came to a successful conclusion.

Fewer of the Jewish MPs were deeply involved in communal affairs. With many, their adherence to the faith of their parents and grandparents was much weaker and the community was diminishing in number. At the same time as this happened, the future of the community was being safeguarded by a large increase in the proportion of Jewish children attending faith schools where they got a far better grounding in the religion than had been the case before. Better taught, deeper in content, the graduates of these schools were committed both to their faith and to Britain. In the arguments about faith schools, they would be a good example of the benefits of such institutions to both the ethnic and the majority community. Much of the credit for this belonged to Lord Jakobovits, who pressed for more faith schools throughout his ministry.

The period also saw a growing concern about the threat of terrorist activity from Muslim extremists. As a result, Jewish MPs focused on the dangers of anti-Semitism, although it is arguable that other ethnic communities were far more the victims of prejudice than the Jewish community. The number of anti-Semitic incidents continued to be minute and the vast majority of them consisted of verbal abuse. While a small number of physical attacks and the defacing of gravestones and some synagogues were rightly and roundly condemned, the overwhelming majority of the community continued to live peaceful lives, and the authorities took swift and effective action whenever there was a need to do so.

The period of New Labour governments did bring some first-class Jewish talent to the House, like the brothers Miliband, and the future may see more coming to the fore. For Jewish Conservative and Liberal Democrat MPs it was to be ten years out of office, though Michael Howard did become Leader of the Opposition and improved on the performance of his two predecessors in trying to steer the Conservatives to electoral success in 2005.

The Jewish MPs elected during these years were:

1997   John Bercow (Conservative), Peter Bradley (Labour), Ivor Caplin (Labour), Harry Cohen (Labour), Louise Ellman (Labour), Michael Fabricant (Conservative), Fabian Hamilton (Labour), Evan Harris (Liberal Democrat), Margaret Hodge (Labour), Michael Howard (Conservative), Gerald Kaufman (Labour), Oona King (Labour), Oliver Letwin (Conservative), Ivan Lewis (Labour), Julian Lewis (Conservative), Peter Mandelson (Labour), Gillian Merron (Labour), Barbara Roche (Labour), Anthony Steen (Conservative), Gerry Steinberg (Labour), David Winnick (Labour)

2001   In the 2001 election all the Jewish MPs elected in 1997 were returned to the House except Peter Mandelson who would become a British Commissioner at the EC. There were two new Jewish MPs: Jonathan Djanogly for the Conservatives and David Miliband for Labour. In addition, Lord Goldsmith was appointed Attorney General.

2005   John Bercow (Conservative), Harry Cohen (Labour), Jonathan Djanogly (Conservative), Louise Ellman (Labour), Michael

Fabricant (Conservative), **Lynne Featherstone** (Liberal Democrat), Fabian Hamilton (Labour), Evan Harris (Liberal Democrat), Margaret Hodge (Labour), Michael Howard (Conservative), Gerald Kaufman (Labour), **Susan Kramer** (Liberal Democrat), Oliver Letwin (Conservative), Ivan Lewis (Labour), Julian Lewis (Conservative), Gillian Merron (Labour), David Miliband (Labour), **Ed Miliband** (Labour), **Brooks Newmark** (Conservative), Malcolm Rifkind (Conservative), **Lee Scott** (Conservative), **Grant Shapps** (Conservative), Anthony Steen (Conservative), David Winnick (Labour)

JOHN BERCOW 1963–

John Bercow's father was a taxi driver, a job which provides that impartial independence which so many people want. His son went to a comprehensive school and on to the University of Essex, achieving a first-class degree in Government. After he left Essex, John Bercow became national chairman of the Federation of Conservative Students, organizing Conservative student support for the 1987 election. After working as a credit manager with Hambros, he joined Rowland Sallingbury Casey, the public affairs arm of the Saatchi & Saatchi group, and became a director. In 1986 he was elected a Lambeth Borough Councillor. He lost two campaigns for the Commons in 1987 and 1992 but in 1997 he was nominated for the secure Conservative seat of Buckingham and has been its member ever since.

Once in the House, Bercow joined the Shadow Cabinet in 2001. He resigned when the Conservatives opposed a provision in a bill to allow unmarried couples to adopt children, since he thought this should have been a free vote. Bercow won the 2005 Channel 4 Opposition MP of the Year award. He believes that opposition must be constructive and, with his party's permission, he agreed to lead a government review of the support available for children who have difficulty in communicating. Communally, in 2000 Bercow said that he identified 'passionately with the Jewish people and the State of Israel', but added, 'I confess that these days I go to synagogue only for funerals'.

IVOR CAPLIN 1958–

Ivor Caplin is a Brighton man. Brighton, Southend and Bournemouth are the three major Jewish communities on the South coast. Caplin went to King Edward's School, Witley, and Brighton College of Technology. From college he moved into marketing with Legal & General Assurance. He started his political career in 1991 when he was elected to the Hove Borough Council. In 1997 he became Leader of the Council and Deputy Leader when Brighton and Hove merged. He became the Labour MP for Hove and Portslade in 1997 with a 16 per cent swing in a traditionally Conservative seat, and remained in the Commons until he stood down in 2005. In the House, he held down a number of appointments including Minister for Veterans at the Ministry of Defence. He was also a Whip. As a keen sportsman, he turned out for the parliamentary football team and scored at least one spectacular thirty-five-yard goal. Communally, Caplin was vice-chairman of the Labour Friends of Israel. When he left parliament, Caplin set up his own political and government affairs business and created a London-based film production company.

LOUISE ELLMAN 1945–

Educated at Manchester High School for Girls and the University of Hull, Louise Ellman studied History and Sociology for her degree in 1967. She gained an MPhil in Social Administration from the University of York and went on to work as a lecturer both at the Open University and at Salford College of Technology from 1970 to 1976. Ellman became a Lancashire County Councillor in 1970 and was Leader of the Labour group by 1977. She also led the Council from 1981 to 1997, which says much about the level of her public support. In 1997 she was elected for the safe Labour parliamentary seat of Liverpool Riverside and has represented the constituency ever since.

In the Commons, Ellman is at the forefront of the efforts to combat racism, terrorism and anti-Semitism. Poale Zion, chaired by Ellman, changed its name to the Jewish Labour Movement in 2004 in order to widen its appeal. She is an active member of the Inter-Parliamentary Council Against Anti-Semitism, and has often attacked Islamist leaders for not being sufficiently robust in condemning terrorism and, in turn, has had her patriotism questioned by them. She is also vice-chair of the Labour Friends of Israel. Ellman has a range of other parliamentary interests and is a prominent member of the Transport Select Committee and Secretary of the All-Party Group against the Trafficking of Women and Children.

FABIAN HAMILTON 1955–

Fabian Uziell-Hamilton's father was a solicitor, and his mother was a barrister at Middle Temple before being appointed a Judge. They sent their son to Brentwood School in Essex and he went on to York University where he studied Politics and Sociology. In order to fund his own graphic design company, he drove taxis in York for a year before working for himself full-time. He left the company after his election to parliament in 1997. Politics attracted Hamilton and he was elected to the Leeds County Council in 1987, the same year that he became chairman of the Leeds West Constituency Labour Party. In 1992 Hamilton lost Leeds North East, Sir Keith Joseph's old seat, but he fought it again in 1997. The candidate originally chosen by the constituency party was vetoed by Labour's National Executive Committee, so Hamilton was nominated in her place. He won with a majority of just under 7,000 and has since remained its MP.

In the House, Hamilton has been a member of the Foreign Office Select Committee since 2001 and is the chairman of the All-Party groups on Business Services, Civil Contingencies, Prison Health and Hospices and Palliative Care. He is also vice-chairman of the All-Party Iran Group. Hamilton represent a highly diverse constituency, but he supports his Leeds Jewish community enthusiastically, particularly in its concerns for Jewish education for its children. As he said at a British Israel Chamber of Commerce breakfast, 'My loyalty is to my home in Leeds and to the Jewish community'.

EVAN HARRIS 1965–

When querying the inclusion of a question on religion in the 2001 census, Evan Harris said he would have difficulty in answering it: 'I consider myself Jewish culturally, but I do not have Jewish belief'. Harris comes from South African Jewish stock. South Africa was a long way to travel for his European ancestors, but the religious discrimination they suffered in Europe made South Africa a popular alternative for what became a substantial community. Harris went to the Blue Coat School in Liverpool and to Wadham College, Oxford. He qualified as a doctor and eventually became a registrar in public health with the Oxfordshire Health Authority.

He joined the Social Democrats in 1985 and the Liberal Democrats in 1988. In 1997, he stood as a Liberal Democrat for Oxford West and Abingdon and won the seat from the Conservatives. He almost immediately became a front-bench spokesman on health and moved from there to education. He became the Liberal Democrat Shadow Secretary of State for Health after the 2001 election, but resigned the post to look after his very sick girlfriend. He remains a hard worker on a number of medical committees. Harris's views have aroused opposition. He believes in voluntary euthanasia and is a vice-president of the Gay and Lesbian Humanist Association. In 2007 he spoke at a debate in the Oxford Union against the leader of the British National Party and an academic who denies the Holocaust. As he said at the time, 'The response must be to argue against them or to ignore them, but not to play into their hands by trying to ban them'. Harris became the Lib Dem spokesman on science after the 2005 election. Communally, he is much involved with the Society of Christians and Jews.

OONA KING 1967–

1997 saw the election of Oona King as Labour MP for Bethnal Green and Bow in the heart of the East End of London. King was the first Jewish black MP. As her mother was an Orthodox Jewess, she was always fully accepted as a member of the faith. She was only 30 years old at the time of her election. King retained the seat in 2001 but lost it in 2005 in a contest which, unhappily, was marred by attacks on both her race and religion. The constituency had been the home of a large number of Jewish immigrants at the end of the nineteenth century but now has a substantial Muslim electorate. It was generally agreed that King had suffered from a substantial degree of anti-Semitic comment. It also didn't help her cause that she had loyally supported the government's invasion of Iraq. Even so, King only lost the seat by some 800 votes. She is currently a special adviser to the Prime Minister.

King's father was an American civil rights activist and her mother was deeply involved in social justice causes. She is the niece of Miriam Stoppard, the famous broadcaster on medical matters, and Tom Stoppard, the playwright. In keeping with her Anglo-American background, King has degrees in politics from the University of York and Berkeley, California. She became one of the youngest recruits to the Labour Party when she joined at the age of 14. She also gained considerable political experience when working in the European Parliament Economic and Monetary Affairs Committee, as a political assistant to Glyn Ford, the Labour Party Leader in the European parliament and later for Glenys Kinnock, another MEP.

King was only the second black woman to be elected to the Commons. As she once said, she had been called a yid, nigger, half-caste and mongrel, but she had always tried to act as a bridge between the communities. When the weather gets really stormy, even the most solid bridges can come under great pressure. As Jewish parliamentarians have always stood for equality before the law, King has maintained that position with outstanding courage both in and out of the House.

OLIVER LETWIN 1956–

Born in Hampstead, son of an Emeritus Professor at the London School of Economics and a Conservative academic mother, Oliver Letwin was educated at Eton College, Trinity College, Cambridge and the London Business School. He also has a PhD – yet his grandparents were refugees from the Ukraine. Letwin was awarded a research fellowship at Princeton from 1980 to 1981 and he became a member of Margaret Thatcher's Conservative Policy Unit from 1983 to 1986. He has a seriously fine brain, especially recognized as such by the firm N.M. Rothschild, who made him a non-executive director. He failed to win Hampstead from the famous actress, Glenda Jackson, but was adopted by West Dorset and won the seat in 1997. He became Shadow Home Secretary in 2001 and Shadow Chancellor of the Exchequer in 2003, and remains an active constituency MP.

In 2001, Letwin attracted controversy over recommendations to cut public expenditure but had more success in getting the government to abandon a plan for making the incitement to religious hatred an offence. He argued that Muslims would feel persecuted if a law of that nature was passed. After the 2005 election, Letwin was given Environment, Food and Rural Affairs, which took up less of his time than the Treasury, but he wanted to concentrate more on his work in the City, and he only stayed seven months. In 2005, Letwin backed his fellow Old Etonian, David Cameron, for the leadership of the Conservatives and is now the head of the Policy Review for the Party and of the Conservative Research Department. Communally, he is always ready to help good causes but is tactfully described as a secular Jew.

IVAN LEWIS 1967–

Ivan Lewis was just 30 when he won his hometown seat of Bury South for Labour in the 1997 election. Since then he has held office in the Treasury and the Departments of Education and Skills. He is now Parliamentary Under-Secretary of State for Health with responsibility for Care Services, and the sole survivor in the Health team after Gordon Brown's 2007 reshuffle. He is the latest in a string of Jewish MPs from Manchester. Lewis studied at William Hulme School and Bury College before spending his entire working life, until he entered parliament, in the social care voluntary sector. At 24 he became chair of Bury Council's Social Services Committee and was appointed the youngest ever chief executive of Manchester Jewish Social Services, at the age of 25. Before becoming a Minister, he was vice-chairman of the Labour Friends of Israel and is currently a trustee of the Holocaust Educational Trust. Only 41, Lewis has held ministerial office for seven years and is highly respected with a bright future ahead of him.

JULIAN LEWIS 1951–

Julian Lewis identifies himself as a third-generation immigrant. Many of his family were killed in the Holocaust. He went to Dynevor

Grammar School in Swansea and on to Balliol College, Oxford, where he read Philosophy and Politics before gaining a DPhil in Strategic Studies at St Anthony's College. A former seaman in the Royal Naval Reserve, he became a military historian and a professional campaigner on defence and security issues.

Lewis has always been an opponent of left-wing groups, especially the Campaign for Nuclear Disarmament. He used his doctorate to good effect on behalf of various research organizations before joining the Conservative Research Department as deputy director from 1990 to 1996. He resigned to campaign against joining the Euro before this was Conservative policy. In 1997, Lewis was elected for New Forest East and has retained the seat ever since. He has been Shadow Minister for the Cabinet Office and is now a Shadow Defence Minister, He is considered an effective right-winger in his party. In 2005 and 2007 he won the annual essay prize of the Royal United Services Institute – a leading military think-tank. In 2007, he resigned his life membership of the Oxford Union after thirty-seven years in protest at its decision to invite the British National Party (BNP) and a leading Holocaust-denier to speak.

GILLIAN MERRON 1959–

Gillian Merron believes in the possibility of an individual being able to make a difference. She doesn't just observe inadequacies, but joins in to sort them out. Merron went to Wanstead High School and on to the University of Lancaster where she read Management Sciences, after spending some of her gap year on a kibbutz in Israel. Before becoming an MP, she worked as a business development adviser, local government officer and full-time official for UNISON, formerly the National Union of Public Employees.

In 1997 she was elected as the Labour MP for Lincoln, a crucial seat for Labour to win in that election. She won with a majority of 11,000 and held it at the next two elections. Until a member defected to Labour in recent years, she was Lincolnshire's only Labour MP and the first since 1979. Currently an International Development Minister, she has also served as a Government Whip and as Lords Commissioner to the Treasury, Transport Minister, Cabinet Office Minister and Minister for the East Midlands. Merron is also very active in her community. She is the first sitting MP to join up with Voluntary Services Overseas, where she worked in Guyana. She has been on the board of the Westminster Foundation for Democracy and is actively involved with the Holocaust Education Trust. Communally,

Merron is a member of Lincoln's fifty-strong Jewish community where she says: 'I feel accepted, valued and extremely welcome.'

JONATHAN DJANOGLY 1965–

When John Major retired from Parliament in 2001, he was succeeded in his Huntingdon constituency by Jonathan Djanogly. The Djanogly family are Sephardim who built a textile business based in Nottingham. Djanogly was brought up in Nottingham but completed his studies at University College School in London. He went on to Oxford Polytechnic, now Oxford Brookes University, where he read read Law and Politics, becoming a solicitor in 1990. His articles were with the City practice of S.J. Berwin, and he has been a corporate finance partner in the firm since 1998. In 2004, he was promoted by Michael Howard to be an Opposition spokesman on Home Affairs. He has also since served as Shadow Solicitor General and a Shadow Trade and Industry Minister. In 2005, Djanogly held Huntingdon.

LORD GOLDSMITH 1950–

Lord Goldsmith was a member of the Blair government but, owing to his peerage, was not elected to the House of Commons, and his entry is included in Appendix A.

DAVID MILIBAND 1965–

David Miliband has shot to public prominence in the last couple of years. He was influential behind the scenes with the Labour Party's 1997 election manifesto and in 2001 was elected for Labour for the constituency of South Shields, Tyne and Wear. In 2005 he was promoted to Minister of Communities and Local Government and in 2006, Secretary of State for the Environment, Food and Rural Affairs. In 2007 he was appointed Secretary of State for the Foreign and Commonwealth Office by Gordon Brown.

Miliband's parents were split up during the war when the Germans invaded Belgium. His father came to Britain and his Polish mother survived when so many others did not, and they were, happily, reunited. Miliband received his education in London, Leeds and Boston, Mass. He eventually moved on to Corpus Christi College, Oxford and gained a First in PPE. From 1989 to 1994 he was a research fellow at the National Council for Voluntary Organisations. With his brother, Ed, also in the Cabinet, the Milibands are likely to have an important role in the future of Labour governments, representing the younger generation of politicians. Miliband is the third Jewish Foreign Secretary, after Herbert Samuel and Malcolm Rifkind. Miliband was not brought up in the heart of the Jewish community but, as he says, 'My commitment to equality, social justice, freedom of expression and solidarity must in so many ways reflect my origins.'

LYNNE FEATHERSTONE 1951–

Lynne Featherstone went to South Hampstead High School and Oxford Polytechnic, now Oxford Brookes University. After college, she worked in the fashion design industry for twenty years and had her own company. Featherstone was elected as a councillor for Haringey in 1998 and she was one of the first three Liberal Democrats to win in the borough. 'Haringay makes Parliament look like a doddle', she once said. She was Leader of the Opposition on the Council.

She first tried unsuccessfully to win the Hornsey and Wood Green constituency from the Labour member, Barbara Roche, at the general election in 1997, failed again in 2001, but managed it in 2005. In 2006, she was promoted to number two in the Liberal Democrats' home affairs team. Communally, Featherstone represents a constituency with a large number of Jewish electors, but she says she 'hasn't practised the religion for years', though 'I have an affection for the traditions I grew up with'.

SUSAN KRAMER 1950–

Being president of the Oxford or Cambridge Union is a good preparation for speaking in the Commons. Arthur Cohen was the first Jew to be elected to the office in 1852 and Leslie Hore-Belisha, Leon Brittan, Michael Howard and Helene Hayman were just four of those who followed suit. Kramer was president of the Oxford Union in 1971. She is the daughter of an illegal immigrant who was a survivor of the Holocaust from Hungary. So it isn't only legal immigrants from whom the country eventually benefits. Kramer went to St Paul's Girls' School and took her MBA at the University of Illinois. As a former vice-president of Citibank, Chicago, she is highly qualified for office in the government, but as she is a Liberal her opportunities at present are limited. Kramer lost in previous elections to both the Commons and the European Parliament, but was elected MP for Richmond Park in 2005.

Kramer has been prominent in London politics, standing against the incumbent Mayor in 2000. She was against the Iraq war and has criticized Israel for its policies on the West Bank and in Gaza. She was appointed her party's Shadow International Development Secretary and later Shadow Trade and Industry Secretary followed by Shadow Transport Secretary. She is now the Liberal Democrat's Spokesperson for Families and a member of her party's Shadow Cabinet.

ED MILIBAND 1969–

Outside Labour Party circles, the names of Ed and David Miliband were not well known politically at the turn of the millennium. Today they are the first brothers in the Cabinet since Edward and Oliver Stanley in 1938. Miliband's parents fled Belgium in the Second World War and his grandparents were from Poland. His father, Ralph Miliband, was a distinguished Marxist academic. Miliband read PPE at Corpus Christi, Oxford, and went on to the LSE. It was as an adviser for Harriet Harman in 1993 and then for Gordon Brown that he moved into the political sphere, becoming a special adviser at the Treasury in 1997. He spent a year's sabbatical at Harvard as a visiting lecturer in government in 2003/4 and even before he entered parliament he was made chairman of the Council of Economic Advisers to the Treasury. In 2005, he was elected for Doncaster North.

In 2006 he was appointed Parliamentary Secretary to the Cabinet Office and in 2007, he was promoted to Chancellor of the Duchy of Lancaster; he is also a Privy Councillor. Milliband is heavily involved in drafting Labour's manifesto for the next general election, a task previously performed by Manny Shinwell and Peter Mandelson. Communally, Miliband holds no offices, but supports the community.

BROOKS NEWMARK 1958–

Brooks Newmark is a City man. Educated at Bedford School, he went on to Harvard College and has an MBA in finance from the Harvard Business School. He was also a politics research graduate at Worcester College, Oxford. He was a senior partner of Apollo Management, a leading private equity firm, having gained his training at Lehman Brothers in New York. He has also served on advisory boards at Harvard, the London Business School and Tel Aviv University.

Standing as a Conservative, it was perhaps not surprising that he didn't win Newcastle Central in 1997. He was also defeated for

Braintree in 2001, but won the seat in 2005. He was quickly appointed to the Science and Technology Select Committee and then to the Treasury Select Committee, both appropriate for a former venture capitalist; in 2007 he joined the Conservative front bench as Treasury Whip. Newmark considers himself a 'progressive modern Conservative' and is very concerned about the most vulnerable of his constituents. He remarked when seeking election that, 'I should be spending 90 per cent of my energies on the 10 per cent who are the most vulnerable'.

Locally, Newmark is known to stand up for the community and actively defends its interests. In 2007, he called a debate on anti-Semitism in British universities. He described the proposed boycott of Israeli academics by the University and College Union 'myopic, morally repugnant and intellectually bankrupt'. He has visited Israel several times since being elected to parliament and believes that 'any comprehensive peace settlement in the Middle East must ensure that Israel lives within secure borders'.

LEE SCOTT 1956–

To hold Aylesbury for at least thirty years in the early days of Jewish emancipation, the candidate needed to be a local man with a good record of service in the community and well known for his charity work. That was what the Rothschilds provided in full measure. In the twenty-first century, to win Ilford North you needed exactly the same attributes, and Lee Scott follows in the fine old tradition. Scott was born and raised in the area, knows it like the back of his hand and understands all the local problems. He is by profession a fundraiser, an occupation at which many Jews have always excelled. From the earliest days of Palestine, there were constant appeals for funds. The Joint Palestine Appeal (JPA) turned into the JIA after the creation of the state and Scott spent some years working for it. From 1988 to 1992 he was considered good enough to be a fundraiser for George Bush Senior on his road to the White House. For several years he was a Redbridge Councillor and has worked voluntarily for many local charities. In 2005, he won the Ilford North seat for the Conservatives. In parliament he joined the Cornerstone Group of Tory MPs and is a member of the Transport Select Committee and the Health Select Committee. He works voluntarily for many non-Jewish charities.

GRANT SHAPPS 1968–

Grant Shapps went to Watford Grammar followed by Manchester Polytechnic and in 1990, when he was 21, he set up his own business. It is a design and printing company called PrintHouse Corporation, and he remains the chairman. In 1997 when he was 29 he turned his attention to politics and was beaten for North Southwark and Bermondsey. He survived cancer in 1999, lost Welwyn Hatfield in 2001 but took the seat in 2005 on a 9 per cent swing from Labour to Conservative. It was a very good performance and led to his promotion to vice-chairman of the party under David Cameron, whom he seconded for leadership. In July 2007 he was promoted to Shadow Housing Minister and attends the Shadow Cabinet in that role. Communally, Shapps was national president of the Bnai B'rith youth organization when he was 17, and he is a member of the Potters Bar Synagogue. He also supports the Holocaust Educational Trust. During Christmas 2007, his decision to spend the holidays sleeping rough in a car park to better understand the problems of the homeless was widely reported. Shapps is much in favour of local initiatives to solve the problems of housing rather than simply relying on central government, and housing will be a key issue at the next general election.

So there you are. That's what just under 200 Jewish MPs have accomplished over 150 years. The community has never numbered more than the population of Nottingham. Yet its members have filled every office of state except that of Prime Minister – unless you count Disraeli. Jewish MPs elected over these 150 years have been highly enough regarded for thirty-three of them to be made peers at the end of their time in the Commons. Another thirty-six have been knighted – approximately 40 per cent in all. If you wanted to form a government from their ranks over the years, you could choose from positions that they held or hold, which are – or were – these:

Assistant Government Whip	Maurice Miller
Attorney General	Rufus Isaacs, Sam Silkin, Peter Goldsmith
Chairman of the Kitchen Department	Alfred Jacoby
Chancellor of the Duchy of Lancaster	Herbert Samuel, Harold Lever, Ed Miliband
Chancellor of the Exchequer	Nigel Lawson
Chief Secretary to the Treasury	Joel Barnett, John Diamond
Chief Whip	John Silkin, Leon Brittan,
Colonial Secretary	Leopold Amery
Deputy Leader of the Commons	John Silkin
Deputy Speaker	Myer Galpern
Education Minister for Universities	Margaret Hodge
Financial Secretary to the Treasury	Edwin Montagu, Arthur Samuel, Harold Lever, Robert Sheldon, Nigel Lawson, Barbara Roche
Financial Secretary to the War Office	Manny Shinwell
First Commissioner of Works	Alfred Mond
First Lord of the Admiralty	Leopold Amery
Foreign Secretary	Rufus Isaacs, Malcolm Rifkind, David Miliband

Home Secretary	Herbert Samuel, Leon Brittan
Junior Minister of Health	Edwina Currie
Junior Minister of International Development	Gillian Merron
Liberal Chief Whip	Percy Harris
Lord Chancellor	Farrer Herschel
Lord Commissioner at the Treasury	Irvine Patnick, Gillian Merron
Minister of Agriculture and Fisheries	John Silkin
Minister of Aircraft Production	George Strauss
Minister at the Cabinet Office	Gillian Merron
Minister of Civil Aviation	Harry Nathan
Minister of Defence	Manny Shinwell
Minister for the East Midlands	Gillian Merron
Minister of Employment	Edmund Dell, Michael Howard, David Young
Minister for the Environment	Michael Howard, David Miliband
Minister of Health	Alfred Mond
Minister of Immigration	Barbara Roche
Minister of Mines	Manny Shinwell
Minister for Northern Ireland	Peter Mandelson
Minister of Overseas Trade	Arthur Samuel
Minister for Planning and Local Government	John Silkin
Minister for Roads	Helene Hayman
Minister of Supply	George Strauss
Minister for Tourism	John Lee
Minister of Town and Country Planning	Lewis Silkin
Minister of Trade and Industry	David Young, Leon Brittan
Minister of Transport	Leslie Hore-Belisha
Minister for Veterans at Ministry of Defence	Ivor Caplin
Minister of State for Agriculture and Fisheries	Helene Hayman
Minister of State for Children	Margaret Hodge
Minister of State for the Civil Service	Robert Sheldon
Minister of State for Consumer Affairs	Sally Oppenheim
Minister of State, Dept of Culture, Media and Sport	Margaret Hodge

Minister of State, Department of Economic Affairs	Austen Albu
Minister of State for Employment	Edmund Dell
Minister of State for Health	Ivan Lewis
Minister of State at the Home Office	Leon Brittan, Barbara Roche
Minister of State for Housing and Urban Affairs	Reg Freeson
Minister of State for Industry and Information Technology	Spencer Batiste
Minister of State for Trade	Edmund Dell
Parliamentary Secretary, Board of Trade	Henry de Worms
Parliamentary Secretary to the Cabinet Office	Ed Miliband
Parliamentary Secretary for Education	Ivan Lewis
Parliamentary Under Secretary for War	Henry Nathan
Paymaster General	Edmund Dell
Postmaster General	Herbert Samuel
Parliamentary Private Secretary (PPS) to Attorney General	David Sumberg
PPS to Chancellor of the Exchequer	Philip Oppenheim
PPS to Minister of State at the Commonwealth Office	David Kerr
PPS Ministry of Defence Procurement	Spencer Batiste
PPS for Department of Education and Science	Philip Oppenheim
PPS to Financial Secretary for the Treasury	Michael Fabricant
PPS to the Leader of the House	Ivor Caplin
PPS to Lord Privy Seal	Martin Brandon-Bravo
PPS to Minister of Defence	Stormont Mancroft
PPS to Minister of Health	Barnett Stross
PPS to Minister of Housing	Arnold Shaw
PPS to Minister of State for Housing	Martin Brandon-Bravo
PPS to Home Secretary	Martin Brandon-Bravo
PPS to Minister of State for Scotland	Michael Marcus
PPS to Minister of Supply	Jimmy de Rothschild
PPS to the Paymaster General	Michael Stern
PPS to Minister of Power	Reg Freeson
PPS to Secretary of State for the Colonies	Frank Allaun

Joint PPS to the Minister of Technology	Edmund Dell
PPS at the Department of Trade and Industry	Spencer Batiste, Barbara Roche
PPS to Minister of Transport	Reg Freeson, Paul Rose
PPS to Minister of Works	John Diamond
President of the Board of Trade	Edmund Dell
Secretary of State for Defence	Malcolm Rifkind
Secretary of State for Energy	Nigel Lawson
Secretary of State for India	Edwin Montagu
Secretary of State for Social Services	Keith Joseph
Secretary of State for Scotland	Malcolm Rifkind
Secretary of State for Trade	Edmund Dell, Peter Mandelson
Secretary of State for Transport	Malcolm Rifkind
Secretary of State for War	Leslie Hore-Belisha
Solicitor General	Farrer Herschel, Sir George Jessel, Rufus Isaacs, Sir Henry Slesser
Under-Secretary of State for Air	Sir Phillip Sassoon
Under-Secretary for the Colonies	Baron de Worms
Under-Secretary of State for Economic Affairs	Edmund Dell
Under-Secretary of State at Dept of Education	Geoffrey Finsberg, Edmund Dell.
Under-Secretary of State at the Dept of Employment	John Lee
Under-Secretary of State at Dept of the Environment	Geoffrey Finsberg, Gerald Kaufman
Under-Secretary of State at Dept of Health and Social Security	Geoffrey Finsberg, Ivan Lewis
Under-Secretary of State at Dept of Health	Helene Hayman
Under-Secretary of State at the Home Office	Herbert Samuel
Under-Secretary of State at the India Office	Edwin Montagu

Deputy Chairman of the Ways and Means Committee	Sir Myer Galpern
Whip	Ivor Caplin, Gillian Merron
Leader of the Conservative Party	Michael Howard
Leader of the Liberal Party	Rufus Isaacs
Chairman of the Liberal Party	Herbert Samuel
Deputy Leader of the Liberal Party	Sir Percy Harris
Chairman of the Labour Party	Manny Shinwell
Vice-President, National Association of Conservative Associations	Lionel Cohen

The following Jewish MPs were made peers:

Joel Barnett, Leon Brittan, Alex Carlile, Stanley Clinton-Davis, John Diamond, Alf Dubs, Myer Galpern, Leslie Haden-Guest, Helene Hayman, Farrer Herschel, Leslie Hore-Belisha, Rufus Isaacs, Barnett Janner, Greville Janner, Keith Joseph, Nigel Lawson, John Lee, Harold Lever, Harry Morris, Alfred Mond, Samuel Montagu, Harry Nathan, Sally Oppenheim, Nathaniel Rothschild, Arthur Samuel, Herbert Samuel, Sam Segal, Robert Sheldon, Manny Shinwell, Lewis Silkin, Sam Silkin, Sydney Stern, Henry de Worms.

The following were knighted:

Benjamin Cohen, Jack Brunel Cohen, Geoffrey Finsburg, Leonard Franklin, Walter de Frece, Clement Freud, Louis Gluckstein, Francis Goldsmid, Julian Goldsmid, Percy Harris, Charles Henry, George Jessel, Gerald Kaufman, Ivan Lawrence, Herbert Leon, Arthur Levy, Maurice Levy, Marcus Lipton, Philip Magnus, Sigismund Mendl, Frank Meyer, Gerald Nabarro, Irvine Patnick, Herbert Raphael, Malcolm Rifkind, Isidore Salmon, David Saloman, Harry Samuel, Stuart Samuel, Edward Sassoon, Philip Sassoon, John Simon, Henry Slesser, Barnett Stross.

Not a bad effort, but the important point to recognize is that they were able to achieve all this because they lived in Britain. They weren't all born in the UK and many of their ancestors certainly weren't, but they all received equal treatment. The consistent position of the British government over the 150 years was summed up by Gladstone before the Jews were even emancipated. In a debate in the House of Commons in 1851 he declared to general approval:

> I say fearlessly whatever may be the difference of opinion in this
> House as to the admission of Jews to political privilege, that no
> person could dare to stand up among us and allege his religion
> as a ground for mistrust or for the denial of justice, without
> drawing down upon himself, from all quarters of the House
> alike, universal scorn and indignation.

The original Jewish MPs were rich because you had to be rich to afford
to sit in parliament. Six of the early members had been to University
College London because it was the best English university that would
take them. When they were able to get into Oxford and Cambridge on
their merits, out of the total 200, thirty-three went to Oxford and
twenty-five to Cambridge. Over 60 per cent of the MPs went to university, including twenty-two to London, three to Harvard, nine to
universities on the continent and twenty to provincial universities, of
which seven went to Manchester. One went to Sandhurst and one to
a Yeshivah. Four went to Scottish universities and two to Welsh.

When MPs started to receive a salary it became possible for people
without private means to enter the Commons, and nine of the Jewish
MPs went to elementary school and left in their early teens. They
include such famous names in the Commons as Manny Shinwell, Reg
Freeson and Phil Piratin. The best speakers in the Commons have
often been past presidents of the Oxford and Cambridge Unions, and
seven Jewish MPs have had that distinction: Arthur Cohen, Leon
Brittan, Helen Hayman, Greville Janner and Michael Howard at
Cambridge, and Leslie Hore-Belisha and Susan Kramer at Oxford.

The Jewish community has always been grateful for the consideration it received and has responded with loyalty to the Crown and by
making its maximum contribution to the life of the nation. Happily,
they have proved that it is possible for a small ethnic community to
serve our parliament and to preserve its own religious and cultural
traditions, along with those of other British minorities. Long may this
continue. As far as their own community is concerned, the ranks of
Jewish MPs have seldom been filled by men and women who devoted much time to religious observance. The early MPs were more
closely allied to their synagogues but, as the years have gone by, the
influence of Judaism has been on their behaviour and cultural beliefs
rather than on their obedience to Jewish law.

From this point of view, the Jewish MP today seldom reflects the
religious position of the majority of the community. For British Jews
today are either moving towards a greater degree of Orthodoxy or
they are moving out of the religion altogether. It is still difficult for

Orthodox Jews to stand as MPs. Their political responsibilities and their religious practices come into conflict, and the two sets of demands make the circle difficult to square. The importance to the Orthodox Jew of keeping the festivals can well clash with the requirement to be in the Division Lobby when the votes are cast. Saturday remains the most convenient day for surgeries for most constituents, but the religious Jew does no work on the Sabbath.

So it follows that the Orthodox Jews are happy to let the non-Orthodox take the lead in representing them. What is ironic is that the Judaism of the Jewish parliamentary candidates may be a memory of the past, associated with their family life long ago. They may wish to have no connection with a synagogue until they die and many would wish to then be cremated rather than buried according to the Orthodox law. Nevertheless, they are categorized by the public as Jews, just as if they were as committed as the Orthodox rabbis. And not only are they categorized as such. They are often criticized for simply being Jews, stereotyped by those prejudices that have followed Jews down the millennia. Do they stand up for the only democracy in the Middle East? It is held by many that this cannot be simply because Britain, their own nation, believes that democracy is superior to dictatorship. It must be because they are Jews, and the majority of the Israelis are Jews. Do Jews support political parties financially? Many will believe that this must be because of the favours they seek from the politicians.

How this argument can be advanced when Jewish MPs have benefited everything from the National Gallery and the Shakespeare Memorial Theatre to St Thomas' Hospital, The Evelina Rothschild Hospital and the George Borrow Museum is not explained. The community watches as the good is sometimes forgotten and the suspect is played up. And yet the truth remains that Britain is one of the least racist counties in the world. It might have lunatic fringes who make snide remarks and a few who vandalize Jewish cemeteries, the occasional club which doesn't like too many Jewish members and the occasional school which takes little account of the religious needs of its Jewish pupils. This is aggravating but hardly noticeable by comparison with a Nazi Germany, a Syrian dictatorship, Russian prejudice under Stalin and the treatment of Jewish communities in so many other lands. It fades totally into insignificance compared to a Pol Pot, the horrors of Rwanda and the Sudan, the situation in Zimbabwe or the corruption of South America. If you keep a sense of proportion, the 150th anniversary of Jewish emancipation is a further opportunity for both the Christian community and the Jews to congratulate each other on a bargain which has worked out extremely well for both sides.

Appendix A: Jewish Non-Elected Ministers 1858–2008

During the past 150 years three Jews were appointed to government posts without, initially, having been elected members of the House of Commons.

LORD MANCROFT 1914–1987

Arthur Samuel was made Lord Mancroft in 1937, and his son, Stormont Mancroft, succeeded to the title when his father died in 1942. He is one of two Jews who held office in Conservative administrations without having been elected as MPs, the other being Lord David Young when Margaret Thatcher was Prime Minister. Mancroft is remembered by all who knew him as one of the wittiest after-dinner speakers of his time. He once said of one of his millionaire friends who was feigning sickness in the West Indies, 'Well, you wouldn't expect him to fall ill in Willesden Green'. There was, however, a more serious side to Mancroft. He had gone to Winchester School and Christ Church, Oxford at a time when you had to have an excellent brain to get into either. He was called to the Bar in 1938 and during the war held the rank of Lieutenant Colonel, was mentioned in dispatches twice and won the Croix de Guerre.

Mancroft was a Lord-in-Waiting to the Queen from 1952 to 1954, a Government Whip in both Churchill's and Eden's administrations, and he became Parliamentary Secretary to the Minister of Defence and then Minister without Portfolio in Macmillan's government from 1954 to 1958. After leaving office, Mancroft concentrated on his business interests, which included a seat on the board of Norwich Union. He was also a director of Great Universal

Stores, whose chairman, Sir Isaac Wolfson, was a great supporter of Israel. In 1963 the Arab League informed Norwich Union that they would no longer deal with the company because Mancroft was on both boards. Mancroft therefore resigned from a company both he and his father had been very closely associated with for many years. The Norwich Union protested that they were not anti-Semitic but the *cause célèbre* left a bad taste in everybody's mouth. Mancroft died in 1987 at the age of 73.

LORD YOUNG 1932–

There are rare occasions when a non-political individual is so effective that he even reaches the Cabinet. One such was David Young, who in 1984 was created a peer and put into the Cabinet by Margaret Thatcher as Minister Without Portfolio to help deal with the current problems of serious unemployment. The Prime Minister explained, 'Where others come to me with problems, David comes to me with solutions'. David Young rose from a typical Jewish background. His father manufactured children's coats and Young went to Christ's College in Finchley, which also educated the present Chief Rabbi. He went on to University College London and became a solicitor in 1954. He decided not to practise, however, and joined Great Universal Stores. He became personal assistant to Sir Isaac Wolfson, the head of the company, and if you wanted a first-class training in commercial and company activities, this was the best seat in the house.

Young was Orthodox and involved in a number of Jewish charities. He was particularly interested in the work of British ORT which seeks to establish vocational training in the Diaspora (including the UK) and Israel. He was also chairman of the International Council of Jewish Social and Welfare services from 1981.

Until 1964 Young voted Labour but in 1977 he became a member of the management board of the Centre for Policy Studies, a Conservative think-tank. By then he had made a fortune in property and could devote time to voluntary political activity. ORT does much work on job creation and in 1981, Norman Tebbitt, Secretary of State for Employment, drafted Young in to head up the British Manpower Services Commission to see what his experience could do for that organization. In 1985, now Lord Young, he was made Secretary of State for Employment, and in 1987 moved to Trade and Industry. He played a major part in the 1987 election campaign, which the Conservatives won handsomely. As he said at the time, 'the ethics of Conservatism strike a chord in Judaism'. In fact, all ethics strike chords in Judaism.

Young was responsible for the last elements of privatization in Thatcher's years but announced his retirement from the government in 1989. In his commercial life he has continued to be very successful.

LORD GOLDSMITH 1950–

Peter Goldsmith was made Attorney General by Tony Blair in 2001 and was the only Jew to sit in that parliament's Cabinet. He resigned his post on the same day that Blair left 10 Downing Street. During his years in office, Goldsmith had the responsibility for advising the government as to whether a decision to go to war with Iraq would be legal, according to the resolutions already passed by the United Nations. He submitted a report that confirmed the legality of the action, and argument has raged ever since.

Goldsmith was the son of a solicitor, born in Liverpool and educated at Quarry Bank School and Caius College, Cambridge. He was called to the Bar in 1972, took silk in 1987 and in 1995 became the youngest ever chairman of the Bar of England and Wales. In 1999, he was created a Life Peer. Robert Mugabe, President of Zimbabwe, said that ancestral baronial blood coursed through Goldsmith's veins; Goldsmith retorted that 'the accusation would have surprised my ancestors in the shtetl'.

In 1996, Goldsmith founded the Bar Pro Bono Unit, of which he remains president. He has said that he considers Guantanamo Bay a 'symbol of injustice', and as Attorney General he agreed to the Serious Fraud Office halting their investigation into irregularities in the 'Al Yamami' Saudi Arabian arms contract on the grounds of national security. Goldsmith considers that his most important contribution during his time in office was the reform of the Crown Prosecution Service, turning it into a much more confident and effective body with greater powers and responsibilities. He wanted to create an organization at the centre of the justice system, championing the interests of the public and of victims and bringing more effective prosecutions. Now that he has left government,

Goldsmith is the European Head of European Litigation at the London office of Debevoise & Plimpton, a United States legal practice.

Appendix B: Jewish MPs in the House of Commons 1858–2008 by Party

[* By-election]

	Liberals	Conservatives	Labour	Independent	Communist
1858	2				
1859	3				
*1860	1				
1865	7				
*1866	1				
1868	7				
*1869	1				
*1870	1				
1874	7	1			
1880	5	2			
*1880	1				
*1882	1				
1885	5	3			
*1885	1				
1886	6	3			
*1891	2				
1892	6	3			
*1892	1				
1895	5	5			
*1896	1				
*1897	1				
*1898	1				
*1899	2				
1900	4	7			
*1902	1				
*1904	1				
1906	14	4			
1910 (i)	12	7			

	Liberals	Conservatives	Labour	Independent	Communist
1910 (ii)	11	8			
*1911		2			
*1912	1				
*1913	1				
*1916	1				
1918	5	7			
*1919		1			
1922	7	6	1		
1923	6	5	3		
1924	2	10	2		
*1927	1				
*1928		1			
1929	7	8	5		
1931		7	11	1	
*1934		1	1		
1935	4	10	3		
*1936			1		
*1937	1		1	1	
*1942			1		
1945			27	1	1
*1948			1		
1950		1	23		
1951		1	18		
1955		2	17		
*1956	1				
*1957		1			
*1958		2			
1959		3	21		
*1963		1			
1964		3	36		
1966		3	39		
1970		10	32		
*1971			1		
*1973		1			
1974 (i)	1	12	34		
1974 (ii)		1	10	36	
1979		1	13	24	
1983		2	19	12	
1987		1	18	6	
1992		1	13	9	

	Liberals	Conservatives	Labour	Independent	Communist
*1994			1		
1997		1	6		14
2001		1	7		14
2005		3	11	10	
Elections won:	159	215	329	2	1

Total: 706

Year	Name	Party	Constituency
1858	Lionel de Rothschild	Liberal	City of London
1859	Lionel de Rothschild	Liberal	City of London
	Mayer Amschel Rothschild	Liberal	Hythe
	David Salomons	Liberal	Greenwich
1860	Francis Goldsmid	Liberal	Reading
1865	Frederick Goldsmid	Liberal	Honiton
	Lionel Rothschild	Liberal	City of London
	Nathaniel Rothschild	Liberal	Aylesbury
	David Salomons	Liberal	Greenwich
	Joseph D'A. Samuda	Liberal	Tavistock
1866	Julian Goldsmid	Liberal	Honiton
1868	Francis Goldsmid	Liberal	Reading
	George Jessel	Liberal	Dover
	Mayer Amschel Rothschild	Liberal	Hythe
	Nathaniel Rothschild	Liberal	Aylesbury
	David Salomons	Liberal	Greenwich
	John Simon	Liberal	Dewsbury
1869	Lionel de Rothschild	Liberal	City of London
1870	Julian Goldsmid	Liberal	Rochester
1874	Francis Goldsmid	Liberal	Reading
	Julian Goldsmid	Liberal	Rochester
	Farrer Herschell	Liberal	Durham
	Saul Isaac	Conservative	Nottingham
	Lionel Rothschild	Liberal	City of London
	Nathaniel Rothschild	Liberal	Aylesbury
	John Simon	Liberal	Dewsbury
1880	Arthur Cohen	Liberal	Southwark
	Farrer Herschell	Liberal	Durham
	Lionel de Rothschild	Liberal	City of London
	Nathaniel de Rothschild	Liberal	Aylesbury
	John Simon	Liberal	Dewsbury
	Henry de Worms	Conservative	Greenwich
	Sydney Woolf	Conservative	Pontefract

1882	Lewis Isaacs	Conservative	Newington
1885	Lionel Cohen	Conservative	Paddington South
	Julian Goldsmid	Liberal	St Pancras South
	Lewis Isaacs	Conservative	Newington
	Alfred Jacoby	Liberal	Mid Derbyshire
	Samuel Montagu	Liberal	Whitechapel
	Ferdinand de Rothschild	Liberal Unionist	Aylesbury
	John Simon	Liberal	Dewsbury
	Henry de Worms	Conservative	Greenwich
1886	Lionel Cohen	Conservative	Paddington South
	Julian Goldsmid	Liberal	St Pancras South
	Lewis Isaacs	Conservative	Newington
	Samuel Montagu	Liberal	Whitechapel
	Ferdinand de Rothschild	Liberal Unionist	Aylesbury
	John Simon	Liberal	Dewsbury
	Henry de Worms	Conservative	Greenwich
1891	Lewis Isaacs	Conservative	Newington
	Herbert Leon	Conservative	North Bucks
	Sydney Stern	Conservative	Stowmarket
1892	Benjamin Cohen	Conservative	Islington East
	Julian Goldsmid	Liberal	St Pancras South
	Herbert Leon	Conservative	Bucks
	Samuel Montagu	Liberal	Whitechapel
	Ferdinand de Rothschild	Liberal Unionist	Aylesbury
	Sydney Stern	Conservative	Stowmarket
	Gustav Wolff	Conservative	Belfast East
	Henry de Worms	Conservative	Greenwich
1895	Benjamin Cohen	Conservative	Islington East
	Julian Goldsmid	Liberal Unionist	St Pancras South
	Harry Marks	Conservative	St Georges, Tower Hamlets
	Samuel Montagu	Liberal	Whitechapel
	Ferdinand de Rothschild	Liberal Unionist	Aylesbury
	Harry Samuel	Conservative	Limehouse
	Arthur Strauss	Liberal Unionist	Camborne
	Gustav Wolff	Conservative	Belfast East
	Henry de Worms	Conservative	Greenwich
1896	Herbert Jessel	Liberal Unionist	St Pancras South
1897	Louis Sinclair	Conservative	Romford
1898	Sigismund Mendl	Liberal	Plymouth
1899	Walter Rothschild	Liberal	Aylesbury
	Edward Sassoon	Unionist	Hythe

1900	Benjamin Cohen	Conservative	Islington East
	Herbert Jessel	Liberal Unionist	St Pancras South
	Maurice Levy	Liberal	Loughborough
	Francis Lucas	Conservative	Lowestoft
	Henry Norman	Liberal	Wolverhampton South
	Walter Rothschild	Liberal	Aylesbury
	Stuart Samuel	Liberal	Whitechapel
	Edward Sassoon	Unionist	Hythe
	Louis Sinclair	Conservative	Romford
	Gustav Wolff	Conservative	Belfast East
1902	Herbert Samuel	Liberal	Cleveland
1904	Rufus Isaacs	Liberal	Reading
	Harry Marks	Conservative	Thanet
1906	Charles Henry	Liberal and Labour	Wellington
	Rufus Isaacs	Liberal	Reading
	Arthur Lever	Liberal	Harwich
	Maurice Levy	Liberal	Leicestershire
	Philip Magnus	Unionist	London University
	Harry Marks	Conservative	Thanet
	Edwin Montagu	Liberal	Chesterton
	Alfred Mond	Liberal	Chester
	Horatio Myer	Liberal	Lambeth North
	Herbert Raphael	Liberal	South Derby
	Walter Rothschild	Liberal	Aylesbury
	Herbert Samuel	Liberal	Cleveland
	Stuart Samuel	Liberal	Tower Hamlets
	Edward Sassoon	Unionist	Hythe
	Bertram Strauss	Liberal	Mile End
	Edward Strauss	Liberal	Southwark
	Gustav Wolff	Conservative	Belfast East
1910	Charles Goldman	Unionist	Falmouth and Penryn
Jan.	Frank Goldsmith	Conservative	Stowmarket
	Charles Henry	Liberal and Labour	Shropshire
	Rufus Isaacs	Liberal	Reading
	Herbert Jessel	Liberal Unionist	St Pancras South
	Maurice Levy	Liberal	Leicestershire
	Ignatius Trebitsch-Lincoln	Liberal	Darlington
	Philip Magnus	Unionist	London University
	Alfred Mond	Liberal	Swansea
	Edwin Montagu	Liberal	Cambridgeshire
	Herbert Raphael	Liberal	South Derby
	Walter Rothschild	Unionist	Aylesbury

	Harry Samuel	Unionist	Lambeth North
	Herbert Samuel	Liberal	Cleveland
	Stuart Samuel	Liberal	Whitechapel
	Edward Sassoon	Unionist	Hythe
	Arthur Strauss	Unionist	Paddington North
	Edward Strauss	Liberal	Abingdon
1910	Frank Goldsmith	Conservative	Stowmarket
Dec.	Felix Cassel	Conservative	St Pancras West
	Charles Henry	Liberal and Labour	Shropshire
	Rufus Isaacs	Liberal	Reading
	Herbert Jessel	Liberal Unionist	St Pancras South
	Maurice Levy	Liberal	Leicestershire
	Ignatius Trebitsch-Lincoln	Liberal	Darlington
	Philip Magnus	Unionist	London University
	Alfred Mond	National Liberal	Swansea
	Edwin Montagu	Liberal	Cambridgeshire
	Herbert Raphael	Liberal	South Derby
	Walter (Lionel) Rothschild	Unionist	Aylesbury
	Harry Samuel	Unionist	Lambeth North
	Herbert Samuel	Liberal	Cleveland
	Stuart Samuel	Liberal	Whitechapel
	Edward Sassoon	Unionist	Hythe
	Arthur Strauss	Unionist	Paddington North
	Edward Strauss	Liberal	Abingdon
1911	Leopold Amery	Conservative	Birmingham South
	Maurice de Forest	Conservative	North West Ham
1912	Philip Sassoon	Unionist	Hythe
1913	Sam Samuel	Unionist	Wandsworth Putney
1916	Percy Harris	Liberal	Harborough
1918	Leopold Amery	Conservative	Birmingham South
	Jack Brunel Cohen	Unionist	Liverpool Fairfield
	Charles Henry	Liberal	Shropshire
	Philip Magnus	Unionist	London University
	Alfred Mond	National Liberal	Swansea West
	Edwin Montagu	Liberal	Cambridgeshire
	Lionel Rothschild	Conservative	Aylesbury
	Arthur Samuel	Conservative	Farnham
	Philip Sassoon	Conservative	Hythe
	Edward Strauss	National Liberal	Southwark
1919	Thomas Myers	Labour	Spen Valley
	Sam Samuel	Conservative	Putney

1920	Sir Walter de Frece	Coalition Unionist	Ashton-under-Lyne
1921	Robert Gee	Conservative	Woolwich East
1922	Leopold Amery	Conservative	Birmingham South
	Jack Brunel Cohen	Conservative Unionist	Liverpool Fairfield
	Walter de Frece	Unionist	Ashton-under-Lyme
	Percy Harris	Liberal	Bethnal Green South West
	Arthur Lever	National Liberal	Hackney Central
	Alfred Mond	National Liberal	Swansea West
	Lionel Rothschild	Conservative	Aylesbury
	Arthur Samuel	Conservative	Farnham
	Sam Samuel	Conservative	Wandsworth Putney
	Philip Sassoon	Conservative	Hythe
	Manny Shinwell	Labour	Linlithgow
	George Spero	Liberal	Stoke Newington
	Edward Strauss	National Liberal	Southwark
1923	Leopold Amery	Conservative	Birmingham South
	Jack Brunel Cohen	Conservative Unionist	Liverpool Fairfield
	Leonard Franklin	Liberal	Hackney Central
	Walter de Frece	Unionist	Ashton-under-Lyme
	Leslie Haden-Guest	Labour	Southwark North
	Percy Harris	Liberal	Bethnal Green South West
	Leslie Hore-Belisha	National Liberal	Devonport
	Henry Mond	Conservative	Toxteth East
	Arthur Samuel	Conservative	Farnham
	Sam Samuel	Conservative	Wandsworth Putney
	Philip Sassoon	Conservative	Hythe
	Manny Shinwell	Labour	Linlithgow
	Henry Slesser	Labour	Leeds South East
	George Spero	Liberal	Stoke Newington
	Joseph Sunlight	Liberal	Shrewsbury
	Moss Turner-Samuels	Labour	Durham Barnard Castle
1924	Leopold Amery	Conservative	Birmingham South
	Jack Brunel Cohen	Conservative Unionist	Liverpool Fairfield

	Name	Party	Constituency
	Harry Day	Labour	Southwark Central
	Walter de Frece	Conservative	Blackpool
	Sam Finburgh	Conservative	Stratford North
	Robert Gee	Labour	Bosworth
	Percy Harris	Liberal	Bethnal Green South West
	Leslie Hore-Belisha	National Liberal	Devonport
	Frank Meyer	Conservative	Great Yarmouth
	Alfred Mond	Conservative	Carmarthen
	Isidore Salmon	Conservative	Harrow
	Arthur Samuel	Conservative	Farnham
	Sam Samuel	Conservative	Wandsworth Putney
	Philip Sassoon	Conservative	Hythe
	Henry Slesser	Labour	Leeds South East
1927	Edward Strauss	Liberal	Southwark North
1928	Manny Shinwell	Labour	Linlithgow
1929	Leopold Amery	Conservative	Birmingham South
	Jack Brunel Cohen	Conservative Unionist	Liverpool Fairfield
	Harry Day	Labour	Southwark Central
	Walter de Frece	Conservative	Blackpool
	Percy Harris	Liberal	Bethnal Green South West
	Leslie Hore-Belisha	National Liberal	Devonport
	Michael Marcus	Labour	Dundee
	Henry Mond	Conservative	Toxteth East
	Harry Nathan	Liberal	Bethnal Green
	Marion Phillips	Labour	Sunderland
	Jimmy Rothschild	Liberal	Isle of Ely
	Isidore Salmon	Conservative	Harrow
	Arthur Samuel	Conservative	Farnham
	Herbert Samuel	Liberal	Darwen
	Sam Samuel	Conservative	Wandsworth Putney
	Philip Sassoon	Conservative	Hythe
	Manny Shinwell	Labour	Linlithgow
	George Spero	Liberal	Stoke Newington
	Edward Strauss	Liberal	Southwark North
	George Strauss	Labour	Lambeth North
1931	Leopold Amery	Conservative	Birmingham South
	Alfred Chotzner	Conservative	West Ham Upton

	Louis Gluckstein	Conservative	Ely
	Albert Goodman	Conservative	Islington North
	Percy Harris	Liberal	Bethnal Green South West
	Leslie Hore-Belisha	National Liberal	Devonport
	Barnett Janner	Liberal	Whitechapel and St Georges
	Dudley Joel	Conservative	Dudley
	Thomas Levy	Conservative	Elland
	Abraham Lyons	Conservative	Leicester East
	Harry Nathan	Liberal	Bethnal Green
	Marion Phillips	Labour	Sunderland
	Jimmy Rothschild	Liberal	Isle of Ely
	Isidore Salmon	Conservative	Harrow
	Arthur Samuel	Conservative	Farnham
	Herbert Samuel	Liberal	Darwen
	Sam Samuel	Conservative	Wandsworth Putney
	Philip Sassoon	Conservative	Hythe
	Edward Strauss	Liberal	Southwark North
1934	George Strauss	Liberal	Lambeth North
	Marcus Samuel	Conservative	Wandsworth Putney
1935	Leopold Amery	Conservative	Birmingham South
	Harry Day	Labour	Southwark Central
	Dan Frankel	Labour	Mile End
	Louis Gluckstein	Conservative	Nottingham East
	Albert Goodman	Conservative	Islington North
	Percy Harris	Liberal	Bethnal Green South West
	Leslie Hore-Belisha	National Liberal	Plymouth Devonport
	Dudley Joel	Conservative	Dudley
	Thomas Levy	Conservative	Elland
	Abraham Lyons	Conservative	East Leicester
	Jimmy Rothschild	Liberal	Isle of Ely
	Isidore Salmon	Conservative	Harrow
	Arthur Samuel	Conservative	Farnham
	Marcus Samuel	Conservative	Wandsworth Putney
	Philip Sassoon	Conservative	Hythe
	Manny Shinwell	Labour	Sealham

	Sidney Silverman	Labour	Nelson and Colne
	Edward Strauss	Liberal	Southwark North
1936	Lewis Silkin	Labour	Peckham
1937	Daniel Lipson	Independent	Cheltenham
	Harry Nathan	Liberal	Central Wandsworth
1942	John Mack	Labour	Newcastle-under-Lyme
1945	Herschel Austin	Labour	Stretford
	Louis Comyns	Labour	West Ham Silvertown
	John Diamond	Labour	Manchester Blackley
	Maurice Edelman	Labour	Coventry West
	Mont Follick	Labour	Loughborough
	Barnett Janner	Labour	Leicester West
	George Jeger	Labour	Winchester
	Santo Jeger	Labour	St Pancras South East
	Harold Lever	Labour	Manchester Exchange
	Benn Levy	Labour	Eton and Slough
	John Lewis	Labour	Bolton
	Daniel Lipson	Independent	Cheltenham
	Marcus Lipton	Labour	Lambeth Brixton
	John Mack	Labour	Newcastle-under-Lyme
	Ian Mikardo	Labour	Reading
	Harry Morris	Labour	Sheffield Central
	Maurice Orbach	Labour	Willesden East
	Phil Piratin	Communist	Stepney Mile End
	Sam Segal	Labour	Preston
	Manny Shinwell	Labour	Seaham
	Lewis Silkin	Labour	Peckham
	Julius Silverman	Labour	Birmingham Erdington
	Sidney Silverman	Labour	Nelson and Colne
	Leslie Solley	Labour Independent	Essex Thurrock
	George Strauss	Labour	Lambeth North
	Barnett Stross	Labour	Stoke-on-Trent Hanley
	Moss Turner-Samuels	Labour	Gloucester
	David Weizman	Labour	Stoke Newington
	Lyall Wilkes	Labour	Newcastle-on-Tyne Central
1948	Austen Albu	Labour	Edmonton
1950	Austen Albu	Labour	Edmonton
	John Diamond	Labour	Manchester Blackley
	Maurice Edelman	Labour	Coventry West
	Barnett Janner	Labour	Leicester West

	George Jeger	Labour	Goole
	Santo Jeger	Labour	St Pancras South East
	Harold Lever	Labour	Manchester Exchange
	Leslie Lever	Labour	Manchester Ardwick
	John Lewis	Labour	Bolton
	Marcus Lipton	Labour	Lambeth Brixton
	John Mack	Labour	Newcastle-under-Lyme
	Ian Mikardo	Labour	Reading
	Harry Morris	Labour	Sheffield Central
	Gerald Nabarro	Conservative	Kidderminster
	Maurice Orbach	Labour	Willesden East
	Manny Shinwell	Labour	Easington
	Julius Silverman	Labour	Birmingham Erdington
	Sidney Silverman	Labour	Nelson and Colne
	George Strauss	Labour	Lambeth North
	Barnett Stross	Labour	Stoke-on-Trent Hanley
	Moss Turner-Samuels	Labour	Gloucester
	David Weizman	Labour	Stoke Newington
	Lyall Wilkes	Labour	Newcastle-on-Tyne Central
1951	Austen Albu	Labour	Edmonton
	Maurice Edelman	Labour	Coventry West
	Barnett Janner	Labour	Leicester West
	George Jeger	Labour	Goole
	Santo Jeger	Labour	St Pancras South East
	Harold Lever	Labour	Manchester Exchange
	Leslie Lever	Labour	Manchester Ardwick
	Marcus Lipton	Labour	Lambeth Brixton
	Ian Mikardo	Labour	Reading
	Harry Morris	Labour	Sheffield Central
	Gerald Nabarro	Conservative	Kidderminster
	Maurice Orbach	Labour	Willesden East
	Manny Shinwell	Labour	Easington
	Julius Silverman	Labour	Birmingham Erdington
	Sidney Silverman	Labour	Nelson and Colne
	George Strauss	Labour	Lambeth North
	Barnett Stross	Labour	Stoke-on-Trent Hanley
	Moss Turner-Samuels	Labour	Gloucester
	David Weizman	Labour	Stoke Newington
1955	Austen Albu	Labour	Edmonton
	Frank Allaun	Labour	Salford East
	Henry d'Avigdor Goldsmid	Conservative	Walsall South

	Maurice Edelman	Labour	Coventry West
	Barnett Janner	Labour	Leicester West
	George Jeger	Labour	Goole
	Harold Lever	Labour	Manchester Cheetham
	Leslie Lever	Labour	Manchester Ardwick
	Marcus Lipton	Labour	Lambeth Brixton
	Ian Mikardo	Labour	Reading
	Gerald Nabarro	Conservative	Kidderminster
	Maurice Orbach	Labour	Willesden East
	Manny Shinwell	Labour	Easington
	Julius Silverman	Labour	Birmingham Erdington
	Sidney Silverman	Labour	Nelson and Colne
	George Strauss	Labour	Lambeth North
	Barnett Stross	Labour	Stoke-on-Trent Hanley
	Moss Turner-Samuels	Labour	Gloucester
	David Weizman	Labour	Stoke Newington and Hackney North
1956	Keith Joseph	Conservative	Leeds North East
1957	John Diamond	Labour	Gloucester
1958	Leo Abse	Labour	Pontypool
	Michael Cliffe	Labour	Shoreditch and Finsbury
1959	Leo Abse	Labour	Pontypool
	Austen Albu	Labour	Edmonton
	Frank Allaun	Labour	Salford East
	Henry d'Avigdor Goldsmid	Conservative	Walsall South
	Joel Barnett	Labour	Heywood and Royston
	Michael Cliffe	Labour	Shoreditch and Finsbury
	John Diamond	Labour	Gloucester
	Maurice Edelman	Labour	Coventry North
	Myer Galpern	Labour	Glasgow Shettleston
	David Ginsburg	Labour	Dewsbury
	Barnett Janner	Labour	Leicester North West
	George Jeger	Labour	Goole
	Keith Joseph	Conservative	Leeds North East
	Harold Lever	Labour	Manchester Cheetham
	Leslie Lever	Labour	Manchester Ardwick
	Marcus Lipton	Labour	Lambeth Brixton
	John Mendelson	Labour	Peniston
	Manny Shinwell	Labour	Easington
	Gerald Nabarro	Conservative	Kidderminster
	Julius Silverman	Labour	Birmingham Erdington
	Sidney Silverman	Labour	Nelson and Colne

	George Strauss	Labour	North Lambeth
	Barnett Stross	Labour	Stoke-on-Trent Hanley
	Moss Turner-Samuels	Labour	Gloucester
	David Weizman	Labour	Stoke Newington and Hackney North
1963	John Silkin	Labour	Deptford
1964	Leo Abse	Labour	Pontypool
	Austen Albu	Labour	Edmonton
	Frank Allaun	Labour	Salford East
	Henry d'Avigdor Goldsmid	Conservative	Walsall South
	Joel Barnett	Labour	Heywood and Royton
	Edmund Dell	Labour	Birkenhead
	John Diamond	Labour	Gloucester
	Jack Dunnett	Labour	Nottingham Central
	Maurice Edelman	Labour	Coventry North
	Reg Freeson	Labour	Willesden East
	Myer Galpern	Labour	Glasgow Shettleston
	David Ginsburg	Labour	Dewsbury
	Barnett Janner	Labour	Leicester North West
	George Jeger	Labour	Goole
	Keith Joseph	Conservative	Leeds North East
	David Kerr	Labour	Wandsworth Central
	Harold Lever	Labour	Manchester Cheetham
	Leslie Lever	Labour	Manchester Ardwick
	Marcus Lipton	Labour	Lambeth Brixton
	Robert Maxwell	Labour	Buckingham
	John Mendelson	Labour	Peniston
	Ian Mikardo	Labour	Poplar
	Maurice Miller	Labour	Glasgow Kelvingrove
	Gerald Nabarro	Conservative	Kidderminster
	Maurice Orbach	Labour	Stockport South
	Paul Rose	Labour	Manchester Blackley
	Arnold Shaw	Labour	Ilford South
	Robert Sheldon	Labour	Ashton-under-Lyme
	Manny Shinwell	Labour	Durham Easington
	Renée Short	Labour	Wolverhampton North East
	John Silkin	Labour	Deptford
	Sam Silkin	Labour	Dulwich
	Julius Silverman	Labour	Birmingham Erdington
	Sidney Silverman	Labour	Nelson and Colne
	Henry Solomons	Labour	Kingston upon Hull North

George Strauss	Labour	Lambeth Vauxhall
Barnett Stross	Labour	Stoke-on-Trent Hanley
Raphael Tuck	Labour	Watford
David Weizman	Labour	Stoke Newington and Hackney North

1966	Leo Abse	Labour	Pontypool
	Austen Albu	Labour	Edmonton
	Frank Allaun	Labour	Salford East
	Henry d'Avigdor Goldsmid	Conservative	Walsall South
	Joel Barnett	Labour	Heywood and Royston
	Arthur Davidson	Labour	Accrington
	Edmund Dell	Labour	Birkenhead
	John Diamond	Labour	Gloucester
	Jack Dunnett	Labour	Nottingham Central
	Maurice Edelman	Labour	Coventry North
	Reg Freeson	Labour	Willesden East
	Myer Galpern	Labour	Glasgow Shettleston
	David Ginsburg	Labour	Dewsbury
	Stanley Henig	Labour	Lancaster
	Barnett Janner	Labour	Leicester North West
	George Jeger	Labour	Goole
	Keith Joseph	Conservative	Leeds North East
	Harold Lever	Labour	Manchester Cheetham
	Leslie Lever	Labour	Manchester Ardwick
	Marcus Lipton	Labour	Lambeth Brixton
	Edward Lyons	Labour	Bradford East
	Robert Maxwell	Labour	Buckingham
	John Mendelson	Labour	Peniston
	Ian Mikardo	Labour	Poplar
	Maurice Miller	Labour	Glasgow Kelvingrove
	Eric Moonman	Labour	Billericay
	Gerald Nabarro	Conservative	South Worcestershire
	Maurice Orbach	Labour	Stockport South
	Paul Rose	Labour	Manchester Blackley
	Arnold Shaw	Labour	Ilford South
	Robert Sheldon	Labour	Ashton-under-Lyme
	Manny Shinwell	Labour	Durham Easington
	Renée Short	Labour	Wolverhampton North East
	John Silkin	Labour	Deptford
	Sam Silkin	Labour	Camberwell Dulwich

Julius Silverman	Labour	Birmingham Aston
Sidney Silverman	Labour	Nelson and Colne
George Strauss	Labour	Lambeth Vauxhall
Raphael Tuck	Labour	Watford
Raphael Tuck	Labour	Watford
David Weizman	Labour	Stoke Newington and Hackney North
David Winnick	Labour	Croydon South

1970	Leo Abse	Labour	Pontypool
	Robert Adley	Conservative	Bristol North East
	Austen Albu	Labour	Edmonton
	Frank Allaun	Labour	Salford East
	Henry d'Avigdor Goldsmid	Conservative	Walsall South
	James d'Avigdor Goldsmid	Conservative	Lichfield and Tamworth
	Joel Barnett	Labour	Heywood and Royston
	Stanley Clinton-Davies	Labour	Hackney Central
	Arthur Davidson	Labour	Accrington
	Edmund Dell	Labour	Birkenhead
	Jack Dunnett	Labour	Nottingham Central
	Maurice Edelman	Labour	Coventry North
	Michael Fidler	Conservative	Bury and Radcliffe
	Geoffrey Finsburg	Conservative	Hampstead
	Reg Freeson	Labour	Willesden East
	Myer Galpern	Labour	Glasgow Shettleston
	David Ginsburg	Labour	Dewsbury
	Stanley Henig	Labour	Lancaster
	Greville Janner	Labour	Leicester North West
	George Jeger	Labour	Goole
	Toby Jessel	Conservative	Twickenham
	Keith Joseph	Conservative	Leeds North East
	Gerald Kaufman	Labour	Manchester Ardwick
	Harold Lever	Labour	Manchester Central
	Marcus Lipton	Labour	Lambeth Brixton
	Edward Lyons	Labour	Bradford East
	John Mendelson	Labour	Peniston
	Ian Mikardo	Labour	Poplar
	Maurice Miller	Labour	Glasgow Kelvingrove
	Gerald Nabarro	Conservative	South Worcestershire
	Sally Oppenheim	Conservative	Gloucester
	Maurice Orbach	Labour	Stockport South

	Paul Rose	Labour	Manchester Blackley
	Robert Sheldon	Labour	Ashton-under-Lyme
	Renée Short	Labour	Wolverhampton North East
	John Silkin	Labour	Lewisham
	Sam Silkin	Labour	Dulwich
	Sidney Silverman	Labour	Nelson and Colne
	Harold Soref	Conservative	Ormskirk
	George Strauss	Labour	Vauxhall
	Raphael Tuck	Labour	Watford
	David Weizman	Labour	Stoke Newington and Hackney North
1971	Neville Sandelson	Labour	Hayes and Harlington
1973	Clement Freud	Liberal	Isle of Ely
1974	Leo Abse	Labour	Pontypool
Feb.	Robert Adley	Conservative	Christchurch and Lymington
	James d'Avigdor Goldsmid	Conservative	Lichfield and Tamworth
	Frank Allaun	Labour	Salford East
	Joel Barnett	Labour	Heywood and Royston
	Leon Brittan	Conservative	Cleveland and Whitby
	Stanley Clinton-Davies	Labour	Hackney Central
	Arthur Davidson	Labour	Accrington
	Edmund Dell	Labour	Birkenhead
	Jack Dunnett	Labour	Nottingham East
	Maurice Edelman	Labour	Coventry North
	Michael Fidler	Conservative	Bury and Ratcliffe
	Geoffrey Finsberg	Conservative	Hampstead
	Reg Freeson	Labour	Brent East
	Clement Freud	Liberal	Isle of Ely
	Myer Galpern	Labour	Glasgow Shettleston
	David Ginsburg	Labour	Dewsbury
	Greville Janner	Labour	Leicester North West
	Toby Jessel	Conservative	Twickenham
	Keith Joseph	Conservative	Leeds North East
	Gerald Kaufman	Labour	Manchester Ardwick
	Ivan Lawrence	Conservative	Burton-on-Trent
	Nigel Lawson	Conservative	Blaby
	Harold Lever	Labour	Manchester Cheetham
	Marcus Lipton	Labour	Lambeth Central

Edward Lyons	Labour	Bradford West
John Mendelson	Labour	Peniston
Ian Mikardo	Labour	Bethnal Green
Maurice Miller	Labour	East Kilbride
Eric Moonman	Labour	Basildon
Sally Oppenheim	Conservative	Gloucester
Maurice Orbach	Labour	Stockport South
Malcolm Rifkind	Conservative	Edinburgh Pentlands
Paul Rose	Labour	Manchester Blackley
Neville Sandelson	Labour	Hayes and Harlington
Harry Selby	Labour	Glasgow Govan
Arnold Shaw	Labour	Ilford South
Robert Sheldon	Labour	Ashton-under-Lyme
Manny Shinwell	Labour	Durham Easington
Renée Short	Labour	Wolverhampton North East
John Silkin	Labour	Lewisham
Sam Silkin	Labour	Southwark Dulwich
Julius Silverman	Labour	Birmingham Erdington
Anthony Steen	Conservative	Liverpool Wavertree
George Strauss	Labour	Lambeth Vauxhall
Raphael Tuck	Labour	Watford
David Weizman	Labour	Stoke Newington and Hackney North

1974 Oct.	Leo Abse	Labour	Pontypool
	Robert Adley	Conservative	Christchurch and Lymington
	Frank Allaun	Labour	Salford East
	Joel Barnett	Labour	Heywood and Royston
	Leon Brittan	Conservative	Cleveland and Whitby
	Stanley Clinton-Davies	Labour	Hackney Central
	Arthur Davidson	Labour	Accrington
	Edmund Dell	Labour	Birkenhead
	Jack Dunnett	Labour	Nottingham East
	Maurice Edelman	Labour	Coventry North
	Geoffrey Finsberg	Conservative	Hampstead
	Reg Freeson	Labour	Brent East
	Clement Freud	Liberal	Isle of Ely
	Myer Galpern	Labour	Glasgow Shettleston

David Ginsburg	Labour	Dewsbury
Greville Janner	Labour	Leicester North West
Toby Jessel	Conservative	Twickenham
Keith Joseph	Conservative	Leeds North East
Gerald Kaufman	Labour	Manchester Ardwick
Ivan Lawrence	Conservative	Burton-on-Trent
Nigel Lawson	Conservative	Blaby
Harold Lever	Labour	Manchester Cheetham
Marcus Lipton	Labour	Lambeth Central
Edward Lyons	Labour	Bradford West
John Mendelson	Labour	Peniston
Helen Middleweek (Hayman)	Labour	Welwyn and Hatfield
Ian Mikardo	Labour	Bethnal Green
Maurice Miller	Labour	East Kilbride
Millie Miller	Labour	Ilford North
Eric Moonman	Labour	Basildon
Sally Oppenheim	Conservative	Gloucester
Maurice Orbach	Labour	Stockport South
Malcolm Rifkind	Conservative	Edinburgh Pentlands
Paul Rose	Labour	Manchester Blackley
Neville Sandelson	Labour	Hayes and Harlington
Harry Selby	Labour	Glasgow Govan
Arnold Shaw	Labour	Ilford South
Robert Sheldon	Labour	Ashton-under-Lyme
Manny Shinwell	Labour	Durham Easington
Renée Short	Labour	Wolverhampton North East
John Silkin	Labour	Lewisham
Sam Silkin	Labour	Southwark Dulwich
Julius Silverman	Labour	Birmingham Erdington
Anthony Steen	Conservative	Liverpool Wavertree
George Strauss	Labour	Lambeth Vauxhall
Raphael Tuck	Labour	Watford
David Weizman	Labour	Stoke Newington and Hackney North
1979 Leo Abse	Labour	Pontypool
Robert Adley	Conservative	Christchurch and Lymington
Frank Allaun	Labour	Salford East

Joel Barnett	Labour	Heywood and Royston
Leon Brittan	Conservative	Cleveland and Whitby
Stanley Clinton-Davies	Labour	Hackney Central
Arthur Davidson	Labour	Accrington
Alf Dubs	Labour	Battersea and Wandsworth
Jack Dunnett	Labour	Nottingham East
Sheila Faith	Conservative	Belper
Geoffrey Finsberg	Conservative	Hampstead
Reg Freeson	Labour	Brent East
Clement Freud	Liberal	Isle of Ely
David Ginsburg	Labour	Dewsbury
Greville Janner	Labour	Leicester West
Toby Jessel	Conservative	Twickenham
Keith Joseph	Conservative	Leeds North East
Gerald Kaufman	Labour	Manchester Ardwick
Ivan Lawrence	Conservative	Burton-on-Trent
Nigel Lawson	Conservative	Blaby
John Lee	Conservative	Pendle
Edward Lyons	Labour	Bradford West
Ian Mikardo	Labour	Tower Hamlets, Bethnal Green and Bow
Maurice Miller	Labour	East Kilbride
Sally Oppenheim	Conservative	Gloucester
Malcolm Rifkind	Conservative	Edinburgh Pentlands
Neville Sandelson	Labour	Hayes and Harlington
Robert Sheldon	Labour	Ashton-under-Lyme
Renée Short	Labour	Wolverhampton North East
John Silkin	Labour	Lewisham
Sam Silkin	Labour	Southwark Dulwich
Julius Silverman	Labour	Birmingham Erdington
Anthony Steen	Conservative	Liverpool Wavertree
David Weizman	Labour	Stoke Newington and Hackney North

1983	Leo Abse	Labour	Pontypool
	Robert Adley	Conservative	Christchurch and Lymington
	Spencer Batiste	Conservative	Elmet

	Martin Brandon-Bravo	Conservative	Nottingham South
	Leon Brittan	Conservative	Richmond
	Alex Carlile	Liberal Democrat	Montgomery
	Harry Cohen	Labour	Leyton
	Edwina Currie	Conservative	South Derbyshire
	Alf Dubs	Labour	Battersea
	Geoffrey Finsberg	Conservative	Hampstead
	Cecil Franks	Conservative	Barrow and Furness
	Reg Freeson	Labour	Brent East
	Clement Freud	Liberal	Cambridgeshire
	Michael Howard	Conservative	Folkestone and Hythe
	Greville Janner	Labour	Leicester North West
	Toby Jessel	Conservative	Twickenham
	Keith Joseph	Conservative	Leeds North East
	Gerald Kaufman	Labour	Manchester Ardwick
	Ivan Lawrence	Conservative	Burton-on-Trent
	Nigel Lawson	Conservative	Blaby
	John Lee	Conservative	Pendle
	Ian Mikardo	Labour	Tower Hamlets, Bethnal Green and Bow
	Maurice Miller	Labour	East Kilbride
	Phillip Oppenheim	Conservative	Amber Valley
	Sally Oppenheim	Conservative	Gloucester
	Malcolm Rifkind	Conservartive	Edinburgh Pentlands
	Robert Sheldon	Labour	Ashton-under-Lyme
	Renée Short	Labour	Wolverhampton North East
	John Silkin	Labour	Lewisham
	Anthony Steen	Conservative	South Hams
	Michael Stern	Conservative	Bristol North West
	David Sumberg	Conservative	Bury South
	David Winnick	Labour	Walsall North
1987	Robert Adley	Conservative	Christchurch and Lymington
	Spencer Batiste	Conservative	Elmet
	Peter Bradley	Labour	Manchester Withington
	Martin Brandon-Bravo	Conservative	Nottingham South
	Alex Carlile	Liberal Democrat	Montgomery
	Harry Cohen	Labour	Leyton
	Edwina Currie	Conservative	South Derbyshire

	Geoffrey Finsberg	Conservative	Hampstead
	Cecil Franks	Conservative	Barrow in Furness
	Mildred Gordon	Labour	Bow and Poplar
	Michael Howard	Conservative	Folkestone and Hythe
	Greville Janner	Labour	Leicester North West
	Toby Jessel	Conservative	Twickenham
	Gerald Kaufman	Labour	Manchester Ardwick
	Ivan Lawrence	Conservative	Burton-on-Trent
	Nigel Lawson	Conservative	Blaby
	John Lee	Conservative	Pendle
	Phillip Oppenheim	Conservative	Amber Valley
	Irvine Patnick	Conservative	Sheffield Hallam
	Malcolm Rifkind	Conservative	Edinburgh Pentlands
	David Shaw	Conservative	Dover
	Robert Sheldon	Labour	Ashton-under-Lyme
	Anthony Steen	Conservative	South Hams
	Gerry Steinberg	Labour	Durham City
	Michael Stern	Conservative	Bristol North West
	David Sumberg	Conservative	Bury South
	David Winnick	Labour	Walsall North
1992	Spencer Batiste	Conservative	Elmet
	Alex Carlile	Liberal Democrat	Montgomery
	Harry Cohen	Labour	Leyton
	Edwina Currie	Conservative	South Derbyshire
	Michael Fabricant	Conservative	Mid Staffordshire
	Mildred Gordon	Labour	Bow and Poplar
	Michael Howard	Conservative	Folkestone and Hythe
	Greville Janner	Labour	Leicester West
	Toby Jessel	Conservative	Twickenham
	Gerald Kaufman	Labour	Manchester Gorton
	Ivan Lawrence	Conservative	Burton-on-Trent
	Peter Mandelson	Labour	Hartlepool
	Phillip Oppenheim	Conservative	Amber Valley
	Irvine Patnick	Conservative	Sheffield Hallam
	Malcolm Rifkind	Conservartive	Edinburgh Pentlands
	Barbara Roche	Labour	Hornsey and Wood Green
	Robert Sheldon	Labour	Ashton-under-Lyme
	Anthony Steen	Conservative	South Hams

	Gerry Steinberg	Labour	Durham City
	Michael Stern	Conservative	Bristol North West
	David Sumberg	Conservative	Bury South
	David Winnick	Labour	Walsall North
1994	Margaret Hodge	Labour	Barking
1997	John Bercow	Conservative	Buckingham
	Peter Bradley	Labour	The Wrekin
	Ivor Caplin	Labour	Hove and Portslade
	Harry Cohen	Labour	Leyton and Wanstead
	Louise Ellman	Labour	Liverpool Riverside
	Michael Fabricant	Conservative	Mid Staffordshire
	Fabian Hamilton	Labour	Leeds North East
	Evan Harris	Liberal Democrat	Oxford West and Abingdon
	Margaret Hodge	Labour	Barking
	Michael Howard	Conservative	Folkestone and Hythe
	Gerald Kaufman	Labour	Manchester Gorton
	Oona King	Labour	Bethnal Green and Bow
	Oliver Letwin	Conservative	Dorset West
	Ivan Lewis	Labour	Bury South
	Julian Lewis	Conservative	New Forest East
	Peter Mandelson	Labour	Hartlepool
	Gillian Merron	Labour	Lincoln
	Barbara Roche	Labour	Hornsey Wood Green
	Anthony Steen	Conservative	Totnes
	Gerry Steinberg	Labour	Durham City
	David Winnick	Labour	Walsall North
2001	John Bercow	Conservative	Buckingham
	Peter Bradley	Labour	The Wrekin
	Ivor Caplin	Labour	Hove
	Harry Cohen	Labour	Leyton and Wanstead
	Jonathan Djanogly	Conservative	Huntingdon
	Louise Ellman	Labour	Liverpool Riverside
	Michael Fabricant	Conservative	Mid Staffordshire
	Fabian Hamilton	Labour	Leeds North East
	Evan Harris	Liberal Democrat	Oxford West and Abingdon
	Margaret Hodge	Labour	Barking
	Michael Howard	Conservative	Folkestone and Hythe
	Gerald Kaufman	Labour	Manchester Gorton

Oona King	Labour	Bethnal Green and Bow
Oliver Letwin	Conservative	Dorset West
Ivan Lewis	Labour	Bury South
Julian Lewis	Conservative	New Forest East
Gillian Merron	Labour	Lincoln
David Miliband	Labour	South Shields Tyne and Wear
Barbara Roche	Labour	Hornsey Wood Green
Anthony Steen	Conservative	Totnes
Gerry Steinberg	Labour	Durham City
David Winnick	Labour	Walsall North
2005 John Bercow	Conservative	Buckingham
Harry Cohen	Labour	Leyton and Wanstead
Jonathan Djanogly	Conservative	Lichfield
Louise Ellman	Labour	Liverpool Riverside
Michael Fabricant	Conservative	Mid Staffordshire
Lynne Featherstone	Liberal Democrat	Hornsey and Wood Green
Fabian Hamilton	Labour	Leeds North East
Evan Harris	Liberal Democrat	Oxford West and Abingdon
Margaret Hodge	Labour	Barking
Michael Howard	Conservative	Folkestone and Hythe
Gerald Kaufman	Labour	Manchester Gorton
Susan Kramer	Liberal Democrat	Richmond Park
Oliver Letwin	Conservative	Dorset West
Ivan Lewis	Labour	Bury South
Julian Lewis	Conservative	New Forest East
Gillian Merron	Labour	Lincoln
David Miliband	Labour	South Shields Tyne and Wear
Ed Miliband	Labour	Doncaster North
Brooks Newmark	Conservative	Braintree
Malcolm Rifkind	Conservative	Kensington and Chelsea
Lee Scott	Conservative	Ilford North
Grant Shapps	Conservative	Welwyn and Hatfield
Anthony Steen	Conservative	Totnes
David Winnick	Labour	Walsall North

Index